Acute Crisis Leadership in Higher Education

This book explores higher education leadership during times of extreme pressures and limited, changing information.

Organized around different functional units in higher education institutions, chapters describe the ways in which campus communities were affected by and responded to the early pandemic crisis. By unpacking observations of real leaders from American institutions of higher education during the COVID-19 pandemic, this book provides lessons learned and takeaway strategies for complex decision-making during a crisis. This edited collection explores the unique moment when leaders and teams must make, implement, and adjust plans rapidly to assure delivery of their missions, while still addressing the needs of students, parents, employees, and stakeholders.

Shining a bright light on decision-making in the early acute stage of a crisis, this book prepares higher education educators to be effective leaders and successful decision-makers.

Gabriela Cornejo Weaver is Assistant Dean of Student Success Analytics and Professor of Chemistry, University of Massachusetts, Amherst, USA.

Kara M. Rabbitt is Associate Provost for Academic Initiatives at William Paterson University, USA.

Suzanne Wilson Summers is Assistant Vice President for Teaching and Learning at Ivy Tech Community College System, USA.

Rhonda Phillips is Dean, Purdue University John Martinson Honors College and Professor of Agricultural Economics at Purdue University, USA.

Kristi N. Hottenstein is Owner of Compass Counseling & Coaching, PLLC and has served as Vice Chancellor for Enrollment Management at the University of Michigan-Flint, as Vice President of Student Services at Jackson College, and as Dean of Students at Adrian College, USA.

Juanita M. Cole is Dean of the College of Arts, Humanities and Social Sciences at California State University Monterey Bay (CSUMB), USA.

Acute Crisis Leadership in Higher Education
Lessons from the Pandemic

Edited by
Gabriela Cornejo Weaver,
Kara M. Rabbitt,
Suzanne Wilson Summers,
Rhonda Phillips,
Kristi N. Hottenstein, and
Juanita M. Cole

NEW YORK AND LONDON

Cover image: © Getty Images

First published 2023
by Routledge
605 Third Avenue, New York, NY 10158

and by Routledge
4 Park Square, Milton Park, Abingdon, Oxon, OX14 4RN

Routledge is an imprint of the Taylor & Francis Group, an informa business

© 2023 selection and editorial matter, Gabriela Cornejo Weaver, Kara M. Rabbitt, Suzanne Wilson Summers, Rhonda Phillips, Kristi N. Hottenstein, and Juanita M. Cole; individual chapters, the contributors

The right of Gabriela Cornejo Weaver, Kara M. Rabbitt, Suzanne Wilson Summers, Rhonda Phillips, Kristi N. Hottenstein, and Juanita M. Cole to be identified as the authors of the editorial material, and of the authors for their individual chapters, has been asserted in accordance with sections 77 and 78 of the Copyright, Designs and Patents Act 1988.

All rights reserved. No part of this book may be reprinted or reproduced or utilised in any form or by any electronic, mechanical, or other means, now known or hereafter invented, including photocopying and recording, or in any information storage or retrieval system, without permission in writing from the publishers.

Trademark notice: Product or corporate names may be trademarks or registered trademarks, and are used only for identification and explanation without intent to infringe.

Library of Congress Cataloging-in-Publication Data
Names: Weaver, Gabriela C., editor.
Title: Acute crisis leadership in higher education : lessons from the
pandemic / edited by Gabriela Cornejo Weaver, Kara M. Rabbitt, Suzanne
Wilson Summers, Rhonda Phillips, Kristi N. Hottenstein, Juanita M. Cole.
Description: First Edition. | New York : Routledge, 2023. | Includes
bibliographical references and index. | Identifiers: LCCN 2022019972 (print) | LCCN
2022019973 (ebook) | ISBN 9781032145556 (Hardback) | ISBN 9781032145549 (Paperback) |
ISBN 9781003239918 (eBook)
Subjects: LCSH: Education, Higher--United States--Administration. |
Universities and colleges--United States--Administration. | Crisis
management--United States. | Educational leadership--United States. |
Communication in higher education--United States. | COVID-19 Pandemic,
2020--Influence.
Classification: LCC LB2341 .C29 2023 (print) | LCC LB2341 (ebook) | DDC
378.1/010973--dc23/eng/20220706
LC record available at https://lccn.loc.gov/2022019972
LC ebook record available at https://lccn.loc.gov/2022019973

ISBN: 978-1-032-14555-6 (hbk)
ISBN: 978-1-032-14554-9 (pbk)
ISBN: 978-1-003-23991-8 (ebk)

DOI: 10.4324/9781003239918

Typeset in Perpetua and Bell Gothic
by SPi Technologies India Pvt Ltd (Straive)

We dedicate this book to our late colleague, friend, and co-author, James Wilson. James provided a guiding vision as we embarked on this project. His inspiration and wisdom helped us complete this book.

Contents

Foreword		ix
Acknowledgments		xiii
About the Authors		xiv

1   Introduction and Overview: 'Embedded' Across the Higher Education Landscape   1
Suzanne Wilson Summers, Gabriela Cornejo Weaver, and Kara M. Rabbitt

PART I
Centrality of the Institutional Mission   17

2   Communications   19
Elizabeth Orwin, Ann T. S. Taylor, and Jay W. Roberts

3   Global Mobility and International Programs   33
Sharon Nagy

4   Continuity of the Academic Mission   51
Gabriela Cornejo Weaver and Rosalyn Hobson Hargraves

5   Equity and Resilience in Academic Research   74
Elizabeth Orwin and Nicholas S. Wigginton

PART II
Community and Operations   89

6   Student Services, Housing, and Dining   91
Kristi N. Hottenstein

7   Athletics   107
Ann T. S. Taylor and Rhonda Phillips

CONTENTS

8   Information Technology Leadership   122
    Juanita M. Cole

9   Operations Facilities and Auxiliaries   138
    Kristi N. Hottenstein and Rachael A. Kipp

10   Human Resource Leadership: Meeting the Needs of Faculty and Staff in the Early Pandemic   155
    Rachael A. Kipp, Kara M. Rabbitt, and Suzanne Wilson Summers

PART III
Planning and Preparation for a Post-COVID World   **177**

11   Admissions and Enrollment   179
    Kristi N. Hottenstein and Rosalyn Hobson Hargraves

12   Advancement through a Pandemic   195
    Kara M. Rabbitt and Jennifer A. Ostergren

13   Moving the Institution Forward: Contingency Planning in Extreme Unpredictability   213
    Suzanne Wilson Summers and Gabriela Cornejo Weaver

14   Reflections on Leadership through Crisis   230
    Gabriela Cornejo Weaver, Suzanne Wilson Summers, Kara M. Rabbitt, and Rhonda Phillips

    Index   241

Foreword

TED MITCHELL, PRESIDENT, AMERICAN COUNCIL ON EDUCATION

This is a book about leadership ... in at least three ways.

First, it is, as the authors intend, an incredibly insightful and nuanced look at how leaders of America's colleges and universities navigated the first, tumultuous months of the COVID-19 pandemic. It is a story of making decisions in a world of uncertainty, imperfect information, and constant, unrelenting pressure over a sustained period.

Second, it is a story of the incredible generosity of a group of host presidents and chancellors who, despite the crisis, saw fit to welcome the American Council on Education's (ACE) 2019–2020 Fellows into their most confidential and often wrenching discussions and debates. In so doing, these presidents and chancellors demonstrated a commitment to building and developing the next generation of leaders by exposing their own leadership to observation, criticism, and learning by the individual Fellow in residence on each of their campuses. They regularly and courageously opened up their own thinking, peeled back their own assumptions, and let the Fellows in not just to the rooms where decisions were thrashed out but into their own minds, enabling them to see executive leadership happening in real time. This openness and generosity are also true of those higher education leaders who, while they were in the thick of their own pandemic responses, engaged in interviews via Zoom with the Fellows. To these generous leaders, I want to say a profound thank you. The experiences you curated for our Fellows stands as testimony to your own dedication to education and learning and to our future as a field.

Finally, this is a story of the Fellows themselves, as leaders who are exploring and understanding avenues they might pursue in their professional journeys. Like the presidents with whom they worked, at both their home and host institutions, and like all of us, this cohort of Fellows managed the crisis of the pandemic as experienced in their own lives, exhibiting an openness to new insights and new learnings while the fire raged all around them. The result is not just this amazing volume, but a cohort of leaders annealed in the crucible of the pandemic and prepared for any challenge. We have high aspirations for all our Fellows, but this class will forever stand apart for its dedication, resilience, and initiative.

Like the institutions we have the honor to represent, ACE worked from the pandemic's first weeks to meet two central objectives: keeping our people safe and sustaining our ability to assist our institutions navigate uncharted waters. Our Board of Directors, used to meeting three times a year, began to gather virtually every week. We engaged public health experts, learned from each other's planning and decision-making, and just kept leaders in touch with others in the same boat. We mobilized the Washington Higher Education Secretariat as an information hub for our collective membership and the field, and, of course, we sent everyone home and operated remotely like the rest of the world.

Our Government Affairs team, which works flat out on a normal day, found another gear, meeting daily with peers in other associations. Together we worked to develop a regulatory and legislative agenda that could help our institutions and those they serve. We pressed on everything from telehealth to emergency funds for students to institutional relief dollars to make up, in part, for lost revenues. Thanks to clear and frequent communication and long, honest negotiations, the field spoke with one voice and achieved successes on nearly every front to help institutions mitigate the realities of the pandemic. I only wish we'd had a Fellow embedded at ACE to be able to tell the story of our responses—the good, the bad, and the in-between—to the events of the last several years.

But the good news is that the 2019–2020 cohort of Fellows WAS embedded in a wide variety of institutions representing a broad diversity of institution types and communities. Their work to distill important learnings from their experiences is "participant-observer" inquiry at its best. It is thorough and incredibly timely, serving as one of the first national scope analyses of how various institutions and leaders managed in a setting of near-complete uncertainty. I am confident that this volume, in addition to providing valuable lessons from the authors' time in the field, will also put many researchable questions on the table for scholars of higher education and organizational leadership.

The stories the Fellows tell combine careful insights about issues that were common across institution types and those that had a differential impact on some institutions, for example residential colleges. Thus, these insights avoid any kind of "one size fits all" narrative about "higher education's response," but in a way that does not fall into the hodge-podge of individual institutional storytelling. This is a fine line, but one the authors have trod with skill.

Similarly, the chapters to follow offer careful guidance in two important areas. The first, and likely expected, are sections in each chapter called "Lessons Learned." These are parsimonious and carefully gauged to the relevant

FOREWORD

observations and research findings. Uniformly, the authors have refrained from *ad hominem* suggestions, instead reflecting the limits of their data and the range of their own learnings. By means of these "lessons learned" we gain insight into practices that led to good outcomes. We also learn what lessons the Fellows themselves are taking from the experiences they relate. Their sagacity bodes well for them and through them, for us.

Less expected are each chapter's "Equity Insights." The existence of these carve-outs signals an important theme of the book and reinforces a major point of reference for us readers. Make no mistake, the authors understand a central role of American higher education as an engine of social and economic mobility and further understand that racial and gender equity are essential components of a quality education. They, like most of us, were heartbroken but not surprised to see the ways that the pandemic deepened social divides between the economic, cultural, and technological haves and have-nots and privileged the privileged: traditional-aged white, middle-class class students.

In each section, the authors pay special attention to ways in which the pandemic and some early responses to the crisis exacerbated already extant inequities. Some of these were unintended consequences of decisions, based on assumptions about "all students," that were really only opportunities available to those with economic and social capital. Early on we all recognized that some students did not have laptops or broadband access, but it took longer to understand the impact of the economic downturn on working students, student parents, and other students who needed to generate income for now-unemployed family members. The authors illuminate these issues with clarity and empathy both for students and for the leaders who, with the best of intentions, often found themselves catching up to the circumstances on the ground that impacted low-income, first-generation students and students of color in disproportionate ways.

Among the many virtues of this volume is its success in combining the multiple narratives of the crisis on campus. Rightly, primary attention is paid to students. But the authors remind us that universities are communities made up also of faculty, administrators, and support staff. While even these groups are not monolithic (the experience of contingent faculty was markedly worse than that for their tenured colleagues), the authors have done their best to portray not only the experience of each group but also the interplay between their experiences, their narratives, and their needs. This is right conceptually, but it is even more significant in the context of a book about campus leadership, where one of the hallmarks of the pandemic was its universal nature. Leaders had to account for multiple communities with multiple and sometimes orthogonal interests, weigh them, find common ground, and make tough calls. That's the stuff of this wonderful book, watching from alongside leaders as they navigated the prolonged crisis of the past several years.

FOREWORD

While it feels premature to talk about the pandemic in the past tense, it is not too early to examine the work that has gone on at campuses during the "hot" phase of the disease. Some of that work has yielded surprising innovations: students AND staff prefer virtual office hours for financial aid, enrollment, and even advising. Some of that work has reminded us of what we already knew, but now understand: it's impossible to overcommunicate; the silos within an institution impede rapid crisis management; lack of engagement of broad teams over time are nearly guaranteed to create local, unit solutions and general chaos. And, most important, trust is everything.

Have no doubt, we have much to repair, much to replace, and more to rethink as we emerge from the COVID-19 crisis. We risk losing a generation of talented low-income, first-generation and minoritized college students; we risk compromising the work of a generation of scholars disrupted by the pandemic; we are challenged ever more to provide meaningful and valuable programs of study to part-time students and the "new normal" adult learner; and we remain a bitterly divided country in need of grace, compassion, and understanding.

I remain convinced, as do all of us at ACE, that America's colleges and universities will continue to rise to the challenges of today and tomorrow and will provide a pathway to social mobility, an example of a just and fair community, and the seeds of a truly inclusive democracy. All of these will require, above all, sound and wise leadership in our institutions. This volume identifies important leadership lessons that will help achieve these goals and highlights just a few of the leaders who will take us there in the coming years.

Acknowledgments

The editorial team wishes to acknowledge as primary inspiration for this project the American Council on Education Fellowship program, with particular thanks to our sages and guides, the very wise Ronald Carter, Theodora Kalikow, Chuck Middleton, Val Moeller, Sara Jayne Steen, and Peggy Williams, and to our ACE Fellows Program Director Sherri Lind Hughes and the dedicated Juanita Banks, ACE Associate Director of Professional Learning. We are each grateful, as well, to our home and host mentors during the ACE fellowship experience and to the many higher education leaders across the country who took the time to share their stories with us through the early pandemic and during the drafting of this book. We gratefully acknowledge, as well, our families and partners who supported us during this learning voyage. Finally, we wish to thank the contributing authors and the other ACE fellows from our 2019–2020 class. We continue to be bolstered, inspired, and challenged by this fellowship of the best class ever.

About the Authors

Juanita M. Cole

Dean, College of Arts, Humanities, and Social Sciences, California State University, Monterey Bay

ACE Host Institution: University of Maryland–College Park
ACE Home Institution: The National Defense University–Washington, DC

Dr. Juanita M. Cole is the Dean of the College of Arts, Humanities and Social Sciences at California State University Monterey Bay (CSUMB). She is a transformative academic professional with over 25 years of experience in higher education as an administrator, professor, researcher and mentor. Prior to joining CSUMB, she served as Deputy Provost at National Defense University. A developmental psychologist by training, Dr. Cole is a champion of innovation—leveraging her research expertise to create accessible educational experiences for all individuals. Dr. Cole was the first in her family to graduate from a university and earned degrees from San Diego State University (BA), Pepperdine University (MA), and Howard University (PhD) in psychology.

Rosalyn Hobson Hargraves

Professor of Electrical and Computer Engineering, Virginia Commonwealth University; Division Director for the Division of Undergraduate Education (DUE) at the National Science Foundation Directorate for Education and Human Resources

ACE Host Institution: William & Mary (W&M)
ACE Home Institution: Virginia Commonwealth University (VCU)

Dr. Hargraves' research interests span science, technology, engineering, and mathematics (STEM) education, diversity, equity, and inclusion in higher education, machine learning, biomedical signal and image processing, and the role of science and technology in international development. As the NSF's DUE

ABOUT THE AUTHORS

Division Director, Dr. Hargraves leads the Foundation's efforts in undergraduate STEM education at 2-year and 4-year institutions of higher education. During her 25 years at VCU, Dr. Hargraves has served in numerous leadership roles. She currently is elected to serve on the American Council on Education Council of Fellows board, the Bon Secours Richmond Health System Board, and as a Richmond Memorial Health Foundation Trustee.

Kristi N. Hottenstein

Owner of Compass Counseling & Coaching, PLLC

ACE Host Institution: The University of Michigan–Ann Arbor
ACE Home Institution: The University of Michigan–Flint

Dr. Kristi Hottenstein has two decades of experience in counseling and higher education. She has served as Vice Chancellor for Enrollment Management at the University of Michigan-Flint, as Vice President of Student Services at Jackson College, and as Dean of Students at Adrian College. Dr. Hottenstein serves as a peer reviewer for the Higher Learning Commission and is a member of the Michigan Mental Health Counselors Association Board of Directors. She earned a doctorate in higher education administration from the University of Toledo, a master's in Counseling from the University of La Verne and a bachelor's in Sociology from Alma College.

Rachael A. Kipp

Assistant Provost for Academic Planning and Accreditation and Associate Professor of Chemistry, Suffolk University

ACE Host Institution: University of Rhode Island
ACE Home Institution: Suffolk University

Dr. Rachael Kipp serves on the University's Integrated Response Team and COVID Taskforce, two committees that coordinate the University's response to COVID-19. She contributed to the University's emergency response plans over the past seven years as a department chair and chaired the Safety Committee several years prior to that. She also leads the accreditation efforts for the University as a whole. Prior to joining the Provost's office, Dr. Kipp was the Chair of the Division of Physical Sciences. Her research is in the field of environmental chemistry.

Sharon Nagy

Associate Provost, Clemson University

ACE Host institution: New Jersey City University
ACE Home institution: Clemson University

ABOUT THE AUTHORS

Dr. Sharon Nagy identifies as an ethnographer, anthropologist, and advocate for global engagement and internationalization of higher education. Her ethnographic research is focused on the social diversity, labor migration and urbanization in the Arabian Gulf States. She has served in leadership roles, creating strategy for comprehensive internationalization and the delivery of global learning outcomes through education abroad, virtual exchange and global service learning. She has served on the board of the Association of International Education Administrators (AIEA) and the American Council on Education's advisory commission for internationalization.

Elizabeth Orwin

Dean, School of Engineering and Computer Science, University of Pacific

ACE Host Institution: California Institute of Technology (Caltech)
ACE Home Institution: Harvey Mudd College
Dr. Liz Orwin's scholarship is in the areas of tissue engineering and biomedical device design, specifically applied to the study and development of an artificial corneal construct. Dr. Orwin also runs several industry-sponsored research projects involving tissue engineering and wound healing in skin and neural models. She has had consulting relationships with a variety of companies, most recently Optics Medical. She is active in the Society of Women Engineers, in implementing best practices and pedagogies for recruiting and retaining a diverse student body, and in developing a more inclusive culture in engineering groups.

Jennifer A. Ostergren

Dean, College of Education, Health and Human Service, California State University, San Marcos

ACE Host institution: Arizona State University
ACE Home institution: California State University, Long Beach
Dr. Jennifer A. Ostergren is the Dean of the College of Education, Health, and Human Services (CEHHS) at California State University, San Marcos (CSUSM). She has received specialized training and certification in the area of futures thinking. Her work in this area focuses on the futures of higher education, work, and health. Dr. Ostergren is a licensed speech-language pathologist who specializes in the care of individuals with cognitive-communicative disorders due to traumatic brain injury and stroke.

Rhonda Phillips

Dean, Purdue University John Martinson Honors College and Professor, Agricultural Economics

ABOUT THE AUTHORS

ACE Host Institution: University of Arizona
ACE Home Institution: Purdue University

Dr. Rhonda Phillips is the inaugural dean of Purdue's only academic residential college, overseeing the design and building of the university's interdisciplinary college serving students from all majors. She also serves as co-director of the Happiness & Well-Being Learning Collaborative, and co-chair of the Purdue Innovation Council, an initiative for research on transformative undergraduate education. Rhonda has served as an administrator and faculty member at several R1 institutions, including Arizona State University and the University of Florida. She was the first woman to receive a doctorate in city and urban planning from the Georgia Institute of Technology and has been inducted into the College of Fellows of the American Institute of Certified Planners for career achievements.

Kara M. Rabbitt

Associate Provost for Academic Initiatives, William Paterson University of New Jersey

ACE Host Institution: Sonoma State University
ACE Home Institution: William Paterson University of New Jersey

Dr. Kara Rabbitt currently oversees program development and support for adult and online learners and strategies for inclusive student success. She previously served first as Associate Dean and then Dean of Humanities & Social Sciences. A professor of Languages & Cultures and an allied faculty member in Africana World Studies, she is a scholar of French and Francophone literatures and has published in related journals as well as in the field of higher education administration. She serves on the ACE Council of Fellows Board. Dr. Rabbitt earned her doctorate in Romance Studies from Cornell University and her undergraduate degree in Languages Studies and Comparative Literature from the University of California–Santa Cruz.

Jay W. Roberts

Provost, Warren Wilson College

ACE Host institution: Lawrence University
ACE Home institution: Earlham College

Prior to Warren Wilson College, Dr. Jay Roberts spent twenty years at Earlham College as a Professor of Education, serving for seven years as the Associate Vice President for Academic Affairs. He also served for four years as a Teagle Teaching Fellow with the Great Lakes College Association. Dr. Robert's scholarship focuses on engaged pedagogy, experiential learning, and place-based learning. He is the author of three books: *Risky Teaching: Embracing the power of uncertainty in higher*

ABOUT THE AUTHORS

education (2021); *Experiential Education in the College Context: What it is, how it works, and why it matters* (2016); and, *Beyond Learning by Doing: Theoretical currents in experiential education* (2011), all published by Routledge. He serves on the Editorial Board for the *Journal of Experiential Education*.

Suzanne Wilson Summers

Assistant Vice President for Teaching and Learning, Ivy Tech Community College–Columbus

ACE Host Institutions: SUNY Rockland Community College; Valencia College
ACE Home Institution: Austin Community College
Having begun her own higher education journey at a community college, Dr. Summers spent over 30 years as a faculty member in access-oriented, rural and urban Hispanic Serving Institutions. Currently, she serves as the Assistant Vice President for Teaching and Learning for Ivy Tech Community College system in Indiana. Her focus is on increasing college going, completion, and transfer rates in a mixed urban/suburban/rural service region. Dr. Summers also served in the US Army, where she led a military history unit to the Pentagon immediately after 9/11. A commitment to service is at the core of her leadership philosophy.

Ann T. S. Taylor

Senior Associate Dean of the College and Professor of Chemistry, Wabash College

ACE Host Institution: Ball State University
ACE Home Institution: Wabash College
While COVID-19 interrupted her cohort's ACE Fellowship, it provided Dr. Ann Taylor an amazing project opportunity at her home institution, where she served as Special Assistant to the President for COVID Planning and Response. She worked with all units of the college to develop and implement mitigation practices necessary for the 2020–21 and 2021–22 school years. Dr. Taylor's research focuses on reinforcing prerequisite knowledge and scaffolding learning to both strengthen knowledge of introductory concepts as well as new material.

Nicholas S. Wigginton

Assistant Vice President for Research, University of Michigan

ACE Host institution: Stanford University
ACE Home institution: University of Michigan
Dr. Nicholas Wigginton works with faculty and staff at the University of Michigan and the broader research community to identify strategic priorities,

administer funding programs, and increase research competitiveness. Before joining U-M, Dr. Wigginton was a senior editor at *Science*, one of the world's premier scientific journals, published by the American Association for the Advancement of Science.

Gabriela Cornejo Weaver

Assistant Dean of Student Success Analytics and Professor of Chemistry, University of Massachusetts, Amherst

ACE Host Institution: Boston University
ACE Home Institution: University of Massachusetts, Amherst

Dr. Weaver's scholarship is in the area of STEM education innovation toward the goal of increasing access to higher education and student success. Her work has included: researching how students learn specific concepts using different pedagogies or tools, engaging in curricular reform at the program or department level, providing professional development for K-12 teachers and higher education faculty, researching and supporting institutional-level change, engaging in national-level policy work, and developing networks for practitioners and researchers of higher education STEM reform. She is a Fellow of the American Association for the Advancement of Science.

Chapter 1

Introduction and Overview

'Embedded' Across the Higher Education Landscape

Suzanne Wilson Summers, Gabriela Cornejo Weaver, and Kara M. Rabbitt

In the spring of 2020, the impact of COVID-19 on US college and university campuses aptly fit every adjective that filled headlines and announcements—"unprecedented," "unimaginable," "destabilizing," "dramatic"—as campus operations shut down rapidly in response to the virus's spread across the nation. Higher education institutions braced for what most expected to be an intense but brief crisis as public health officials called for lockdowns of two weeks to a month. Shortly after the health dangers of the virus became evident, the pandemic also pulled back a curtain on deep inequities that existed across different communities, including different groups within the higher education landscape. These disparities led to uneven impacts not only of the virus itself, but of the decisions intended to help our institutions respond to the virus. For those who work in and feel a deep commitment to the mission of higher education, it seems critical that we capture the history of, and learn from, the response to this crisis—one that affected the US higher education enterprise on a scale never before experienced.

A line coined by Damian Barr in early 2020 (Barr, 2020; Haley, 2020; Noonan, 2020) neatly summed up the complex situation: "We are not all in the same boat. We are all in the same storm." Prior to the COVID-19 pandemic, leaders, researchers, and observers were already grappling with the need for higher education to adjust to and effectively meet the demands of a changing global economy and shifting stakeholder demographics. The pandemic intensified these deliberations by presenting many institutions with a truly existential threat. Reflecting on the lessons about the role of leadership in guiding institutions of higher education (IHEs) through crises, as well as on the lessons that higher education can draw from this period about the complexities of diversity and equity across their communities, can help current and future higher education leaders and their institutions develop greater capacity for resilience (Duchek, 2020). We hope that this book will be a contribution toward that development.

WHO WE ARE

The authors of this book served as part of the 2019–2020 American Council on Education (ACE) Fellows cohort. The ACE Fellows program is the oldest higher education leadership program in the US (ACE, n.d.). One of its invaluable features is that it brings together promising leaders from across all sectors of higher education and different regions. During gatherings of the cohort, Fellows receive training on key higher education issues and mentorship from retired senior leaders who serve as "sages" to teams of Fellows. Much of the learning, however, comes from being embedded at a host institution for all or part of an academic year with a designated mentor, often the CEO or CAO, whom the Fellow shadows. Fellows attend cabinet sessions and other senior team meetings, interact with other campus leaders, and spend time with a variety of decision-makers at their host institution. Regular meetings with their host mentors provide Fellows with an opportunity to learn directly from those living the day-to-day challenges, and joys, of IHE leadership.

By the time our host institutions began planning to shut down in March 2020, our class had nearly completed our Fellowship year. As disorienting as the experience was for our cohort of Fellows, we all realized that we were living through a historically significant moment for the field we were actively studying. Some of us remained at our host institutions, while others returned home. Most, however, continued to sit through senior-level meetings, albeit now held remotely, as institutional leaders planned for what most assumed would be a short-term shutdown. Unlike those employed at our home and host institutions who were knee-deep in daily crisis planning and decision-making, as Fellows we had the unique opportunity to observe and to reflect individually and collectively on what we were witnessing.

During a typical ACE Fellowship year, Fellows would make short visits to institutions outside of their host institution, where they would tour campuses and meet with senior leaders to learn about the missions and challenges of a wide array of colleges and universities. Once the pandemic began, however, the Fellows in the 2019–2020 cohort realized that they could carry out these visits remotely; in fact, we found that a larger number of "visits" became possible when these conversations moved to remote platforms and the barriers of travel time and expense were removed. In an ordinary year, the generosity of senior leaders who make time in their extremely busy schedules to meet and share their leadership insights with Fellows is a highlight of the program. That IHE leaders maintained this willingness even while they were dealing with the onslaught of pandemic-related demands is something for which we are all immensely grateful and demonstrates their commitment to nurturing emerging higher education leaders. In all, members of our class had visits with almost 50 different higher education leaders across dozens of campuses from April to June 2020. A number of these presidents, chancellors, provosts, and other leaders who met with us in late spring 2020 indicated that the occasion to talk with us about decision-making at their institutions during this period offered them their first opportunity for reflection.

As a cohort, we sustained each other through regular virtual meet-ups and shared observations and questions with each other on a mobile messaging platform. Perhaps more so than for any previous class of Fellows, the intensity of this experience connected us with each other and provided an urgency to our discussions together about the types of decisions being made on the various campuses at which we were placed, as well as our observations of the events unfolding across the country in higher education institutions. Many of us were able to assist our own institutions as a result of this shared information by providing perspectives about how other institutions were handling new issues, such as social distancing requirements, adjustments of grading regulations, or planning for new student onboarding. The academic year experience for the 2019–2020 cohort of ACE Fellows moved from over half a year of typical (in-person) academic on-campus leadership observation into four months of intensive and expanded observation from March–June 2020 during the acute phase of the pandemic response in higher education. This book grew out of our recognition that our positions as Fellows provided us a unique vantage point during a chaotic, uncertain, and unfolding situation.

Combining the experiences from our host, home, and visited campuses, the authors and editors of this book represent a considerable swath of the American higher education landscape. Figure 1.1 shows this breadth geographically, by state. In addition, we either visited, were hosted by, or had as our home institutions a range of higher education sectors: two-year/community colleges, four-year institutions, doctoral/research institutions; private and public institutions; large and small institutions (ranging from a few hundred students to over 100,000 students). In writing the chapters for this book, authors and editors alike strived to make the material representative of and applicable across the full higher education landscape, although some chapters may apply more to one sector than others due to their topic (e.g., Chapter 5 about the research mission).

Because this is a book about leadership based on our interviews and observations, we sought to capture a broad range of leadership experiences. At the beginning of our fellowship year, none of us could have imagined that we would write a book on this topic. Once the value of such an analysis became apparent and we began the planning process, it was clear that some of the information we had learned or the activities we had observed would need to remain anonymized, if reported at all. Honoring the need for confidentiality is a commitment that Fellows make to their host institutions and that we held to in the drafting of these chapters. When examples and quotes are included in this book, the institutions and/or individuals listed have explicitly given their permission for them to be

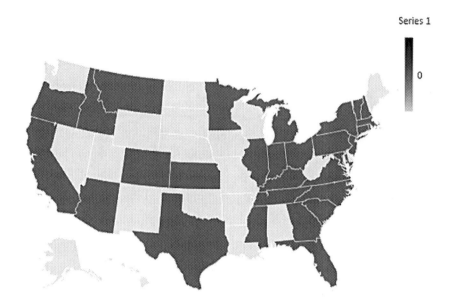

Figure 1.1 States of the home, host and visited institutions of the contributing authors and editors of this book.

identified. Most of the reflections on decision-making included herein came from interviews with leaders at a variety of institutions across the country arranged by the authors rather than out of the cabinet sessions we observed.

THE CONTEXT OF HIGHER EDUCATION'S COVID-19 RESPONSE

Long before the COVID-19 pandemic hit campuses, IHEs had already reached what one scholar described as a "breakpoint" (McGee, 2015) as they faced economic, political, and cultural challenges in defining and delivering their missions. In the Northeast and Midwest, in particular, institutions were also already confronting a demographic "cliff"—declining numbers of high school graduates ready to enter college (Grawe, 2017). The impact of the 2008 recession had created a sea of red ink for IHEs (Selingo, 2015) that was far from resolved on many campuses by the time the outbreak of COVID-19 occurred, particularly for public institutions whose financial situation was further compounded by reductions in state appropriations. For two-year colleges, a robust job market in 2019 resulted in typical counter-cyclical enrollment declines (AACC, 2019). The COVID-19 crisis further deepened these declines (Kyaw, 2021). Subsequent to the election of Donald Trump in 2016, long-simmering political pressures against IHEs within some states gained increased force, propelled by what many higher education administrators saw as a hostile Department of Education, and funding sources for research faced new restrictions and limitations (Schwartz, 2020). Climbing tuition rates, offerings of new certificates and degree options from non-traditional entities, and questions about higher education's ability to promote social and economic mobility fed public skepticism about the value proposition of higher education.

Against this backdrop, institutions of higher education then faced the greatest public health emergency since the influenza epidemic of 1918–1920. Crises are generally "perceived and addressed as time-bounded events," as storms that pass (McGee, 2015, p. 20). The COVID-19 pandemic, however, created a full-fledged and multi-fronted disaster that required, in its early stages, a complete and almost immediate transformation of how higher education institutions carried out their mission. Although emergency planning had become common at many institutions, these exercises tended to focus on public safety threats, such as armed shooter responses, or short-term acts of nature, including fires, hurricanes, and tornadoes. Past public health threats, such as those posed by the H1N1 and Ebola viruses, had been relatively short-term or geographically-bounded episodes with limited impact.

When COVID-19 appeared in the US, it represented not only a new public health threat, but also one that was global in scope, with a high level of lethality. Stories of overwhelmed hospitals and bodies stacked in morgues appeared regularly in the press. During the period reported in this book, late winter through summer of 2020, neither the mechanisms of disease transmission nor its effects were yet well understood. Consequently, the path toward effective treatments and preventative measures was unclear and confusing. Changing public health directives from federal and state authorities exacerbated the public's worries and fears about this new disease: Could you catch it from touching surfaces? If so, for how long? Would the wearing of masks protect or endanger you? These and other questions were still under debate, and vaccinations or treatments were a long way off.

The impact of the COVID-19 crisis quickly spread to the economy which, in turn, affected both students' ability to remain in school and IHEs' capacity to provide needed support for both students and employees. Not only did IHEs close down,[1] but as businesses also shut their doors due to stay-at-home orders, the economic impacts rippled throughout communities. Similarly, the varying political contexts at the local, state, and federal level had distinct and profound consequences for institutional responses (St. Amour, 2020). Public institutions in some conservative states, for example, faced governmental pressures to end social distancing and to reopen quickly. Leaders of these institutions often spent a considerable amount of time and energy navigating these pressures.

In this environment, higher education leaders sought to protect employees and students while maintaining a commitment to their institutional missions.

Their mission-driven goals, however, were often in tension with the fiscal pressures created and exacerbated by the pandemic. As stay-at-home orders spread across the US, unemployment rose, particularly in fields that had historically employed large numbers of low-skilled workers, such as food service and retail. The spreading economic downturn and rising unemployment, in turn, increased the financial difficulties for many students to remain enrolled in college, and the resulting enrollment declines, particularly for students of color, alarmed higher education leaders across the US.

As we write this volume, the US is heading into the third year of the COVID-19 pandemic. Yet, while these continue to be difficult times for many institutions, many in higher education have also noted a level of resiliency and rapid responsiveness that few would have predicted in the fall of 2019. As an AAC&U report noted,

> The pandemic has challenged a number of stubborn assumptions about higher education—e.g., that change is slow, that faculty can't adapt, that student learning can be neatly separated from students' everyday lives, or that all students have the same opportunities to succeed.
>
> (Finley, 2021)

The challenges facing IHEs now include how to build upon the movement toward greater equity awareness and advance the changes needed to ensure that a college education is in reach for all.

This volume provides a means to reflect on lessons learned through the initial period of the pandemic and a chance to draw from them means to advance through future crises. Our institutional missions, regardless of sector, are rooted in a commitment to serve people: students, employees, local communities, civic society, and the national economy. Our ability to adapt to changing conditions—even dramatically changed conditions—will determine our ability to make good on that commitment. We will not return to a pre-pandemic "normal," however nostalgic we may be for that past. Individually, collectively, and institutionally, the pandemic changed and challenged us. It is up to us, therefore, not to squander the lessons this event has provided us about how we may serve more equitably and effectively.

A few words about the goals and limits of this book are in order. This is, above all else, a book about leading higher education institutions through the most dramatic global crisis in memory. Its chronological focus covers the months immediately before campus shutdowns began in March 2020 through the summer of that year as colleges and universities hoped for a return to a pre-pandemic "normal" in the fall. It is a study of both institutional and functional leadership and is rooted in our belief that leadership matters. The book has a dual focus. One part is historical—what happened and how institutions responded—as well as an attempt to understand the landscape through the eyes and experiences of leaders charged with safeguarding their campus communities. The other part is about the ways in which the growing awareness of inequities—for students, faculty, and staff—played out in decision-making and the actions taken in response to the pandemic.

In ordinary times, higher education leadership is taxing, complicated, and meaningful. If the public perception of higher education often centers on the image of unchanging, ivy-covered college campuses, today's leaders know that they, like their counterparts in other industries, operate within a volatile, uncertain, complex, and ambiguous (VUCA) environment. The challenges higher education leaders faced grew exponentially when the COVID-19 pandemic first began to affect IHEs. We hope this book will help current and future leaders in higher education to think ahead about how they will prepare for whatever the future holds.

As many observers have noted, one of the distinctive features of the US higher education system is that it isn't a "system" at all. Instead, it represents a geographically dispersed patchwork composed of multiple sectors, some private and some public. This variety makes it challenging to write about "higher education" as a whole. Yet, although we have not captured every type of post-secondary institution (e.g., we did not cover fully online institutions), we believe it is important to capture the experiences of multiple sectors rather than assuming that the experience of one sector covers all.

ADDRESSING EQUITY DURING A CRISIS

The rapid shutdown of colleges and universities across the country and resulting shift to remote learning in March 2020 had very different effects on low-wealth student populations and students of color. These disparities, in turn, meant that institutions, such as public comprehensives and community colleges, with large numbers of such students, felt an immediate impact as dropout rates threatened to undo a decade of work designed to expand educational access and attainment.

The pandemic responses of IHEs did not form in a historical vacuum, and their responses to the needs of internal and external constituents during the COVID-19 pandemic revealed the impact of recent debates over issues such as how to best support Black, Indigenous and people of color (BIPOC) students, faculty, and staff. Indeed, during the early phase of the pandemic, equity concerns threaded their way through discussions of student homelessness and food insecurity, of faculty promotion and tenure processes, of federal aid to colleges and universities, and of remote work policies for employees. Although this book is not intended as a full analysis of diversity, equity, and inclusion (DEI) issues during the pandemic, the centrality of these concerns for higher education leaders makes the question of how institutions recognized and addressed equity issues a key theme of this book. Perhaps the most challenging leadership imperative of the pandemic came from the need for leaders to balance the at times conflicting and other times overlapping needs of student and employee populations. In this period, we observed that for institutions to advance effectively in the face of their multiple challenges, equity truly had to become everybody's work (Kezar et al., 2021).

Many commentators have pointed to the spring and summer of 2020 as a period in which multiple crises—health, economic, racial—overlapped, and IHEs often struggled to accommodate this reality. Issues related to systemic racism that erupted to national view in spring 2020 had been playing out on campuses for several years, but the differential impact of the pandemic on student populations proved especially stark. The overlap of racially uneven economic standing combined with the racial and class impacts of the pandemic threatened to undo the educational gains of a generation. By June 2020, 50% of Latinx and 42% of Black students reported that COVID had disrupted their educational plans compared to only 25% of White students (NSCRC, 2020). Early national polls showed that 41% of minoritized high school seniors indicated that they were unlikely to attend college in the fall 2020 or that it was "too soon to say" compared to 22% of white students (Simpson Scarborough, 2020). First-generation students, too, worried about their ability to pay for and complete a college degree. Many low-wealth students dropped out of college so that they could work to supplement family incomes as the national economic effects of the pandemic resulted in rising unemployment.

Moreover, a renewed racial justice movement erupted in the late spring and early summer of 2020, fueled by the racialized impacts seen in the high infection and mortality rates for communities of color, along with long-standing anger nationally over patterns of police violence against Black Americans. Groups like Black Lives Matter (BLM) launched national protests from Minneapolis to Houston after the deaths of George Floyd, Breonna Taylor, Ahmed Aubery, and others. Anti-Asian hate crimes also increased, triggered by associations between China and the origin of the COVID-19 outbreak. As these issues erupted on and off college campuses, students, faculty, and staff demanded that institutional leaders address patterns of bias and systemic inequality within their own institutions.

The inequitable impacts of the pandemic arose in numerous dimensions and across student, faculty, and staff populations. For example, women across all three groups were particularly affected by the pandemic. (Some observers noted that the pandemic set off a "she-cession" as female unemployment rose dramatically due to the need to care for children as schools shut down and the service industries that historically employed large numbers of female workers—retail and food service—also closed.) On college campuses, too, female faculty often earned less than their male peers while carrying disproportionate "invisible burdens" of departmental/institutional service and caregiving. As primary caregivers for both children and elderly relatives, women faculty experienced professional impacts in terms of grants, tenure-status, graduate degree completion, and promotion (NASEM, 2021). Although many institutions sought to mitigate the effects of the pandemic by delaying tenure and promotion decisions, some worried about the potential for long-term career mobility and economic effects. If fewer women made it to senior faculty ranks, what would be the impact on the leadership pipeline across higher education? BIPOC faculty and staff faced similar challenges and risks due to disproportionate impacts of the pandemic on their communities, and the complex intersectionality of people's lives was rendered more evident in the multiple challenges different members of the higher education community faced.

Other equity concerns quickly appeared. COVID-19 presented disproportionate health risks for older, essential, and front-line employees and those already suffering underlying health conditions. The move to remote learning and work forced institutions to scramble to provide technological and broadband access for low-wealth and rural students and employees who might not have it. Growing numbers of contingent faculty found themselves laid off as institutions struggled to accommodate the enrollment and budgetary impacts of the pandemic.

The pandemic—overlapped by the racial justice movement and severe economic challenges—presented an unplanned laboratory for crisis leadership strategies. While it challenged and stress-tested those strategies, it also created the conditions for the possibility of fundamental change that had seemed impossible to predict prior to the pandemic.

> Our study of this period finds that in the short term, decision makers sought to balance operational continuity and efficiency with equity considerations, but that one-size-fits-all policies which fail to recognize the differential policy impacts on different segments of communities can reinforce inequities.
> (Hottenstein et al., 2021)

Moreover, decisions that favored one group over another, rather than treating COVID-19 as a campus-wide threat, carried the risk of long-term damage to trust and morale, critical ingredients for IHEs facing an unprecedented crisis.

During the period studied by this book, it became increasingly clear that the pandemic was widening the gaps of inequality. This truth played out, as well, in the ways that different types of IHEs were affected by and dealt with the storm that COVID-19 inflicted on campuses. Regional comprehensives, minority-serving institutions, and community colleges faced and continue to face increased student needs, declines in enrollment, and fiscal challenges. Research-intensive institutions had to reexamine how they evaluate and support the research and scholarship of their faculty and students through profound disruption. Small liberal arts colleges faced intensive pressures in trying to provide a residential "college experience" when the college community was unable to operate fully in person. As we move forward, our institutions must imagine new models and reinvent old methods. How we reevaluate and reimagine our collective work—whether in the classroom, the boardroom, or in spaces such as this book—will be crucial for the ability of our institutions, and our students, to survive and to thrive in a post-pandemic world. As one contemporary observer noted,

> This isn't a "crisis": it is a disaster requiring transformation of our entire infrastructure. … It will be a true disaster if DEI issues are not considered. We can't let go of what's right to do for convenience or expediency during a hard time.
>
> (Pluviose, 2020)

CRISIS LEADERSHIP AS A CRITICAL COMPETENCY

The pandemic presented an unplanned, but critical, laboratory for crisis leadership strategies even as its demands for rapid response challenged the most resilient institutions and leaders. It also created the conditions for levels of fundamental change that seemed impossible to predict prior to the pandemic. If evangelists for higher education reform saw the pandemic as an opportunity for transformational change, many institutional leaders wrestled with how to navigate a highly fluid and threatening situation while communicating care to students and employees. The ability to balance sometimes conflicting and competing priorities with the needs of campus constituents in an environment of information scarcity represented one of the greatest leadership challenges resulting from the COVID-19 pandemic.

In ordinary conditions, leaders constantly attempt to harmonize the need to look ahead while actively tending to operational fires. They rely heavily on their senior functional leaders (CAOs, CIOs, etc.) to help them do so. The ability to achieve a coordinated response effort across institutional silos greatly determined the effectiveness of institutions during early 2020. Institutions facing an unprecedented crisis needed more than charismatic leaders; they needed effective teamwork. One of the most important lessons that arises repeatedly from the observations in this book is that effective crisis preparation and response depends on senior leaders actively fostering an environment that promotes, supports, and holds accountable leadership teams for working across organizational boundaries.

Additionally, many institutional leaders found that they could no longer defer difficult decisions, such as cutting programs with long declining enrollments. The cost of these decisions, however, made more rapidly than many would have wished, to employee morale, trust, and willingness to collaborate is likely to have long-lived consequences just when these elements are essential. The president of one southern HBCU observed that institutional leaders through this period had to balance decision-making between student needs—for community, for a developmental experience, and for mentorship—with fiscal needs. While IHEs with high percentages of at-risk students focused early on equity issues, many institutional leaders felt forced to make decisions based on fiscal realities and to justify them in terms of student needs. The challenge, he observed, was to figure out how to move beyond decision-making based on economic anxiety to a focus on serving in new ways, meeting mission priorities while still balancing the budget.

Crisis leadership requires above all else attention to trust-building across campus constituencies. Many leaders engaged with different units through a regular cadence of online meetings and town halls that gave them the opportunity both to share with students and employees the latest information on institutional plans and to listen to the concerns of these groups. Presidents and other senior leaders needed to be seen and heard from, directly, even as communications offices developed multiple information streams to reach varying audiences. In times of crisis, people need the reassurance of a compassionate and human-centered leadership in order to establish trust.

FRAMEWORK AND ORGANIZATION OF THIS BOOK

This book is certainly not the first to address the topic of leadership during crisis, or even to address this topic within the specific context of the higher education system (Gigliotti, 2019). Our unique situation, however, provided us a lens into the rather sudden organizational changes that were needed in response to the acute stage of the pandemic-imposed crisis. Organizational change is a well-researched topic with a long and deep history of scholarly publications, both for organizations in general and for IHEs more specifically (e.g. Eckel & Kezar, 2003; Kezar, 2005, 2014). The majority of that work deals with the deliberate act of creating, or attempting to create, change at institutions. The situation in spring 2020, however, demonstrated how change was imposed as a result of an overwhelming and unexpected external force.

Central to the frameworks that examine organizational change is the concept of *sensemaking*. Sensemaking is a socio-cognitive process by which individuals and groups of people interpret a situation and their place in it, through ongoing and shared interpretation of information, in order to take action. This construct has been applied to organizational change for many decades, but the work of Karl Weick (1995) has been particularly instrumental for understanding sensemaking in the context of organizational learning (Kezar and Eckel, 2002; Kezar, 2014). Weick (1988) specifically explored sensemaking within crisis situations, and found that

> Crises are characterized by low probability/high consequence events that threaten the most fundamental goals of an organization. Because of their low

probability, these events defy interpretations and impose severe demands on sensemaking. The less adequate the sensemaking process directed at a crisis, the more likely it is that the crisis will get out of control.

The authors of this book were immersed in observation of leadership as COVID-19 emerged, and can now reflect on the "sensemaking processes of scanning, interpretation, and action" (Thomas et al., 1993) taken during the most ambiguous stage of the ongoing pandemic crisis. The efforts by institutional leaders to engage in fruitful sensemaking, and the enactment of plans from that process, are interwoven throughout the descriptions of leadership in the chapters that follow.

As ACE Fellows, we had discussed and dissected the Four Frames theory of Bolman and Deal (2013) from the beginning of our fellowship year. This theoretical framework, described at greater length in Chapter 2, provides a structure for understanding organizational leadership choices through the Structural, Human Resources, Political, and Symbolic frames. The metaphors of these frames are powerful reminders of the complexity of organizational interactions: factory or machine (Structural), family (Human Resource), jungle (Political), temple or theater (Symbolic) (Bolman & Deal, 2013, p. 19). As we observed leaders working to engage, organize, manage, and motivate their teams to respond to the evolving crisis, we noted the ways in which they engaged—or ignored—different leadership frames through the decision-making process. This theoretical grounding underpins many of the observations shared by the different authors of this book.

The following chapters are organized around different functional units in higher education institutions. This organization allows us to describe the ways in which each area was affected by and responded to the early pandemic crisis, although these responses and impacts were not isolated within these individual units. To emphasize the connections across functional areas, we have provided cross-references to other chapters within each chapter. The organization of chapters by institutional area is not intended to instruct a reader about how each of these areas functions in an institution (this book is not a primer for learning about higher education), but only to provide context for our observations about decision-making and organizational response during the early stages of the pandemic within the units acting in response to the unique issues the crisis raised for each.

In Part I, Chapter 2 discusses the role of communications. In the process of initially understanding and dealing with the COVID-19 tsunami, communications were critical and central to mounting a successful response. Chapter 3 addresses the global presence of IHEs and international programs involving both students and faculty. Many weeks before campus operations in the US were affected by the pandemic, global programs officers were deeply engaged in tracking down and finding safe passage for their campus community members who were overseas. Their early activities and insights were invaluable once other campus leaders were also faced with making decisions around pandemic response. The next two chapters address the academic and research missions of higher education, describing the steps that were taken in the early months of the pandemic to buttress these two core areas. The five chapters in Part II address the operational side of campus leadership. The topics addressed in these chapters include, broadly speaking, housing, athletics, information technology, auxiliaries and human resources. Part III explores the functions that are central to moving IHEs forward to the year after the pandemic began. Because we have chosen to limit the focus of this book to roughly the first half of 2020, our discussions of decisions about enrollment, advancement, and financial planning represent what was being done at institutions *at that time*, with the limited knowledge that anyone had about how the virus would progress. Institutional leaders lacked the benefit of hindsight. We conclude this book where we began: with the experiences of emerging leaders from the 2019–2020 ACE Fellows cohort. In Chapter 14, many of our cohort members and a few of our mentors share their reflections on how lessons learned and experiences since early 2020 have shaped their own leadership journeys.

Elements that the reader will see in each chapter include boxed material in which the authors provide additional details for either an Equity Insight or A Close-up Lens on Leadership. These boxes provide a thread throughout the book, linking every chapter to these two foundational themes of this volume. Each chapter also concludes with a section titled Lessons Learned. The concluding chapter then provides a high-level summary of those combined lessons for higher education from this period, framed by the dual foci of the book: leadership and equity.

The story of the impact of COVID-19 on higher education most definitely has not concluded, and probably will be evolving for at least several years. This book is not intended to tell the exhaustive story of how COVID-19 affected or changed higher education over the long run. Instead, it is intended to provide a snapshot of a critical time in decision-making and reflect upon leadership through a period of extreme duress. The pandemic experience has created a clear need to reflect and learn from this crisis for future planning and advancing institutional goals. This book is an effort to engage in and support that process.

NOTE

1 Bryan Alexander, of *Inside Higher Ed*, created a crowd-sourced Google Doc during this period that allowed people to track "Colleges and universities closed/migrating online for COVID-19," which many institutional leaders monitored regularly as closures spread rapidly across the country at an impressive pace (Alexander, 2020).

REFERENCES

Alexander, B. (2020). *Colleges and Universities closed/migrating online for COVID-19.* Google Drive. Retrieved from https://docs.google.com/spreadsheets/d/19wJZekxpewDQmApULkvZRBpBwcnd5gZlZF2SEU2WQD8/htmlview?usp=sharing&lsrp=1%2C+https%3A%2F%2Fwww.insidehighered.com%2Fquicktakes%2F2020%2F03%2F11%2Fcrowdsourced-google-doc-shutdowns

American Association of Community Colleges (AACC). (2019). *Community college enrollment crisis? Historical trends in community college enrollment.* Retrieved from https://www.aacc.nche.edu/wp-content/uploads/2019/08/Crisis-in-Enrollment-2019.pdf

American Council on Education. (n.d.). *ACE Fellows Program. Programs & Services.* Retrieved from https://www.acenet.edu/Programs-Services/Pages/professional-learning/ACE-Fellows-Program.aspx

Barr, D. (2020, May 30). *We Are Not All In The Same Boat. We Are All In The Same Storm. Some Are On Super-Yachts. Some Have Just the One Oar.* Damien Barr blog. Retrieved from https://www.damianbarr.com/latest/https/we-are-not-all-in-the-same-boat

Bolman, L. E. E. G., and Deal, T. E. (2013). *Reframing Organizations: Artistry, Choice, and Leadership.* Jossey-Bass in San Francisco, CA: Jossey-Bass.

Duchek, Stephanie. (2020) "Organizational resilience: A capability-based conceptualization." *Business Research* 13: 215–246.

Eckel, P., and Kezar, A. (2003). *Taking the Reins: Institutional Transformation in Higher Education.* Westport, CT: Greenwood Publishing.

Finley, A. (2021). *Campus Challenges and Strategic Priorities in a Time of Change.* Washington, DC: American Association of Colleges & Universities (AAC&U). Retrieved from https://www.aacu.org/research/campus-challenges-and-strategic-priorities-in-a-time-of-change

Gigliotti, R. A. (2019). *Crisis Leadership in Higher Education: Theory and Practice.* New Brunswick, NJ: Rutgers University Press.

Grawe, N. D. (2017). *Demographics and the Demand for Higher Education.* Baltimore, MA: Johns Hopkins University Press.

Haley, E. D. (2020, June 9). *We Are Not in the Same Boat.* Inside Higher Education. Retrieved from https://www.insidehighered.com/blogs/gradhacker/we-are-not-same-boat

Hottenstein, K., Phillips, R., Rabbitt, K., Summers, S. W., and Weaver, G. (2021, May 24). *Rethinking the Academy: Lessons From Higher Ed's Response to Equity Concerns During COVID-19.* Higher Education Today. Retrieved from https://www.higheredtoday.org/2021/05/24/rethinking-academy-lessons-higher-eds-response-equity-concerns-covid-19

Kezar A. (2005). *Organizational Learning in Higher Education; New Directions for Higher Education*, No. 131. San Francisco, CA: Jossey-Bass.

Kezar, A. (2014). *How Colleges Change: Understanding, Leading, and Enacting Change.* New York, NY: Routledge.

Kezar, A., and Eckel, P. (2002). Examining the institutional transformation process: The importance of sensemaking, inter-related strategies and balance. *Research in Higher Education* 43(3): 295–328.

Kezar, A., Holcombe, E., Vigil, D., and Dizon, J. P. M. (2021). *Shared Equity Leadership: Making Equity Everyone's Work*. Washington, DC: American Council on Education; Los Angeles: University of Southern California, Pullias: Center for Higher Education. Retrieved from https://www.acenet.edu/Documents/Shared-Equity-Leadership-Work.pdf

Kyaw, A. (2021, June 3). *Reports: Two-Year Colleges Hit Hard by Declining Enrollment*. Diverse Issues in Higher Education. Retrieved from https://www.diverseeducation.com/institutions/community-colleges/article/15109370/reports-two-year-colleges-hit-hard-by-declining-enrollment

McGee, J. (2015). *Breakpoint: The Changing Marketplace for Higher Education*. Baltimore, MA: Johns Hopkins University Press.

National Academies of Sciences, Engineering, and Medicine (NASEM). 2021. *The Impact of COVID-19 on the Careers of Women in Academic Sciences, Engineering, and Medicine*. Washington, DC: The National Academies Press. Retrieved from https://doi.org/10.17226/26061

Noonan, P. (2020, April 23). What comes after the coronavirus storm? *Wall Street Journal*. Retrieved from https://www.wsj.com/articles/what-comes-after-the-coronavirus-storm-11587684752

NSCRC. (2020, June 30). *Term Enrollment Estimates Spring 2020: A COVID-19 Supplement*. National Student Clearinghouse Research Center. Retrieved from https://nscresearchcenter.org/wp-content/uploads/CurrentTermEnrollmentReport-Spring2020Supplement.pdf

Pluviose, D. (Executive Editor and Host). (2020, March 27). Three big diversity-related questions resulting from the COVID-19 Crisis [Webcast Episode]. In *Diverse Talk Live!*. Diverse: Issues in Higher Education. Retrieved from https://www.diverseeducation.com/webinars/webinar/15114129/three-big-diversityrelated-questions-resulting-from-the-covid19-crisis

Schwartz, N. (2020). October 29). *How Has the Trump Administration Changed Higher Education?* Higher Ed Dive. Retrieved from https://www.highereddive.com/news/how-has-the-trump-administration-changed-higher-education/588044

Selingo, J. J. (2015). *College (Un)Bound: The Future of Higher Education and What It Means for Students*. Las Vegas, NV: Amazon Publishing.

Simpson Scarborough. (2020, April). *Higher ed and covid-19 national student survey*. Retrieved from https://f.hubspotusercontent30.net/hubfs/4254080/SimpsonScarborough%20National%20Student%20Survey%20.pdf

St. Amour, M. (2020, September 3). *State Politics Influenced College Reopening Plans, Data Show*. Inside Higher Ed. Retrieved from https://www.insidehighered.com/news/2020/09/03/state-politics-influenced-college-reopening-plans-data-show

Thomas, J.B., Clark, S. M., and Gioia, D. A. (1993). Strategic sensemaking and organizational performance: Linkages among scanning, interpretation, action, and outcomes. *Academy of Management Journal* 36: 239–270.

Weick, K. (1988). Enacted sensemaking in crisis situations. *Journal of Management Studies* 25: 305–317.

Weick, K. E. (1995). *Sensemaking in Organizations*. Thousand Oaks, CA: Sage.

Part I
Centrality of the Institutional Mission

Chapter 2
Communications

Elizabeth Orwin, Ann T. S. Taylor, and Jay W. Roberts

Just as crises bring out the best and the worst in people, they also reveal in organizations the strengths and gaps in pre-existing structures and processes. The outbreak of COVID-19 in the spring semester of 2020 required institutions of higher educations (IHEs) to alter operations quickly and to engage in clear communications with their constituents, especially students and employees. This created a high degree of both institutional and personal stress. As such, most prioritized the crafting of effective internal and external communications throughout the early phase of the pandemic. The sudden and all-encompassing nature of the COVID-19 crisis required administrators and communicators to decide quickly what, how, and when to communicate. In the face of broader institutional responses to this evolving crisis, they also needed to figure out how to engage in best practices in crisis communication. These include planning responses before crises occur; listening effectively to constituent concerns; responding with honesty, candor and transparency; collaborating and coordinating with strategic partners and public entities; communicating with compassion, concern and empathy; accepting uncertainty and ambiguity; and incorporating messages of self-efficacy (Seeger, 2006, pp. 232–244).

There is a saying in the emergency responder field that "care not documented is care not given." This pithy phrase suggests that, as important as the actual care itself in a crisis, are the communications used to express it. The American Council on Education (ACE) fellowship provided us the opportunity to observe senior leadership teams in action at several institutions and offered a window into the "dos and don'ts" of communication during a crisis. If communications were an important tool for culture building in normal times, they became critical during the early phases of the COVID-19 pandemic. What follows is a reflection on and analysis of these observations and experiences regarding communication by higher education leaders during the acute phases of the COVID-19 crisis.

The experiences of recent crises of various types, such as Hurricane Katrina, campus violence, and large wildfires, provided Chief Executive Officers (CEOs) and Communications Directors with a rich body of research on how, when, and how often to communicate during the early phases of a crisis. For example, experts on crisis communication point to the need for leaders to understand how the needs of their constituents evolve at various stages of crises. In the earliest phase, people are looking for clear information to help them understand what is going on and how they should respond to stay safe. As a McKinsey & Company report advises, (Mendy, Stewart & Akin, 2021, p.3):

> At a crisis's onset, audience attention is finite; new, disruptive inputs overwhelm a person's ability to process information. High levels of uncertainty, perceived threats, and fear can even lead to "cognitive freezing." Put simply: the more complicated, abstract, or extraneous information is, the more difficult it will be for people to process. Leaders may be inclined to defer to governments and media outlets for clear and simple safety instructions. Don't. Employers often underestimate how much their employees depend on them as trusted sources.

Their recommendations for how to shift approaches to communications are summarized in the McKinsey report according to the stage of a crisis. After the initial stage, employees begin to feel worn down as the crisis progresses. Communications need to provide clarity on plans for moving out of the crisis and positive stories. These communications no longer need to focus solely on instructions but need to begin to include messages about a return to normalcy. Finally, as the crisis is winding down, employees begin feeling ready for change even as they may be dealing with a sense of loss. Communications should begin to look toward the future as well as be supportive of the need to process or grieve the crisis (Mendy, Stewart & Akin, 2021).

Larger institutions generally have a separate office for internal and external communications for advising the CEO on appropriate strategies. However, the creation of a communications strategy that embodied the mission of the institution while communicating care and empathy was one of the most important functions of CEOs in the early months of the pandemic. As students and employees grappled with the implications of such a complex crisis, CEOs worked closely with, and sometimes took on the role of Communications Directors. Their success in this role depended on their understanding of the needs and concerns of the various groups that make up the college community.

APPROACHES TO CRISIS COMMUNICATIONS

Lee Bolman and Terrence Deal's model of leadership (2013) suggests four key frames that a leader or leadership team should consider: Structural, Human

Resource, Political, and Symbolic. The Structural frame involves a focus on the tasks at hand and includes goal setting, strategy, process, and procedures. The Human Resource frame focuses on the people within the organization—their needs, development, and performance. The Political frame, in turn, involves an awareness of conflict and conflict resolution strategies, the interests of multiple stakeholders, and the need to build coalitions. Finally, the Symbolic frame involves making meaning and paying attention to both an individual and a collective sense of purpose, vision, and inspiration. Using Bolman and Deal's model clarifies the ways that a leader or leadership team can use each frame to address specific communications issues or challenges. Each of these frames suggests different strategies and approaches—something we observed across a range of leadership teams throughout the pandemic.

The following sections provide an overview of four areas in which approaches were needed early in the pandemic and have continued to be important throughout the unfolding of shifting and changing communications needs. These include: (1) emergency response protocols and players; (2) new modes of communication; (3) leveraging social media communication outlets; and (4) communicating with Boards.

Emergency Response Protocols and Players

Very early in the pandemic, IHEs drew on the Emergency Operations Center (EOC) model, reflecting the need for quick response times in often-chaotic environments. As the scope of COVID-19's impact upon institutions of higher education began to unfold in early 2020, institutions looked to their emergency response protocols and committees. Institutional pandemic plans and guidance from the Center for Disease Control (CDC) for an anticipated H1N1 flu outbreak in 2009 provided a base from which to begin planning, but these quickly proved insufficient given the magnitude and impact of COVID-19 on all aspects of higher education operations. Existing emergency operating plans (EOPs) offered a starting point for institutions, especially for those institutions that had maintained up-to-date plans and regularly carried out training within their EOC teams (or that had recently had occasion to activate these teams for response to other crises). Even these EOPs, however, required institutions to innovate and adapt to the all-encompassing impact and rapidly changing nature of the worldwide pandemic. For example, while emergency response teams (ERTs) are often centered in institutional public safety offices, as COVID-19 unfolded in spring 2020, this placement proved inadequate. Consequently, CEOs, along with their executive cabinets and/or other senior staff, met on an almost daily basis to make decisions about institutional operations. Both to inform and to alleviate the fears of campus constituents, institutions had to communicate these decisions to operational-level personnel who could then make implementation decisions. They also needed to develop communications plans that reflected the interrelationship between institutional mission, values, and current needs in an environment where understanding of the transmissibility of COVID-19 remained nascent.

Fostering communications among and across teams became an early priority for internal communications. We observed leadership teams focusing on the Structural lens when it came to communications in the first few weeks of the pandemic. One example of this was the issuance of procedures for managers to survey employees on technology needs as IHEs planned to shift to remote work. This choice is not surprising, given the uncertainty about how to conduct campus operations while planning for a shutdown. In the shock of the moment, campus constituents needed clear guidance on what to do and how to do it. Campuses stood up ERTs that went to work developing frequently asked questions (FAQs) pages, memorandums, digests, and other forms of communication that emphasized the "what, where, and how" of emergency response. These modes of communication kept campus constituents informed of events as campuses closed and substantial changes were introduced to once-familiar processes. Moreover, they provided role clarity so that employees and their managers knew who had responsibility for specific procedures.

New Modes of Communication

As the pandemic led to campus shutdowns, the need to make use of new communications media or more extensive use of existing modes became essential. Most leaders employed Zoom "town halls" to disseminate evolving information about COVID-19 and campus operations, to take the pulse of and to reassure campus constituencies, and to answer questions from employees and students. The opportunity for campus members to come together, albeit virtually, and to hear directly from leaders about the emerging situation helped to alleviate the isolation and anxiety experienced by students and employees as a result of uncertainty created by shutdowns of campuses and businesses in March 2020.

Leveraging Social Media Communication Outlets

Acknowledging the importance of social media as the primary purveyor of news to younger audiences, many IHEs also used existing websites and social media, such as Twitter and Facebook, to post the most accurate information available on COVID-19 health and safety measures, as well as evolving federal and state policies. They shared updates regarding emergency student aid, the availability of hardware for remote learning, and sources of academic and mental health counseling. Purdue University, for instance, used YouTube as its preferred social medium, and the number of social media followers grew 42 percent (Braden & Faust, 2020). These and other modes of communication allowed leaders new levels of transparency and connection even as the pandemic forced remote work and learning. In a sense, IHEs learned from a younger generation that had grown up creating online communities on social media.

Experts in higher education social media communications advised IHEs to use a consistent "voice"—be it administrative or more casual—in their social media. Advice included using continuity of voice to amplify confidence in the information shared, so it would more likely be accepted and followed. Additionally, it was advised that a member of the CEO's staff should be assigned the tasks of monitoring the CEO's social media to respond to questions (DeDiemar, 2020).

Another key approach deployed early on was the Symbolic frame. CEOs and senior leadership teams recognized that the pandemic was an unprecedented event in higher education and one that engendered real fear and concern—not just about the health and wellbeing of all members in their communities but also about the long-term consequences to their institutions. Layoffs, furloughs, and a massive shift to remote learning caused many to worry openly about the fate of the residential campus, especially among small, liberal arts schools and already-struggling regional institutions where the loss of revenue from room and board was a significant existential threat.

As faculty and staff worried about how to support students and colleagues who found themselves in vulnerable situations, the need for regular communications became immediately apparent. Communication in this moment required not just technical and tactical problem-solving skills, but also a reminder of institutional missions, commitments, and a sense of community. Most leaders understood that campus shutdowns represented more than an operational issue. These shutdowns raised fundamental questions about what it meant to be an IHE and how to maintain the mission if employees and students could no longer come together as a community physically.

Addressing issues of identity, mission, and purpose transparently represented one of the most important leadership imperatives during the early period of the pandemic. We observed CEOs and senior leadership teams communicating in the Symbolic frame by calling community members back to the identity of the institution, balancing the more Structural communication about process and procedure with the more Symbolic language of vision, inspiration, meaning, and purpose.

While most institutions we observed communicated effectively in this frame, not all did. Some senior leadership teams appeared to get bogged down in the procedural details of emergency response (the Structural frame) and neglected to communicate effectively in other frames. Symbolic communication of this sort often depends on the interpersonal skills of the CEO and other senior leaders, which varied widely. Not all felt comfortable expressing personal vulnerability and acknowledging the uncertainties inherent in the situation. Without sufficient attention to the Symbolic frame, we heard from employees who felt as though leadership failed to "get it" in terms of the challenges employees were feeling on the ground and worried that their institutions were floundering. On the other hand, leaders who employed the Symbolic frame effectively seemed to have their finger on the pulse of the campus community, communicating with emotional intelligence in ways that galvanized campus constituents with reassurance, empathy, and care.

Communicating with Boards

CEOs generally collaborated closely with their boards—often people with important community, political, and business connections—in setting internal and external communication goals. The purpose of a board of trustees or regents at most institutions of higher education is to approve college policies, oversee fiscal health of the institution, and attend to diverse stakeholder interests. In public institutions where they are appointed by government leaders, they represent the interests that political entities have in the institution. They also serve as advocates for the institution and are often involved in fundraising efforts. Their supervisory and public facing roles made it imperative that IHEs kept board members well informed about the impact of COVID-19 on campus operations, even where bylaws limited boards' operational influence.

In turn, CEOs leaned on board members as a source of advice and counsel, as well as for advocacy, particularly when controversial decisions arose such as the decision to shut down campus operations. Institutions implemented numerous strategies to keep their boards informed during the initial phase of the crisis. Regular phone calls by the CEO with the board chair and frequent emails to board members kept them apprised of the rapid decision-making that was happening on campuses. IHEs created two-way communication avenues through frequent teleconferences with executive committees or full boards that allowed for input as IHEs decided when and how to close campuses. Sometimes these steps required waiving or revising institutional bylaws to allow meetings to happen via telephone or video conference, although worries about "Zoom bombing" (Zigterman, 2020) led to elaborate processes to keep the discussions secure. These new processes involved a learning curve for people who were accustomed to more formal, in-person Board meetings, but were necessary for two-way communications.

A Close-Up Lens on Leadership

Communications officers recognized the role that their offices would play in communicating vital information and in shoring up morale among employees and students. One of the most important roles that communications leaders played was to work with the CEO and senior team members to coach them and to ensure that they communicated the right information transparently and effectively. As Jay Galbraith, Vice President for External Relations at Valencia College in Orlando, Florida explained, "Crisis communication is a muscle—not a manual." Galbraith drew on decades of experience in the field of crisis response in the corporate world.

In his role, which included external communications, beginning in early February 2020 he worked closely with the VP of Organizational Development, who had responsibility for internal communications, to research COVID-19 and its possible impact on the college. They continued to work daily during the first months of the pandemic to decide on "the message of the day." This coordination helped to avoid contradictory and confusing messaging that might undermine employee and student confidence. They also engaged the college's CEO, who headed the board of a local hospital system, to learn what little was known about the virus' medical impact. "COVID bubbled up so fast there wasn't time to overthink," he noted. This connection, widely known among employees, helped to create confidence in the leadership's guidance.

By mid-March, the college shut down as COVID-19 spread. This decision required new messaging to students and daily coordination with local school districts, due to the importance of dual credit relationships, and with the local university, the University of Central Florida. In early March, the college hired a national communications expert for advice given the large number of unknowns. He provided advice about what and how to communicate through the developing phases of the pandemic.

The college's previous shutdown experience due to hurricanes proved helpful. "We're over-communicators in normal times," Galbraith explained. To emphasize that they were sharing the most up-to-date advice in a constantly changing landscape, they prefaced their communications with "Based on the best information currently available." Early on, to reinforce a message of care for both students and employees, the CEO and senior team made a public commitment that the college would put the health and safety of the college community first and to ensure that there would be no layoffs.

TOWARD A NOT QUITE "NORMAL"

As the pandemic extended into the summer of 2020 and higher education leaders began turning their attention to a potential fall restart, we observed more communication from the Human Resource and Political frames as institutions and campus leaders moved from immediate emergency response to managing a longer-term crisis. Throughout the late spring and into summer, we observed units headed by provosts and deans collaborating and communicating with faculty committees and working groups to plan the fall restart. From a Political frame, leaders recognized the necessity and desirability of shared governance as a means to capture faculty perspectives and ensure their support for reopening plans. Campuses that communicated effectively using the Political frame seemed to think carefully about how to bring faculty and staff perspectives and concerns into the planning process as well as how to involve them in communicating with their peers and fellow community members. Conversely, institutions that did not pay sufficient attention to the Political frame found themselves struggling at times with push-back on a variety of issues—from the safety of the classroom environment to the policies around remote learning and working, and a host of issues in between.

Finally, the Human Resource frame of communication was perhaps the greatest lightning rod of all throughout the early stages of the pandemic. Because this frame directly addressed issues of employee needs, support, development, and performance, it proved the most challenging for institutional leaders. It was also the one that we observed to have the greatest variation across the higher education sector, due to the context specificity of this frame. For example, by the summer of 2020, it was becoming clear that the pandemic would be a longer-lived phenomenon than anyone could have imagined in spring and would likely stretch into the fall. At some IHEs, CEOs spoke proudly about reopening plans featuring in-person instruction, seemingly to reassure students and the marketplace. While such pronouncements proved popular with students, their families, and political leaders, faculty and staff expressed growing concern that these would come at their expense and safety given renewed COVID-19 surges across the country. Some CEOs went so far as to indicate publicly that faculty and staff who refused to resume work on-campus might find their jobs in jeopardy. Implicitly, these types of remarks sent the message to faculty and staff that although they might be part of the "campus community," their welfare was of lesser concern (Calonge et al., 2021). The nature of the COVID-19 pandemic eroded the distinction between the needs and concerns of students, their families, and campus-based employees—any of whom might experience health impacts from it. Communications that granted legitimacy to the concerns of one group, but not others, increased tensions rather than creating unity of purpose. Given the historical memories of campuses, this may have a long-term impact on efforts to create positive cultures.

Before the start of the academic year in fall 2020, one university released a memo sharply limiting remote work by employees with school-aged children. This was described as tone deaf to the needs and challenges of those who were attempting to work while caring for their children who were still learning remotely. The reaction on campus and nationally was immediate and robust. On this campus, the senior leadership team quickly convened a meeting to address the concerns, apologized, and adjusted the policy. While the policy was perhaps appropriate for campus operations in a Structural sense, it lacked sufficient awareness of the Human Resource lens and, as a result, it resonated poorly with the campus community. This example also serves to demonstrate how the same communication might need to include all four of Bolman and Deal's (2013) frames. Rarely, in our observations, did campus leadership only communicate in one of the four frames. However, just as importantly, when one frame was clearly missing in a communication that called for it, negative community reaction was likely.

Creating Opportunities to Listen

Another dynamic we observed on a variety of campuses: a shift from only communicating *at* constituents toward spending more time listening *to* them. The sheer volume of issues and problems that needed to be addressed in the spring and summer of 2020, and the fact that many campuses were closed, made it extraordinarily challenging for senior leaders to stay connected with campus constituents. Shortly into the pandemic, leaders at all levels began to make wider use of technologies such as Zoom to hold college- and department-wide "town halls" and "happy hours" to maintain connection among co-workers in a remote environment. Many found that virtual meetings could be called and organized more efficiently and allowed for wider participation of stakeholders than had in-person versions of such forums. We observed that senior leaders who moved effectively into this new modality were able to provide multiple opportunities for listening to community members' concerns and feedback, contributing to a sense of trust and relationship that helped institutions move through uncertainty more effectively.

EXTERNAL COMMUNICATIONS

Institutional leaders recognized the need for transparent and timely communications with current students and employees, and they also considered how and what to communicate with external audiences. IHEs needed to carefully consider the communications for groups such as parents of current and prospective students, state and federal agencies, news media, and community organizations. Three areas of communications observed are in the following sections: university websites and statements; public dashboards; and governmental agencies and entities.

University Websites and Statements

Existing communication forums such as institutional websites and newsletters increased in importance as sources of information on emerging policies and processes as conditions evolved. Many IHEs quickly prepared COVID-19 websites to house the latest information, copies of messages to the community, FAQs for parents, students, faculty and staff, and guidelines for safety practices adopted by the campus. Some schools included targeted messages to different audiences. For example, the California Institute of Technology (Caltech, n.d.) organized its messages into three categories: (1) students and parents; (2) faculty, postdocs, and staff; and (3) general announcements. Other schools sent out general community messages to all constituencies.

Public Dashboards

COVID-19 case counts represented one of the most sensitive issues for public dissemination, given growing sensitivities about the pandemic's impact on enrollments. Yet internal and external calls for caseload transparency prompted many IHEs to publish them. Without uniform standards of how to count caseloads, institutions differed significantly in how they counted and reported them. The decision to provide this information often reflected both the local political environment and the budgetary health of the institution. For IHEs in states where there was strong political resistance to long-term shutdowns and/or weak public health and safety regulations, public reporting on caseloads came with political peril. At others, the financial implications of disclosure on future enrollments and budgets weighed on leaders' minds. Yet, in many IHEs, both employees and students demanded transparent data about the institutional situation. Balancing these external and internal risks with the demand for transparency and accountability proved one of the thorniest issues for institutional leaders through the early phases of the pandemic.

Governmental Entities and Agencies

Communication with government agencies, particularly public health departments, became extremely important throughout the pandemic and especially so in the early months as information changed rapidly. IHEs needed to take the initiative to contact public health agencies and to articulate the unique and specific needs of higher education to them. Dependent upon these agencies for guidelines that would allow them to operate safely, IHEs needed to solidify relationships with state and county health officials as a key part of their overall communication strategy. Some schools partnered with other institutions in their region to help articulate the needs of higher education settings to health officials and to explain how those needs varied across sectors. For example, research universities needed to ensure that health officials understood their research activities, as well as classroom needs, in order to establish guidelines for resuming research activities (Legend Labs, 2020).

LESSONS LEARNED

Although many IHEs have highly skilled communications officers, the role of the CEO as Chief Communications Officer proved critical in the early days of the pandemic. As one study of crisis communications explained, "When a crisis hits, people feel betrayed, distressed, uncertain, and scared, and they also feel they have been naive and vulnerable to deceit" (Hutson & Johnson, 2016). Campus stakeholders look to CEOs as the representatives of stability and response for their institutions. CEOs need to respond quickly, transparently, and empathetically to avoid disengagement and hostility. Failure to do so or shifting this responsibility to others undermined confidence in the ability of institutions to survive through the crisis. "The best leaders embrace their responsibilities as truth tellers," even as they reassured their campuses that they were working effectively to address the myriad issues that arose in the pandemic response (Hutson & Johnson, 2016).

In times of confusion, the need for consistent messaging—even when the message is "this is what we know so far"—becomes critical. Although CEOs had important roles to play as the visible leadership voice on campuses, other leaders too engaged in communications. The need to disseminate consistent information is critical to preserving the trust necessary to engage the campus in shifting operations, as was needed early in the pandemic.

The four communication lenses discussed previously (Structural, Symbolic, Human Resource, and Political) provide a framework to ensure that communications addressed the broad range of concerns and relationships of campus and external groups. When these frames were not carefully considered in the crafting of communications, we observed many instances where campus leadership fell into a variety of what we will term "communication traps" that we believe are important to highlight as we consider the broader implications and lessons learned of communicating during crisis.

Trap 1. Ready-Fire-Aim: Communicating Too Quickly

Across a range of institutions, one trap we observed was the tendency for communication to go out too soon. Leaders during crises want to demonstrate that they are "in control" and to reassure the campus community. This can result in a desire to address problems and issues as quickly as possible before they get bigger. This is particularly the case in our instant feedback, social media age. However, rushing a communication out can do real damage and sometimes make things worse. We observed wise leaders putting the hand brakes on cabinet-level discussions where vice presidents argued for "getting out in front" of a given problem. These leaders made sure they had all the information they needed, and the right people in the room assisting with the communication strategy, before sending anything out.

Trap 2. Analysis Paralysis: Communicating Too Slowly

The opposite of "ready-fire-aim" is "analysis paralysis." We observed some institutions and leaders who would occasionally become paralyzed by a need for more data, consultation, or certainty before communicating. Memoranda and college-wide emails would need to be reviewed and approved by multiple departments and offices, which slowed the process and left the campus community without important and timely information. The tendency to become more conservative regarding communication was understandable, especially if a campus leader had received negative feedback about prior attempts. Rarely is a campus-wide communication perfect, and sometimes it is more important to put out information in a timely manner than it is to wait until everyone agrees with every sentence. Letting recipients know that IHEs were sharing the most current information helped maintain transparency balanced with the reality that the information IHEs had was often partial and incomplete. Campuses that seemed to succeed in this strategy issued consistent messages and occasionally corrected information in subsequent communication. Campus constituents seemed to appreciate a consistent flow of information rather than "one and done" immaculate memorandums.

Trap 3. Too Long–Didn't Read: Communicating Too Much Detail

In the world of information technology, there is a shorthand for this particular trap: "TL; DR"–too long, didn't read. We observed some campus communications that were simply too long and too detailed and, as a result, did not effectively connect with the intended audience. Academics and their institutional leaders tend to write essays when short paragraphs will do. Yet the judicious use of bolded subtopics, underlines, and other forms of attention-grabbing typographical methods could help readers manage the sheer volume of information, especially in an age where almost all communications were relayed via email or through a website. Campuses that avoided this trap best included executive summaries with embedded hyperlinks for those who wanted to drill down into the details.

Trap 4. "Who Wrote This!?": Incorrect Audience Analysis

We observed campus communications in a variety of contexts that lacked sufficient audience analysis in advance: messages, for example, that went to both students and employees with the same narrative and tone, or messages sent to faculty and staff without differentiation of their needs. While it is challenging to remember to differentiate communication, especially during a crisis, insufficient audience analysis leaves community members with a sense that senior leaders are not paying attention to *them*. Generic messages miss opportunities to employ the Symbolic and Human Resource lenses. Senior leadership teams that managed this effectively always asked: "who is the intended audience?" for any particular type and mode of communication and consciously responded to the needs and interests of that particular audience as much as possible.

Trap 5. Don't Poke the Bear: Use of Triggering Words and Tone

A final trap we observed was not being aware of specific words, phrases, or tone that had a high likelihood of causing upset within the community. Usually, presidents, cabinet members, and communications specialists are well-versed in ensuring such verbiage and tone is sufficiently scrubbed from communications at the level of the university. However, we observed that during the pandemic, as more offices and groups were communicating, it was not always possible to catch everything that was being sent out on behalf of the institution. For example, areas like public safety, however well-intentioned, might issue emails that landed the wrong way with students. In another example, messages created by a faculty working group that did not understand that they were also communicating with staff members alienated some employees and caused unnecessary polarization. All communications wind up being "owned" by the institution, regardless if they came directly from an office of communications. This can be especially challenging on campuses that do not have a formal and more hierarchical organizational structure when it comes to internal communication. Creating a process for vetting and editing such communications is important for shaping both internal and external perceptions of the institution.

REFERENCES

Bolman, L., & Deal, T. (2013). *Reframing Organizations: Artistry, Choice, and Leadership* (5th ed.). San Francisco, CA: Jossey-Bass.

Braden, E., & Faust, B. (2020, September 24). *Beyond Crisis Communications: Inside Higher* ed. Call to Action: Marketing and Communications in Higher Education. Retrieved from https://www.insidehighered.com/blogs/call-action-marketing-and-communications-higher-education/beyond-crisis-communications

Calonge, D. S., Connor, M., Hultberg, P., & Aguerrebere, P. M. (2021). Were higher education institutions communication strategies well suited for the COVID-19 pandemic? Retrieved from https://files.eric.ed.gov/fulltext/EJ1310339.pdf

Caltech. (n.d.). *Updates.* Coronavirus Information, Resources and Support. Retrieved from https://coronavirus.caltech.edu/updates

DeDiemar, J. (2020, March 18). *Covid-19: Strategies for Communicating and Leading with Certainty.* University Business Magazine. Retrieved from https://universitybusiness.com/strategies-for-communicating-and-leading-with-certainty

Hutson, H., & Johnson, M. (2016). *Navigating an Organizational Crisis: When Leadership Matters Most.* Santa Barbara, CA: Praeger.

Legend Labs. (2020, March 9). *COVID-19: Key Considerations for University Communications and Marketing Teams.* E&I Cooperative Services. Retrieved from https://www.eandi.org/media-room/ei-blog/COVID-19-key-considerations-university-communications-marketing-teams/

Mendy, A., Stewart, M. L., & VanAkin, K. (2021, October 8). *A Leader's Guide: Communicating with Teams, Stakeholders, and Communities During COVID-19.* McKinsey & Company. Retrieved from https://www.mckinsey.com/business-functions/people-and-organizational-performance/our-insights/a-leaders-guide-communicating-with-teams-stakeholders-and-communities-during-covid-19

Seeger, M. W. (2006). Best practices in crisis communication: An expert panel process. *Journal of Applied Communication Research, 34*(3), 232–244. DOI:10.1080/00909880600769944

Zigterman, B. (2020, April 3). *Coronavirus Response: UI, Others Taking Measures to Curtail Zoom-Bombing.* The News-Gazette. Retrieved from https://www.news-gazette.com/coronavirus/coronavirus-response-ui--taking-measures-to-curtail-zoom-bombing/article_114f3678-ad18-5905-b058-a233d8bba50b.html

Chapter 3

Global Mobility and International Programs

Sharon Nagy

The rapid spread of the virus beyond Asia, and particularly its initial impact on Italy and subsequently the rest of Europe, tested institutional preparedness as campuses scrambled to bring students, faculty, and staff back to the US from programs in affected areas. This recall accelerated rapidly, in some cases within a week or two, to bringing home campus members from all overseas locations. The mass recall and closure of education abroad programs proved logistically challenging and costly for institutions. For returning students, this shut down disrupted plans, caused logistical challenges, and created anxiety about potential disruption in their progress to degree. International students in the US found themselves also adversely impacted as campuses and borders closed. The extent of the challenges of responding to the pandemic was greater than most US institutes of higher education (IHEs) had faced previously due to the global nature of the emergency. Extrapolating from previous experiences, reaching across campus and externally to their professional associations, international education professionals effectively repatriated thousands of students and made program adjustments in response to severe disruptions to global mobility and the contraction of global networks.

Prior to COVID-19, many IHEs viewed the expansion of international programming and enrollments as a strategic cornerstone. Yet, as higher education leaders look ahead to the potential for global impacts from climate change, new diseases, and other yet to be identified crises, the lessons from the COVID-19 pandemic make clear the need to recognize potential hazards on a new scale and the consequent need for more extensive and comprehensive contingency planning.

THE SETTING: INTERNATIONALIZATION AND US HIGHER EDUCATION

IHEs have long served as critical nodes of global diversity and engagement in communities throughout the US. From area studies and world language programs to academic exchange and global research collaborations, from the recruitment of international students and study abroad programs to economic development initiatives, IHEs have engaged globally for many decades. These initiatives are supported by the broadly agreed-upon understanding that knowledge of, and competence engaging with, colleagues in other cultures and countries serves the national interest and institutional missions to facilitate the academic and personal growth of our students and faculty and the cultural competence of organizations operating internationally. Those across the political spectrum, whether hawk or dove, isolationist or globalist, generally concur that understanding the world is of value. During the final decades of the 20th century, both international travel and international collaboration without travel became more accessible, contributing to the growth of discipline-spanning, resilient, and well-entrenched networks with neighbors, both near and far. By 2020, a new paradigm of what the American Council on Education terms *comprehensive internationalization* (ACE, n.d.), which moves beyond student exchange and mobility to the engagement of all campus stakeholders into global networks, had become a standard goal across US higher education. For many IHEs, international offerings served as a key tool for recruiting and brand differentiation.

The reality for most institutions, however—and few international education professionals would argue otherwise—is that mobility has remained the key goal for educational efforts in internationalization. Prior to the 2020 pandemic, the number of students moving in and out of the US served as the primary measure of internationalization efforts and as a benchmark for institutional comparisons. The COVID-19 pandemic, however, demonstrated just how vulnerable IHEs dependent on global mobility can be to events or crises that shut down travel and constrict global networks.

COVID-19 OUTBREAK IN CHINA: HOW PREPARED WERE WE?

As the volume of global mobility increased prior to the pandemic, the challenges of keeping participants and programs safe intensified. Systems for tracking and communicating with students in real time as threats emerge, mandatory international health insurance with repatriation coverage, and contracts with emergency response providers and risk analyst services have become *de rigueur* among institutions with broad global program portfolios. The employment of in-house international health, safety and risk specialists have become more common, as has the training of on-site providers and staff to care for students, in compliance with US regulations to which they may or may not be bound in the host country. An entire industry of insurance, risk assessment, and emergency response services has grown out of this need: third-party "program providers" have benefited from the need for location-specific resources to provide the holistic care and education of students while abroad, as well as detailed program logistics and risk mitigation.

At the initial reports of a COVID-19 outbreak in China and neighboring countries, emergency response and risk management teams across higher education campuses activated emergency response protocols developed through previous experience with public health outbreaks (e.g., SARS in 2003, Bird Flu in 2005, Ebola in 2014), natural disasters, political unrest, or terrorist threats. Teams leaned on advice from national associations, such as the Association of International Educators (NAFSA), the Association of International Education Administrators, and the Forum for Education Abroad, which regularly offer consulting and workshops on risk mitigation and crisis management. In response to events such as the COVID-19 outbreak, these organizations serve as important resources for practitioners and provide information and advice as institutions respond to an unfolding crisis.

While responses to crises are neither easy nor desirable, most IHEs were well prepared to address isolated risks by canceling, postponing, or relocating operations and programs from one location or country. Institutions with operations, programs and/or personnel in China acted quickly to postpone the start dates of their spring 2020 semester programs or to relocate students to other locations. The Wuhan lockdown and entry restrictions imposed by the US on non-US citizens arriving from China prevented Chinese students, both current and new, from arriving to conduct their studies on US campuses. Fortunately, the number of Chinese students planning to start their studies in the US in January is always significantly lower than for August or September start dates, and many of those students had been able to depart for the US prior to the US closing its borders to certain travelers from China on January 2, 2020. The Institute of International Education (IIE) reported that 87 of the 234 institutions included in their March 2020 survey indicated that 831 Chinese students enrolled at their institutions were impacted by the travel restrictions. This number accounted for fewer than 0.4% of the Chinese students enrolled at those same institutions for this period (Institute of International Education, 2020a). Though this early number was modest, IHEs had not yet realized the longer-term implications that pandemic-related travel restrictions might have, not only for Chinese students, but also for students from other countries.

The challenge of returning personnel from China extended beyond students and study abroad programs. US faculty and staff were also present in China, visiting family for the Lunar New Year, conducting research, teaching, or processing immigration requirements at US consulates. The travel restrictions in the early pandemic prevented all but those with US citizenship or permanent residency from reentering the US. Through February, few really thought this would be much more than a regional and temporary disruption, however. The complex legal and logistical decisions about having employees performing duties and being compensated while abroad could be postponed until this crisis "passed."

By March, however, it became clear that these issues would become more pressing with time, especially once additional travelers from Europe, Ireland, the UK, Canada, Mexico and Brazil faced restrictions on entering the US. In rapid succession, US consulates closed, countries around the world imposed their own travel restrictions, and commercial travel was substantially reduced. Students and colleagues unable to return from China were rapidly outnumbered by the many others in similar situations around the world. Concerns about students, faculty, visitors, and staff unable to arrive for the start of fall term spread across campuses by late spring 2020.

THE SPREAD OF COVID-19 INTO EUROPE AND THE RUSH TO SAFETY

By late February, attention turned to Italy as officials there worked to contain the spread of the virus by restricting travel to and from the communities where COVID-19 cases were on the rise. This expanding crisis brought senior international officers, education abroad personnel, and risk management offices back to the table at IHEs. US study abroad students have long favored Italy, ranking it consistently among the top three destinations for study abroad enrollment (NAFSA, 2021). The sheer number of students needing to return presented a challenge for many institutions. With eyes now on Italy, IHEs reached out to students and to their families with alerts and invitations to return to campus. Many institutions anticipated, and met with, resistance to their requests to return to the US. With the spring semester close to half-way completed, students initially felt safe and supported by their hosts and did not assess the risk as being as severe as their home institutions indicated. In-country providers and staff also took a "wait-and-see" attitude, speculating that the high numbers of reported cases were the result of extensive testing and that the virus would be contained. However, as the situation in Italy worsened, and cases in both Spain and France started to rise, recommendations to return became urgent and quickly began to shift to "mandatory recalls" by mid-March. Mandatory recalls have been rare in education abroad and have usually been associated with elevated Department of State Travel Advisories, which had not yet been issued at that point in the outbreak.

At many institutions, the rapid-fire decisions and messaging in late February and early March seemed like watching a tennis match on fast-forward. The process at Clemson University provides an example of the rapidity of the recall process playing out at colleges and universities across the US. Clemson's Provost and Associate Provost for Global Engagement sent a message on February 27 to the university's 94 students scattered across Italy in 16 different programs to communicate that the university would support students' choice to return. The next day, as the education abroad office began fielding questions from parents, students, and staff at the program sites, the Centers for Disease Control (CDC) issued a level 3 travel alert for Italy. Within 24 hours of Clemson's first message, the university sent a second message to the same students and their families *requesting* that they prepare to return to the US within seven days. As that message was going out, the university began editing the original "optional" version to send to their students throughout the rest of Europe. On March 2, while executive leadership reviewed this letter, the CDC issued a recommendation to colleges and universities "to consider canceling exchange programs" (ACE, 2020). Clemson University's executive leadership team then took the decision not to offer the "option" to return. Instead, they issued a mandatory recall to 386 students in 26 countries with a one-week deadline for return. The university set up a call center to provide support as students arranged, or resisted, their return to the US.

As the virus spread, European officials began closing schools and universities, and the CDC issued level 3 travel alerts for all of Europe. On March 11, less than two weeks after Clemson's initial letter to its students in Italy, the CDC and the World Health Organization (WHO) declared COVID-19 a "pandemic." The White House issued a restriction on entry to the US for travelers who had been in the Schengen countries in the past 14 days, adding Ireland and the UK to the ban a few days later. On March 19, the US Department of State issued a Global Level 4 Travel Advisory, the highest-level alert advising US citizens to avoid all non-essential travel (Overseas Security Advisory Council, 2020). Such travel advisories are usually specific to a country or region; March 2020 marked the first time a Level 4 Global Advisory had ever been issued admonishing all US citizens abroad to return or be prepared to shelter in place indefinitely. By that point, IHEs across the US were bringing their students back from abroad.

The logic of crisis management is first and foremost to locate your people and get them to safety. In the instance of the COVID-19 pandemic, IHEs widely interpreted this logic as "bring them home." Not everyone agreed, however, with this interpretation during a global health crisis or with the decision to recall students. After all, the virus was already spreading in the US, and travel put students at increased risk of exposure. Some stakeholders—parents, students and on-site providers—debated whether students should shelter in place instead of returning to the US. With no guarantees that the host institutions would remain open, nor any clear forecast if conditions in the host communities would deteriorate or improve, many US institutions assumed that most students would prefer to be among their US-based support network, with access to familiar healthcare and living in a context that they were comfortable navigating. Once closures abroad became a reality, US institutions across the board worked to bring students back to their home communities. IHEs granted few exceptions to remain and then generally only for students with dual citizenship and/or family in the host country or for graduate students in dual degree programs or year-long research placements. Some students insisted on exercising their choice to remain; however, the number of students opting to stay dwindled as the conditions worsened across the globe and universities world-wide shifted to online instruction (Institute of International Education, 2020b). Students who had resisted the earlier requests to return were now sometimes caught behind travel restrictions or canceled flights, resulting in much more challenging logistics than would have been the case earlier.

Bringing students back quickly before borders closed proved difficult. As noted above, IHEs had experience responding to *isolated* emergencies abroad—such as the Tohuko earthquake and tsunami in Japan in 2011, the back-to-back hurricanes Maria and Irma in the Caribbean in 2017, or events of political unrest such as those in Hong Kong beginning in 2019 or in Haiti in 2018. Few education abroad professionals could even have imagined preparing for a crisis that would shut down the entire portfolio of international education programs at the same time. These administrators prided themselves on building, not on dismantling, programs. Furthermore, as institutions learned, many of the constituent units across campus impacted by this recall had limited knowledge of education abroad operations and found themselves unprepared to accommodate returning students.

OPERATIONALIZING THE RECALL: COMPLICATIONS AND CONSIDERATIONS

The intensity of the recall revealed both strengths and weaknesses in IHE organizational infrastructure and protocols. Returning students back to the US required considerable coordination and finesse in the realms of decision-making, communication, logistics, finances, academic continuity, and student support. Once in motion in early to mid-March, the recall created myriad issues and tasks requiring collaboration across the institution, from academic units to student affairs and housing, from financial aid and the bursar to media relations. As such, it foreshadowed the level of campus-wide coordination in support of students, their families, and the staff that IHEs would need later to move constituents through the subsequent campus closures, transition to online instruction, and plan for recovery and reopening.

Making and Communicating Decisions

The rapid pace of necessary decisions in this recall precluded fully working out the related details in advance. Frontline staff, who worked directly with students studying abroad, and academic advisors found themselves unprepared to respond do student and parent questions or arguments, and they could not always reach decision-makers for further details. Stateside decisions, in some instances, conflicted with those of host institutions, increasing confusion. For example, US institutions may have instructed students to inquire with their professors abroad about the possibility of completing courses online when the host institution had already decided that was not a possibility. Exacerbating this confusion, sometimes personnel at the host institutions heard about home institution decisions from students rather than from the international office or university administration, as occasionally occurred when IHEs prioritized quick communication to students ahead of fully consulting in-country partners. Questions about refunds, assurances of academic continuity, and consequences for non-compliance with institutional recalls presented some of the thorniest challenges as these advisors guided students' return. Often, students began to request refunds before those responsible for the financial decisions could finalize guidance. Given the scope and volume of the recalls, many in international programs offices found themselves educating colleagues across their campuses about the intricacies of education abroad operations and working through issues with other units that had previously been deemed the sole purview of one office. As such, the pandemic experience raised awareness of international education issues and forced cross-unit coordination and collaboration.

Reentry: Advising, Mental Health, Logistics and Academic Continuity

The COVID-19 education abroad recall proved sudden, disruptive, and frustrating for students. For students and their families, education abroad represents a major investment of time, planning, and money, and it is often the culmination of years of dreams about traveling to unknown countries. When recalled, students understandably expressed varied responses from acquiescence to defiance, from anger to fear, but also, and overwhelmingly, disappointment and grief. In the first few days of the recall, students and their families needed empathy and information. Returning students, as well as international students remaining on campuses, needed support as their anxiety increased from watching the pandemic spread in their home and host countries. It became necessary to coordinate with campus counseling units and to activate care networks to provide this type of support, as well as to train advising staff working with students through the relocations and transitions.

Institutions varied in their approach to arranging and refunding, or not, the cost of travel back to the country of origin. Study abroad advisors and in-country staff generally talked students through the best options and strategies for return travel. Some international offices work closely with specific travel agencies, particularly those that cater to the education abroad market, and were able to arrange to have the university directly billed for rebooking fees. If students had traveled on a group flight, the international office could more easily work directly with the airline or travel agent to book return flights. These group flights or approved student travel services allowed for a much smoother rebooking process during the recall than did individual arrangements. A small number of very large programs even chartered flights for their students' return (Redden, 2020). Few universities had enough students in single locations to make this option viable, but some partnered with other institutions to make such a solution possible, a collaborative response that may serve as a model in the future for such cases.

The timing of the recall coincided with campus closures and the shift to online instruction. Returning students were, like their stateside classmates, generally expected to return to their homes rather than to campus. This practice limited the number of students needing to be accommodated on campus. However, as addressed in Chapter 6 on Student Services, campuses still faced a need to provide housing to those students most in need due to insufficient social support, limited financial resources, or housing insecurities. Given the diversity of students and the complexity of their lives, IHEs could not assume that with the closure of campus residences that all students had a safe place to live.

SUMMER, FALL AND CONTINUED PROGRAM CANCELLATIONS

As students returned from abroad, IHEs already had study abroad programs planned for spring break, spring quarter, and summer 2020. Faculty had been preparing to teach students in the field, in-country interlocutors were ready to receive them, and courses were already scheduled on both college and student records, for which fees had been collected and payments made. Dismantling these programs represented a complex operation. The comprehensive transitions to online instruction being made across US campuses affected students' ability to progress as planned in their degree programs. A number of educational abroad providers—suddenly faced with empty programs and potentially no work for their staff and faculty usually devoted to teaching US students in the summer—quickly began to offer online options. These included online courses taught by their faculty to students at home in the US, virtual internships, and other creative remote international experiences, though these were not always as attractive to students as would have been the option to travel abroad.

Institutions that made early decisions to cancel summer programs met with resistance from those faculty, providers, and students whose preference was to hold on in the hope that the virus would abate and that their plans could continue. By June 2020, most universities had announced the cancellation of fall 2020 education abroad programs. The continued travel restrictions, closure of passport offices and consulates, uncertainty around local conditions, and ethical obligations to avoid spreading the virus to host communities tempered the resistance experienced in reaction to summer cancellations. Institutions that regularly send large numbers of students abroad now faced challenges in absorbing these students into on-campus housing and in adding additional course sections to replace courses students would have taken abroad. To support overseas partners, some institutions arranged for students to take online courses with the same instructors they would have had while studying internationally. The institutions most challenged by these cancellations were those with overseas operations owned and/or operated by the home campus. As with the on-site providers mentioned above, some universities engaged the faculty from their satellite campuses to teach online. Others used their overseas facilities to accommodate international students unable to travel to the US.

For those IHEs whose study abroad experiences depend upon third-party programs, host institutions, and exchange partners, the primary institutional investment is in the relationships with such partners rather than in physical and organizational infrastructure. In the early pandemic, US institutions grappled with questions regarding their collective responsibility to these partners and relationships. As higher education struggled with the financial impact and other hurdles of recovering from the pandemic, there was an immediate impetus to retract global networks and to protect core operations. However, when education abroad rebounds (as it has after other global health crises), these global networks and partnerships would be needed again. Including partners wherever possible in recovery efforts would accelerate and strengthen recovery, programs, and relationships. Engaging existing partners in virtual programming and exchange began to emerge as a tool for achieving this desired outcome.

The historical resilience of education abroad provided reason for optimism. Education abroad has tended to recover relatively quickly from disruptions due to health crises (Institute of International Education, 2020c). This time around, the global nature of the event, its extended duration, and the resulting economic recession seemed likely to slow the rebound. Consequently, IHEs needed to redesign systems carefully and intentionally to prepare for any future disruptions before resuming full operations. The experience of responding to the pandemic brought changes in the nature of travel, behaviors, and organizational infrastructure and policy. By the summer of 2020, education abroad professionals and their associations had already begun rethinking aspects of programs such as classroom size, frequency of in-country travel, modes of transportation, housing and accommodations, student conduct and behavior, as well as a scaling up of the use of virtual exchange and collaborative online international learning practices.

BEYOND STUDENT MOBILITY: FACULTY AND STAFF TRAVEL

Of course, it is not only students who travel abroad. Faculty and staff do, as well, for research, conferences, consulting, site visits, and many other reasons both professional and personal. The growing number and improved quality of online enrollment management and communication platforms custom-designed for education abroad made tracking students in study abroad programs easier, but it can be more challenging for IHEs to locate student volunteers and mission trips organized outside of the institution's oversight, as well as graduate students. The most challenging by far, however, is tracking travel by faculty and staff.

The mechanisms that IHEs use to track faculty travel include the use of a designated travel vendor and/or travel authorization processes linked to the associated expenditures of travel. Some institutions have taken this a step further and link this form to an automated travel registry. Auburn University, for example, had worked to link the procurement request to Banner (a business process management software specific to higher education that maintains student, faculty, course, alumni, financial, and personnel data), enabling a record of travel. Still, in 2020 few institutions possessed a robust system for tracking employee overseas travel in real time. Challenges to tracking faculty and staff travel include varying organizational structures, institutional culture, policies regarding activities of faculty when not under contract, practices regarding externally funded activities, budget controls, and procurement policies.

While faculty face the same risks as students when traveling, institutions generally afford a higher level of discretion and independence to these employees. As noted in Chapter 10 on Human Resources, many institutions set employee travel or reentry restrictions in March 2020, but not all formally dictated if and where faculty and staff could travel. Many institutions used a case-by-case approach to allowing faculty travel, considering the reason for deployment abroad, and whether the travel could be pursued without disruption or high risk to the employee or the community. Many employees faced the same international travel bans and other obstacles students experienced. For those employees who found their stays abroad extended, whether these "trapped" employees could perform their work and receive compensation while abroad became a question of both practicality and compliance. Some IHEs already had an "employer of record" arrangement for overseas employment. For those without, settling these questions required input from the institution's comptroller, institutional legal counsel, human resources, export control office, international services, tax compliance officer, and in many cases, external legal counsel.

Without a reliable record of employee travel, institutions found themselves scrambling to identify which members of their faculty and staff had traveled abroad. For example, the senior international officer at a large research institution described trying to obtain a list of who was on sabbatical leave during spring 2020 only to learn that no comprehensive list existed in any of the offices for sponsored programs, human resources, or faculty affairs. The incomplete lists that were available did not indicate the location where the faculty members were conducting their sabbatical leaves, whether domestic or international. Aware at the start of the pandemic that a few Fulbright scholars were abroad, he then learned of two more such scholars once Fulbright canceled programs and asked their fellows to return to the US. This administrator was able to piece together what he thought was a relatively accurate list from those provided by the academic colleges in his institution, the provost's office, and human resources. However, by June, with travel into the US becoming more difficult, he received inquiries from yet additional faculty members abroad who had not been on any of these lists. As his institution went fully online for spring and summer, a handful of other faculty members chose to travel and teach from abroad; few faculty members felt it necessary to inform the institution of this relocation. Such cases embody the cultural dynamics on many campuses when faculty do not perceive themselves as institutional employees, but rather as allied scholars and teachers, independent in their decisions and destinations. While this positionality makes sense within the normal functioning of IHEs, it complicated the ability of these institutions to then provide support to faculty abroad when travel itself became dangerous.

Nationally, there simply was no central clearinghouse to track employee travel or faculty mobility in the way that student mobility is tracked by IIE's *Open Doors* report (2020d). Aware of this gap in data collection, one firm, Terra Dotta, a widely used enrollment management platform for education abroad, began to actively market a faculty registry 'add-on' to their existing clients in April 2020. As the pandemic carried on into summer, a number of IHEs implemented new procedures for faculty travel registration requirements, including, in some cases, a requirement that all employee travel be purchased through designated vendors.

IMPACT ON INTERNATIONAL STUDENTS IN THE US

Even as institutions sought to identify employees overseas, they worked to care for international students in the US who provide considerable cultural, social, and economic benefit to their host campuses and communities. As addressed in Chapter 5 on Research Programs, graduate students among this group often serve to support the teaching and research activities of their institutions as teaching and research assistants. Any loss of this population would have a significant impact on the finances and academic activities of IHEs in the US.

International students faced the same challenges as their US counterparts as colleges and universities closed and pivoted to online instruction, yet the pandemic affected them in ways that US students did not experience, despite being on the same campuses. At institutions that closed campus housing, most international students scrambled to find places to live. They found themselves ineligible to apply for CARES Act Emergency Financial Aid Grants in spring 2020 (see Chapter 13 for a discussion of the CARES Act) even as those who were required to leave their campus residences faced unanticipated housing expenses.

Additionally, international students experienced uncertainty about whether their visa status would allow them to enroll in fully online programs or to extend their program duration in the US to complete their studies (Fischer, 2020). Accepted students not yet in the US found themselves unable to obtain the necessary documents and visa stamps to enter the US as consulate offices closed world-wide.

Students and scholars enter the US under a variety of visa programs. The two most common visa programs for students are the F1 student visa program and the J1 exchange visitor program, managed by the US Customs and Immigration Services and the Department of State, respectively. Each of these programs has unique requirements, yet the pandemic context made some of these requirements difficult to meet, and the timing of the governmental agencies' responses to the challenges caused much anxiety for students and their host institutions. Students on an F1 visa, for example, had always been limited in the number of online courses they could take. With the pivot to online learning in March, the US Student Exchange Visitor Program (SEVP) acted quickly to relax this restriction, allowing institutions to seek permission to offer full-time online instruction to international students as they completed the semester. This response solved the problem for the spring term, but its limitations created a lingering anxiety about subsequent terms. J1 exchange visitors, on the other hand, are granted status in the US for defined durations. When foreign students faced restrictions on traveling home, the DOS initially granted 90-day extensions. As with other decisions taken in the first months of the pandemic, federal agencies made these determinations as needed, but often a bit late for the comfort of students, their supervisors, and hosts.

As campuses closed and classes moved online, with the option to complete coursework from anywhere, international students made rapid decisions about whether to remain in the US or to return to their home countries. Some campuses encouraged and even supported these students to return home, assisting with travel arrangements and expenses. This decision to "ride out" the pandemic in their home country held uncertainty regarding whether and when a return to the US would be feasible. Other institutions, therefore, worked to help these students remain in the US for fear that they would be unable to return later, which would result in enrollment declines. The decision to leave proved more likely for undergraduate students residing in on-campus housing at smaller institutions. IIE found in its survey of IHEs in April-May, 2020, that 92% of international students remained in the US, either on- or off-campus. Only three of the 441 institutions responding to the IIE survey in April-May, 2020, reported that 100% of their international students left. All three of these respondents were small institutions with under 5000 total enrollments. Institutions with over 20,000 students reported departure rates between 0% and 20% (Institute of International Education, 2020b). With greater resources, larger institutions could offer housing and other support services to their international students, including additional visa guidance, communications on health and well-being, emergency funding, statements of support, and virtual events for students.

Equity Insights

The rapid decisions and actions required by the unexpected and urgent nature of the COVID-19 pandemic ran the risk of creating DEI challenges on campuses by "othering" certain faculty, staff, and students. International students and employees who may not have had the resources to relocate were separated from their families, and most were under only temporary legal status. In the US, institutional rhetoric extolling the value that global diversity brings to US campuses is often at odds with anti-immigration, xenophobic, and populist rhetoric in the country, particularly during the period leading up to the 2020 presidential election. International students and faculty navigate these contradictions and vulnerabilities throughout their time in the US. Although the pandemic exacerbated these conditions for all international students and faculty, people of Asian descent initially faced the brunt of this, whether they were US citizens or not.

As the virus first emerged in China, Chinese students and Chinese student organizations coordinated the humanitarian response, finding ways to send masks, surgical gloves, and other needed resources to China. As the virus spread to the US, Asian students began reporting increased instances of bias, hate speech, and harassment. The virus's origin in China, along with the repeated reference to COVID-19 by President Trump and others as the "Chinese Virus," the "Wuhan Flu," or even "the Kung Flu," set in motion a wave of fear and rumor that scapegoated peoples of Asian descent for the pandemic. IHEs attempted to correct this misconception, with campus leaders issuing messages in support of Asian students and denouncing any instances of racism (Williams, 2020). Others offered Asian and Asian American students resources and suggestions for responding to racist harassment (Harvard University, 2020).

Some of the most effective and moving responses to the xenophobia and hate speech against Asians came from student organizations, such as the film *Your Bias Hurts Me* made by students in the Graduate School of Education at the University of Buffalo. Conceived and organized by Chinese graduate students, the project features over 100 members of the University of Buffalo community speaking out against racism toward Asian and Asian American people. The group produced two versions of the film, one in English and one in Mandarin (Robinson, 2021).

SHARON NAGY

CLOSED BORDERS, TRAVEL BANS AND SUSPENDED VISA PROGRAMS

In spring 2020, borders began closing around the world like shutters in the face of a storm. The nature of international programs and enrollments gave federal agencies an outsized influence on IHEs' institutional policies during the pandemic. Additional measures taken by the federal government, or rumored to be forthcoming through this period, created further anxiety and obstacles to international enrollments in spring 2020. Professional organizations serving IHEs and advocating on their behalf, such as NAFSA and the American Immigration Lawyers Association (AILA) carefully tracked the presidential proclamations and assisted IHEs in interpreting the compliance implications. On April 22, 2020, the White House issued a 60-day suspension on the processing of Permanent Residency applications (also known as "Green Cards"). May 22 brought a new executive order restricting the granting of F1 visas for graduate students to Chinese citizens with past associations with specific institutions in China. A month later, the April 22 suspension was extended until December 31 and additional non-immigrant visas were added to the list of suspended processes (AILA 2020). The suspension of H1B visa processing created particular concern for IHEs because they are used to recruit top talent from around the world into faculty, research, and other positions. Rumors of potential changes to the post-graduation Optional Practical Training (OPT) benefit afforded to students on F1 visas intensified as unemployment rose in the US, with the Trump administration communicating a connection between preserving the right to work for US citizens and the visa suspensions. The OPT benefit allows recent graduates who secure employment in their field of study to extend their F1 student visa for 1–3 years depending on discipline. The IHE hosting the student maintains the student visa record for the duration of their OPT.

Clemson University provides an example of the international enrollment implications and risks institutions faced in this period. Most accounts would deem Clemson to be rather moderate in terms of international enrollments, but, in many ways, it represented national trends. Unlike many institutions that rely heavily on the tuition and fee revenue from a substantial population of international undergraduates, Clemson's international undergraduate population is small—composed mostly of athletes and short-term exchange students. The focus of Clemson's international recruitment is in its graduate programs, with a graduate student population that aligns with the national average of 30% international and 70% domestic. The countries represented at Clemson likewise match typical international enrollments across the US, with China and India each accounting for close to a third of the international population and the remaining third hailing from more than 90 countries. In 2020, Clemson enrolled approximately 1700 international graduate students, 680 of whom were employed by the university as teaching or research assistants. There were another 740 recent graduates from the university working across the US under the OPT benefit. While the number of J1 visitors—visiting scholars, researchers, instructors, etc.—fluctuated from month to month, the institution averaged between 200–300 at any one time and processed an average of 50 H1B visas for faculty, post-docs and research scholars yearly.

Fortunately for Clemson enrollments, only 54 of its continuing international students left during the spring of 2020. The chances of any new international students arriving from abroad for the following term, however, were grim. The requests for visa documentation from newly accepted students were much lower than in previous years. At the end of June 2020, only 294 of the 600+ international students accepted at Clemson had requested visa documents, and of those only 17 had obtained visas compared to 398 documents issued and 236 visas obtained at the same point in the previous year.

Throughout summer 2020, Clemson's Graduate School and departments expressed concern not only regarding overall enrollments, but also over how to support faculty in teaching and grading the large lecture classes for the fall or meeting research requirements with the anticipated shortage of international teaching and research assistants. As the US changed its restrictions and policies, Clemson, like many US institutions, explored new opportunities to enroll international students in online courses and to compensate them for teaching and research service given labor, licensing, and taxation risks of compensating them for service rendered outside of the US. In addition, the suspension of H1B visas prevented newly hired international faculty from arriving for the new academic year. Although it would take time to understand the long-term impact of these disruptions, the implications for institutional finances and structures were concerning (see Chapter 13 for a detailed discussion of budget impacts and planning). Institutions with far larger international enrollments likewise worked to sort out these same issues and risks, with potentially a much greater impact on institutional revenues and functioning.

LESSONS LEARNED

The impacts of an unprecedented pandemic reach far and wide, and given its global scope, particularly affect international programs at IHEs. The following sections summarize leadership lessons garnered from responding to challenges that emerged quickly beginning from the onset of the COVID-19 pandemic. Seven areas are discussed, ranging from support services to the changing nature of international partnerships.

Leadership and Responsibility for Internationalization

The pandemic revealed challenges to the organizational structure and/or units responsible for internationalization on US campuses – not only in terms of the size and organization of the office/staff directly supporting internationalization efforts, but also regarding the level of access the leadership in those units have to the executive level in a crisis. For example, does the Senior International Officer report to the Provost, the Vice President of Student Affairs, or the President? Is their role advisory, discretionary, or functional? What is the relationship between this office and the academic units? Who makes final decisions about risk management? Who is consulted and who implements?

Integration and Education of Internationalization Activities and Support Services

The pandemic response required collaboration among areas of campus that extended far beyond the offices charged with managing internationalization. With only infrequent experience with collaboration, staff members often required some quick cross training, but the pandemic also revealed the possibility of and need for more intentional and sustained collaboration. Personnel need to be introduced to or trained in tasks that intersect with other areas, and processes previously "owned" by multiple offices/units require streamlining and more effective integration.

Reconsideration of Roles and Responsibilities to Overseas Partners

IHEs engaging the services of third-party providers, partner institutions, or others abroad need to rethink and renegotiate the shared responsibilities for students' well-being and program viability. The purely transactional or "outsourcing" nature of many of these relationships made them vulnerable to misunderstandings and miscommunications during the pandemic response. How can we better communicate the shared and reciprocal needs? How can we support and protect the vulnerabilities of our partners?

Value of Professional Organizations

International education professionals often work in contexts where they are among the few on campus with expertise in internationalization. In smaller IHEs, a single person may have sole responsibility for the operation. During the initial months of the COVID-19 pandemic, professional organizations such as NAFSA and AIEA, and professionalized third-party providers offered webinars, town halls, advocacy templates, immigration advice, and more to those operating in isolation on their campuses. This support became crucial through the early pandemic; institutions should ensure that resources are available to their internationalization offices to access these networks and avail themselves of the professional development opportunities they provide so that they can reach out as needed before and during future crises.

Alternatives to Mobility to Meet Objectives of Internationalization and Global Learning

The prolonged hiatus in travel necessitated a turn to alternative means to internationalize our campuses and to provide global learning outcomes to our students. The pandemic accelerated advances already underway in the use of virtual international exchange, global classroom technology, and collaborative online international learning. Courses that integrate international and intercultural collaboration through on-line interactions have an added potential of increasing accessibility of global learning to students unable to travel for personal or financial reasons. Similarly, virtual engagements provide a means to bring international guests, scholars, and students to our campuses without the time and expense of travel.

Connections Between Internationalization and DEI

For campuses not yet including global diversity and internationalization into their thinking around diversity, equity, and inclusion (DEI), the pandemic likely alerted them to significant overlaps in the two areas. The sharp drop in international students in the US during the 2020–2021 academic year reduced diversity in classrooms and on campuses. International students and scholars in the US faced unique challenges as residence and dining facilities closed, uncertainties arose regarding their status in the US and ability to travel home, and incidents of Asian hate broke out apparently prompted by the association of the virus with Asia. Diversity Abroad, AIEA, and ACE all initiated increased conversations around the intersections of internationalization and DEI in the year after the pandemic.

Risks of International Recruitment as an Enrollment Strategy

Prior to the pandemic, some IHEs banked on international enrollments as an increasingly important source of tuition revenues. There are many positive reasons to encourage such enrollments, but COVID-19 also revealed the risks inherent in this goal as a budget strategy. Embracing this strategy necessitates robust contingency planning and preparation for disruptions that are global in nature.

REFERENCES

American Council on Education. (n.d.). *Comprehensive Internationalization Framework*. Research & Insights. Retrieved from https://www.acenet.edu/Research-Insights/Pages/Internationalization/CIGE-Model-for-Comprehensive-Internationalization.aspx

American Council on Education. (2020, March 2). Colleges continue planning for coronavirus outbreaks as CDC recommends bringing students back from study abroad programs. Retrieved from https://www.acenet.edu/News-Room/Pages/Colleges-Continue-Planning-for-Coronavirus-Outbreaks-as-CDC-Recommends-Bringing-Students-Back-From-Study-Abroad-Programs.aspx

American Immigration Lawyers Association. (2020). Resources related to presidential proclamations temporarily suspending entry of certain immigrants and nonimmigrants from entering the US. Retrieved from https://www.aila.org/advo-media/issues/all/covid-19/eo-temporary-suspension-immigration

Fischer, K. (2020, July 8). As MIT and Harvard Sue, Colleges Scramble to Respond to New Federal Policy on International Students. *The Chronicle of Higher Education*. Retrieved from https://www.chronicle.com/article/as-mit-and-harvard-sue-colleges-scramble-to-respond-to-new-federal-policy-on-international-students

Harvard University. (2020, March 24). Statement on Asian and AAPI COVID-19 related harassment and resources [updated 11/4/21]. *East Asian Languages and Civilizations*. Retrieved from https://ealc.fas.harvard.edu/news/resources-asian-and-aapi-students-experiencing-covid-19-related-harassment

Institute of International Education. (2020a, March). COVID-19 Snapshot Survey Series, *Academic Student Mobility to and from China*. Retrieved from https://www.iie.org/Connect/COVID-19/COVID-19-Snapshot-Survey-Series

Institute of International Education (2020b, May). *COVID-19 Snapshot Survey Series, From Emergency Response to Planning for Future Student Mobility*. Retrieved from https://www.iie.org/Connect/COVID-19/COVID-19-Snapshot-Survey-Series

Institute of International Education. (2020c). Open Doors Infographics. Retrieved from https://www.iie.org/Connect/COVID-19/Infographics

Institute of International Education. (2020d). Open Doors. Retrieved from https://opendoorsdata.org/

NAFSA. (2021). Trends in US Study Abroad. Retrieved from https://www.nafsa.org/policy-and-advocacy/policy-resources/trends-us-study-abroad

Overseas Security Advisory Council (OSAC). (2020, March 3). Global level 4 travel advisory. Retrieved from https://www.osac.gov/Content/Report/0bf863de-8afb-411d-a1b6-183cf466ee2f

Redden, E. (2020, March 24). Stranded Abroad. *Inside Higher Education*. Retrieved from https://www.insidehighered.com/news/2020/03/24/study-abroad-students-caught-international-border-closures

Robinson, M. (2021, April 27). International Students Create Film to Stop Asian Hate. *University of Buffalo News*. Retrieved from http://www.buffalo.edu/ubnow/stories/2021/04/asian-hate-film.html

Williams, D. (2020). *The COVID-19 DEI Crisis Action Strategy Guide: Recommendations to Drive Inclusive Excellence*. Atlanta, GA: Center for Strategic Diversity Leadership & Social Innovation.

Chapter 4

Continuity of the Academic Mission

Gabriela Cornejo Weaver and
Rosalyn Hobson Hargraves

When the onset of the COVID-19 pandemic forced institutions of higher education (IHEs) to remove people from campus buildings in March 2020, administrators initially operated under the belief that this situation would last a short while, perhaps a couple of weeks at most. Faculty, in most cases, they assumed, would be able to make relatively minor adjustments to assignments, due dates and grading for this limited period. Administrators focused their attention primarily on the logistics of emptying the campus, securing the buildings, and creating a safe environment for the campus community. Within a few days of the initial closures, however, it became clear that campus shutdowns would remain in place for the rest of the academic year.

Nationally, over 1,300 colleges and universities across all 50 states ended up canceling in-person classes and moving entirely to online-only instruction in the spring 2020 term (Smalley, 2021). This shift to remote instruction raised the question of how to ensure that students could meet their academic requirements for the remainder of the year. Institutions quickly confronted a range of details regarding *how* academic requirements could be addressed remotely. These included constraints regarding clinical or practicum requirements for certain professional programs; considerations of pass/fail grading and its implication for letter-grade equivalents in future semesters; and challenges in accommodating the subsequent changes in student data systems that such one-term anomalies could entail.

Whether private or public, research-intensive, or two-year colleges, the primary mission of higher education institutions is to educate their students. The closure of campuses put that primary mission in jeopardy in a way that had no historical precedent. Maintaining the continuity of the academic mission became a primary focus of institutions across the nation amid changing health and safety guidelines, mounting uncertainty about the course of the pandemic, and simmering worries by all individuals about the health of their loved ones and their own safety. Although academia can be notoriously slow to change, the acute crisis phase of the pandemic during spring 2020 showed a new capacity in this sector to be resourceful, responsive, and agile in a way never before witnessed on such a large scale in the history of US higher education.

Almost every higher education institution across the US experienced common challenges once campuses faced the prospect of campus shutdowns and a rapid response to ensure academic continuity. Yet institutional mission, student demographics, location, financial positioning, and technological capacity all shaped individual IHEs' experiences in making the transition to remote teaching and learning. The level of experience with online course delivery before the pandemic was quite varied across higher education and was not aligned with a particular sector of the higher education arena (for example, some community colleges had high levels of readiness compared to others, and some research institutions were less prepared to transition to online instruction than others). What seems clear is that the pandemic experience pushed both institutions and faculty from all sectors to expand their online course delivery capacities.

MOVING TEACHING TO AN ONLINE FORMAT: A STUDY IN ACADEMIC AGILITY

In the early morning of Tuesday, March 10, 2020, the president of a private, urban research-intensive university received word of the governor's order that all places of work must close except for essential workers. This news came with instructions for staff, faculty, and students to remain home or to return there immediately. Because spring break would take place the following week, the administration expected only a small fraction of the student body to be on the campus, simplifying the task of sending people away. For the remaining days of the current week, faculty received encouragement to use their learning management system (LMS) or emails to communicate with and to provide coursework to their students to cover the scheduled classes they would miss. In programs requiring practicums, laboratories, clinical experiences, or where no remote options would be possible, instructors were asked to adjust their grading and/or teaching plans to accommodate 2-3 weeks of missed class meetings.

Should the disruption prove particularly long, the administration discussed the possible need to close for an additional week after spring break, as well. Given its location in a section of the country that occasionally experiences winter snowstorms large enough to close the campus, this institution had dealt with interruptions to teaching before. Moreover, in recent years, a city water main problem had caused the university and all surrounding businesses to close for several days, and the university had mobilized campus resources to provide food and safety for its students. The current interruption, then, could borrow from the strategies and lessons of those events.

CONTINUITY OF THE ACADEMIC MISSION

By Friday of that week, however, news about the spread of the pandemic across the country and the world—case counts, fatalities, mechanisms of spread—were hinting at a protracted and nightmarish scenario. Administrative meetings, usually held in person, now moved online. That change alone had a learning curve. Most importantly, however, the pace and gravity of decisions that needed to be made was increasing. If the institution would be unable to teach classes in person, myriad details needed to be planned and executed quickly to ensure students could continue to learn. With the semester past its midpoint, "academic continuity" was critical to ensure that the progress of students toward their degree objectives would continue. For students, a single critical course remaining incomplete could mean a full academic year delay if the course was a necessary step to further requirements in their program, or a delay in graduation if spring 2020 was their final term.

Before making a definite decision to extend remote learning, campus leadership needed to determine the feasibility of various continuity plans. They would need to establish training and support to help faculty transition to online instruction. (See Chapter 13 on finances and contingency planning for a detailed discussion of the financial impacts of implementing support programs of this type and Chapter 8 for technology considerations through this period). This institution held a license for a videoconferencing application but had not previously made use of it extensively for daily operations. Could this system handle a massive increase in traffic? Could the institution's own cyber infrastructure support delivery of all or most of its courses using video conferencing?

By the following Tuesday—one week after the announcement of the initial short-term closure—faculty received a new communication. It was decided that classes would be online for the remainder of the semester, and faculty should be prepared to begin teaching their courses fully online beginning Monday, March 30—one week after the end of spring break. While some faculty had experience with online teaching and the use of various technologies, many others did not, and instead built their courses around traditional in-place, face-to-face modes of instruction. By requiring a transition of these courses to online modalities, campus leaders would need to communicate the parameters needed and support available for that conversion. For example, faculty and staff would need to understand that they were not expected to build an online course of the caliber and instructional design specifications that the institution would expect of "native" online courses, such as those that are part of online degree offerings. In the current scenario, the conversions were intended to happen quickly in order to get students through the material needed for the remainder of the semester in the best way possible. The goal was to ensure that students could meet their academic requirements.

Although the specifics of the above scenario are drawn from a particular institution, they mirror what transpired at most campuses across the country.

As information about the effects of the pandemic shifted rapidly, corresponding decisions by higher education leaders adjusted to anticipate and ameliorate impacts on students, faculty and staff. The pace of required changes by faculty and staff required efforts far beyond what had ever been expected from them in known academic history. The principle of academic freedom in higher education brings with it a culture in which much of what takes place in the instructional environment—whether virtual or in-person—is left to the discretion of the instructor, or at the very least, to the academic department. The arrival of the pandemic and the need for sudden response by institutions required administrators to make decisions that were, on the surface, antithetical to that centuries-old doctrine. By the typical processes of higher education, such changes would generally go through numerous faculty committees, the faculty governing body, and, on unionized campuses, the collective bargaining unit for contract discussions. The exigencies of the pandemic required these normal processes to be superseded by a highly centralized approach to decision-making more closely resembling an emergency operations center or "EOC". (Refer to Chapter 2 for examples of communication and decision-making systems deployed during the early phases of the pandemic.)

Faculty and staff needed both resourcefulness and administrative support to pull off such an effort. At the institution in the scenario above, the central IT unit identified IT points-of-contact in each academic unit (colleges and schools) and provided them with training and resources for supporting faculty with a rapid transition to online teaching. In turn, these IT point-persons monitored course transformation activities and communicated with faculty or with additional IT support personnel. In some cases, individuals who already held these roles assumed these responsibilities but, in others, reassigned personnel took on these roles. Academic affairs leaders needed to communicate expectations clearly, to both faculty and students, particularly in distinguishing natively online courses from those being transitioned to a distance delivery mode in response to the pandemic. Some institutions specifically selected different words for these two versions of online teaching: "remote" rather than "online," for example.

Equity Insights

This juncture was, for many administrators, the first awakening to the differential access to resources for different faculty and staff in their institutional communities. It was, in some cases, a surprise to realize that adjunct faculty, younger faculty, and faculty of color were less likely to have serviceable at-home computer equipment, reliable internet access, or private workspaces in their home environments.

> This realization would be quickly followed by a growing appreciation of the unequal access many students had to hardware, software, and bandwidth when off-campus. Unsurprisingly, uneven access to the internet and computers characterized rural areas. This caused Berea College, a private institution serving many students from rural parts of Appalachia, to make the decision to suspend operations for the duration of the spring semester. However, even many urban institutions grappled with the number of their students who relied on on-campus computer labs and WiFi. Access to broadband and technology, in many ways, became a defining equity issue of the early period of the COVID-19 pandemic, and many institutions devoted a large portion of the CARES Act (see Chapter 13) funds they received to providing loaner laptops and mobile "hotspot" devices to students to ensure that they could continue their coursework.

Preparing Faculty for Remote Instruction

Although many institutions had experience with using LMSs in some fraction of their course offerings, many faculty members had not previously opted to engage with this support if they were teaching entirely in-person classes. Though videoconferencing applications were already common for some types of meetings among administrators, with some faculty likewise having experience with them, familiarity with such platforms as Zoom or Microsoft Teams varied widely across campuses. Utilizing these applications for online teaching involved a scale-up challenge for both technology and teaching support teams. Some institutions only activated these tools once it became clear that there would be no rapid move back to in-person formats. In these cases, they needed to coordinate significant training of users across the academic spectrum. (Refer to Chapter 8 for details about the IT infrastructure during the early pandemic response.)

Different Types of Courses

It was immediately apparent that some types of courses would lend themselves more easily to an online format than others. Courses that were normally taught in a lecture or discussion format in a classroom could utilize already common frameworks such as an LMS in combination with videoconferencing applications. The investment of time to record lectures (in some cases) or the creativity to convert assignments to those that could be carried out away from campus were some of the larger hurdles in these sorts of classes.

The more challenging courses, however, were those that required hands-on, performance, or in-person engagement with other people, specialized equipment, or facilities to achieve course learning outcomes. Laboratory courses in the sciences, engineering, agriculture, and health fields; clinical and practicum courses in professional programs; experiential, studio and performance-based classes in numerous arts and humanities programs: all of these needed to be dealt with individually and creatively. There were numerous examples of laboratory courses in the sciences being translated to online methods by either video-taping an instructor or a graduate assistant in the laboratory carrying out the procedures, or by making use of commercial "virtual laboratory" resources. For example, the online provider of scientific videos, JOVE (jove.com) made all of its resources available free of charge through June of 2020 for this very purpose, one of many examples of companies and organizations helping in this time of crisis by increasing ease of access to their products. Professional societies also made efforts to ease the transition by providing channels through which to access online resources for teaching as well as discussion boards and training sites for teaching laboratory courses online. Overall, these laboratory courses required a great deal more effort to transform to an online format, and some types of laboratory courses could not feasibly be converted. (For a study of the success of various approaches that chemistry faculty, for example, used to deliver instruction remotely through this period, see Mojica & Upmacis, 2021.)

A parallel scenario unfolded for studio courses in the arts and performance classes. Where they could, faculty engaged students via videoconferencing or requested individual recordings of performances. Some art teachers created makeshift at-home recording studios in which to demonstrate techniques in different media, though approximating these materials at home was a challenge in many cases for students. Some institutions permitted instruction in sound studios that could physically isolate a performer from a person in a different room—but allow sound to travel, such as through speakers. Ensuring that students would have a way to complete the requirements justified a sacrifice in fidelity. Shared resources through listservs and websites of such professional associations as the International Council of Fine Arts Deans (ICFAD) or the Council of Colleges of Arts & Sciences (CCAS) assisted faculty in learning from others in their disciplines about strategies to creatively deliver instruction through this period.

Other types of courses that required special attention were clinical and experiential courses related to professional programs, such as nursing, dentistry, or teaching, to name a few. Finding solutions to these was critical for degree completion or certification of students, as these are often the culminating requirements for such programs. Cutting them short or eliminating them was not easily an option, given their important role in preparing students for authentic workplace skills. For these courses, on a case-by-case and state-by-state basis, working with distancing, masking, and cleaning guidelines allowed for some adaptations of the format of these experiences. In some cases, such changes required engaging with state licensing agencies. For example, the California State University system, facing the very real possibility in March 2020 that hundreds of nursing students would be unable to complete their required clinical placement hours to meet license requirements that spring, needed to work with the state licensing board for nursing students who would not have been permitted to earn planned degrees by existing standards—more stringent than in other states. In light of the "anticipated increase in the use of the healthcare system [that would] require an increase in the health care workforce such as nurses," the governor signed an executive order on March 30, 2020, mandating a temporary adjustment of staffing and health and safety standards for health providers and health facilities given that students preparing for the health professions found themselves unable to satisfy professional licensing requirements at a time when they were desperately required (State of California, 2020). Following this executive order, the board ultimately agreed to accept the same standards as in other states (with only 50% of nursing students' required supervised hours needing to be in clinical settings), but it was an arduous negotiation process that left nursing students across the state wondering for several weeks if they would be qualified for their licenses upon completion of their degrees that term. (For additional state nursing board educational adjustments through this period see the National Council of State Boards of Nursing, 2020, overview document.)

In some circumstances, departments needed to waive or delay course requirements that they deemed impossible to deliver in this rapid transition to remote instruction, such as field experiences or culminating group projects that are normally part of a course syllabus. Instead, instructors of subsequent courses were alerted that certain material had not been covered by incoming students who were completing prerequisite courses in spring 2020. This type of solution was problematic for students and institutions alike as it pushed problems into later terms. With so much uncertainty about the duration of the pandemic through this period, or the longer-term impacts on institutions, IHEs avoided, whenever possible, such "kick the can down the road" options. Avoiding them, however, was rarely simple and often required individualized solutions or expenses beyond planned budgets.

From a leadership standpoint, such decisions required a careful balance of encouraging creative solutions to novel challenges and continuously examining the availability of resources to see what was feasible. As described in other sections of this book, most institutions faced unprecedented revenue losses in the first few months of the pandemic, requiring rather large budget cuts in many cases. (Refer to Chapter 13 for details about budgets and financing through the pandemic response.) As such, finding cost-effective ways to continue the academic trajectory of students was a daily—or hourly—juggling act for educational leaders from department chairs to presidents.

The experience of the School of Nursing at the University of Massachusetts, Amherst, demonstrates how all these challenges came together simultaneously and required a rapid and coordinated response. The School's Acting Dean during the spring 2020 semester noted that securing the clinical hours for their students proved the biggest academic challenge:

> Two big things occurred. All the clinical sites we normally work with closed completely to our students. That's about 200 to 300 students across 80 to 90 agencies for placements. But our students must have clinical hours in the 2nd half of the semester for their certification. This required a rapid search for online case-studies that could qualify as replacements for on-site clinical experience. We got information about freely available online resources but prior to [the pandemic] online resources were only a modest part of our teaching. Nobody had been ready to be 100% online. —Cynthia S. Jacelon, Acting Dean of Nursing, University of Massachusetts, Amherst

The team also needed to figure out how to replace the mentoring by clinical faculty who were no longer available to meet with students that had been assigned to them. Based on existing studies, which indicated that up to 50% virtual clinical experience does not affect pass rates on certification exams, the team was able to use a combination of mentored online case studies and reduced in-person clinical time to meet the educational needs of their students. The current Dean of the Elaine Marieb College of Nursing at UMass Amherst, Allison Vorderstrasse, noted that people in the nursing education community across the country were informing each other online about available resources. Being part of state networks helped with this information sharing. However, at the end of the day, "everyone was trying to make their own boat float." The team noted that finding resources and experiences to ensure their students could complete their requirements took a great deal of teamwork and extra effort by the faculty. Jacelon and other nursing school leaders interviewed agreed that "The willingness of our faculty to roll up their sleeves and do what needed to be done was remarkable. There was no whining, no 'I can't do that.'"

Policy Considerations

Many campuses also made rapid and one-time changes to standing academic policies to accommodate the extenuating circumstances created by the pandemic. Institutions modified grading policies, leave policies, and medical policies to respond to the changing landscape of instruction. In a June 2020 survey by the National Institute for Learning Outcomes Assessment (NILOA), 97% of respondents indicated that they had made changes of some kind during spring 2020 in response to COVID-19 by modifying assignments and assessments, changing deadlines, shifting to pass/fail grading, and/or modifying assessment reporting (Jankowski, 2020). Among survey responses summarized in this study, 36% had moved to pass/fail or grade optional policies in the spring 2020 term. Examples of short-term solutions included extending withdrawal deadlines until after course completion to give students an option to withdraw or choose the grade mode that best suited them (see UC Davis Academic Senate, 2020, and PVCC, 2020, which represent just two of many such examples).

Some schools created new pass/fail grading scales (Retta, 2020). In making these decisions, administrators consulted with students, faculty, and advisors—with varying levels of engagement of faculty governance structures at different institutions—and sought review by university legal counsel. In addition, the accrediting bodies had to be consulted to ensure these changes would not adversely impact a program's accreditation. A survey of higher education accrediting organizations shows that only 6 of 47 responding organizations felt that their institutions did *not* have problems accommodating clinical, laboratory, or field experiences (CHEA, 2020). Higher education accrediting organizations proactively introduced flexibilities regarding schedule and grading accommodations (see, for example, HLC, 2020, n.d.), which was encouraged by the United States Department of Education (USDE, 2020):

> … we extended temporary flexibility to institutions to implement distance learning solutions to continue educating students in the event of campus interruptions or the unexpected return of students from travel abroad experiences. We similarly provided flexibility to accrediting agencies to waive routine regular distance learning review requirements and approval processes to allow institutions quickly to switch to distance learning so as to enable currently enrolled students to complete the current term.

These policy-level supports allowed IHEs the freedom to make the most appropriate academic changes for their context in a timely manner, toward the end goal of ensuring academic continuity for their students.

Scheduling

Campus closures meant that many residential students dispersed across the nation, and international students might be in many countries if they had been unable to return to the US due to travel and visa restrictions (see Chapter 3 for a discussion of the pandemic's impact on international students). Thus, many institutions found that their students were spread across many time zones domestically and around the globe. Moving courses online allowed students to continue their studies from any location they might find themselves, but the time zone dilemma became a new and unforeseen challenge for synchronous course delivery.

Moving any single course to a different time in the weekly schedule created a cascade of scheduling conflicts with other required courses and was, therefore, virtually impossible for large courses and at larger institutions. In some cases, instructors elected to offer additional course meeting times to accommodate students in different time zones. These efforts increased the work and contact time for faculty in ways that were rarely directly compensated. For smaller classes, instructors might be able to poll students to find out if a different time during the week could be found that would be able to accommodate everyone in the class. However, in most cases, synchronous online class meetings were kept on the same schedule as they took place in person. This meant that students in distant time zones were forced to keep up their coursework by "attending school" in the middle of the night, or during very late or very early hours—something that would impact not only them but others with whom they might be living. For working students and student-parents, this might simply prove impossible, and many had to withdraw from individual classes if not from school altogether (see Chapter 6 on Student Services and efforts to retain students).

Dual Credit/Dual Enrollment

For many community colleges and regional comprehensive universities, large dual credit and dual enrollment programs in collaboration with high schools are an increasingly important source of enrollment in a growing number of states, including Texas, Florida, New Jersey, and Indiana. These programs are also an important tool for expanding college access. Given that while these students are in college courses they are part of the IHE student body, the institutions had to ensure that they, too, had access to needed technology and student support services to complete the semester. Academic leaders and K-12 offices worked with local school districts to coordinate access for these students, as well as navigating the sometimes-conflicting COVID-19 health protocols and shutdown schedules.

IMPACT ON FACULTY

Scheduling adjustments also had an impact on the instructional staff and faculty in IHEs. Surveys and reporting have demonstrated the toll that the extra work of the online transition to teaching had on instructors of all types (McMurtrie, 2021). Many faculty made scheduling accommodations out of a sense of responsibility and caring for the wellbeing of their students, even if such options could mean teaching two or three times more often during the week than they normally would or holding class meetings at inconvenient times for themselves in order to limit the level of inconvenience for their students. And they were doing so, often while also having families to care for, children completing schooling remotely at home, or older family members needing extra assistance. Women faculty and faculty of color reported that they often felt a special responsibility to take on this work even as they wrestled with increased family caretaking responsibilities

(NASEM, 2021; June, 2015; Pettit, 2020). Such efforts were engaged in by thousands of instructors across the country—whether tenure-track or contingent—with little or no additional compensation.

In the rapid changes implemented in spring 2020, faculty were also often in the position of reacting to circumstances, rather than being able to make plans regarding their teaching. As institutional leadership grappled quickly with vital decisions in those beginning days in response to evolving news about the pandemic, the people whom these decisions would impact waited for guidance. Faculty and staff wondered if their institutions would move completely online, if spring break would be extended to give faculty time to move classes online, or if students who had no other alternatives would be allowed to come back to campus and thus require that courses be taught both in person and remotely. The rapid changes in a compressed time period did not always permit the full deliberative and inclusive dialogues through committees, senates, and councils normally used to determine collective outcomes.

In some cases, proactive faculty and staff, assuming that campus shutdowns were likely, simply began to prepare to teach remotely, just in case that would be the decision, scooping up needed materials and notes from their offices before leaving campus, unsure when they might be back and looking to leverage what they could for a potential transition to remote instruction. Faculty set up home workstations and attempted to determine the tools they would need to adequately teach from home or establish whether they would be able to come to campus and teach from their offices. If they had not previously made use of the LMS for their courses, they needed to decide how they could teach in an effective manner through use of PowerPoint slides or recorded lectures. For many faculty this transition required altering long-standing teaching methods and practices.

As academic affairs leaders made the decision to move courses online, they recognized that many faculty required training in both the technologies and pedagogies to enable remote instruction. Those IHEs with the resources to provide in-house instructional designers helped faculty move their classes online. In smaller and less resourced institutions that lacked these technical experts, faculty with online teaching experience worked with their colleagues to revamp courses. As the spring semester wore on, many higher education organizations responded to the emergency by providing free training to faculty on topics such as how to use Zoom features to engage students.

Assessments

One area that many faculty revised were course assessments. For classes that previously used in-person exams as the primary mode of assessment, faculty needed to reflect on how to adjust formats and expectations for exams taken outside of the classroom. The issue of how to assure the integrity of the students' work led faculty and instructional support staff to explore proctoring and automated grading tools *en masse* (Flaherty, 2020). In courses with a large class-participation component, instructors had to revisit how they could assess participation in an online environment, shifting requirements, for example, to include discussion posts, blogs, or other means for students to demonstrate engagement with material. Faculty also needed to change attendance requirements and grading rubrics and rethink required content given a lost week of instructional time for many as well as new course delivery modalities. In the end, the question often became "What is 'good enough'?" Experts in online pedagogies had long advocated for these measures, which were considered good practices and commonly used in some institutions. The pandemic experience, however, increased faculty exposure and usage across the nation.

Equity Insights: Disparate Impacts across the Faculty

As faculty and staff navigated this period, institutions gained an increasing awareness of the systemic inequities impacting the lives of their employees. As captured in "On the Verge of Burnout," an October 2020 survey report by the *Chronicle of Higher Education* (2020), faculty faced their own health concerns and family needs while also working to adjust their instruction and research expectations, creating enormous physical, mental, and emotional stress and exhaustion. The strain on women faculty and staff as well as those from Black, Indigenous and people of color (BIPOC) communities experiencing a greater impact from COVID-19, created gendered and racialized disparities. When the survey asked how their work–life balance had shifted over 2020, 74 percent of all women faculty surveyed responded that it had deteriorated, compared with 63 percent of men. Eighty-two percent of women professors said their workloads increased, compared with 70 percent of men. Further, the survey found that,

> Overall, the results are consistent with pre-Covid research showing gender disparities in stress and workload and that those differences have gotten worse during the pandemic," says KerryAnn O'Meara, a professor of higher education at the University of Maryland and the 2020 president of the Association for the Study of Higher Education. "It is striking that in every category of faculty, women were more likely than men to say that since the start of 2020, their workload has increased, and their work–life balance has deteriorated. What we

> need to ask is what are the likely factors contributing to making a situation that was already gendered and racialized worse?
> (Chronicle of Higher Education, 2020, pp. 13–14)
>
> The gender disparity prevalent on many campuses, with a higher percentage of women in "teaching faculty positions" as compared to tenured or tenure-eligible faculty positions with often lighter teaching loads (Weissman, 2020), also meant that more female faculty members had a higher number and variety of courses to transition to online or hybrid delivery. Moreover, because women faculty earn less than their male counterparts, they were less likely to be able to afford the kind of services, such as child and elder care, that might alleviate their workload.
>
> Part-time and contingent faculty also faced a far greater disparity in levels of resources (home computers, internet access), previous baseline training, and integration with the campus community and supports. As the pandemic spread, bringing with it severe budget implications, IHEs often responded by not hiring and/or not renewing contracts for part-time, contingent or non-tenure eligible faculty. According to an article by the Executive Committee of Tenure for the Common Good:
>
>> [The] COVID-19 pandemic is beginning to show how fragile the positions of contingent faculty actually are. Reports from campuses across the country attest to the insecurity of all of our nontenured colleagues' positions. Some administrators, understandably frightened by the likely impact that the coming economic downturn will have on their institutions, are already making plans to jettison contingent positions, completely ignoring any past non-contractual commitment to lecturers or even adjuncts. At the very least, the divide between tenured faculty and their casual colleagues is widening and, as *Inside Higher Ed* reported, contingent faculty worry that hiring freezes may soon be used to further reduce the little security they have attained.
>> — Executive Committee of Tenure for the Common Good, 2020

Changes Regarding Assessment of Faculty Performance

The extensive changes to course structures led campuses to consider whether or not to follow existing policies and timeframes for faculty teaching evaluations.

This discussion often came in response to concerns about the differential impact of the pandemic on women and BIPOC faculty. Like many other institutions, UMass Amherst suspended mandatory faculty evaluations. Faculty could request student feedback about their teaching, but assessments from the spring 2020 term would not figure in reappointment or promotion decisions. At this university, a section on the impact of COVID was added to the annual faculty review form where faculty could discuss extenuating circumstances in relation to performance expectations, both for teaching and for research. By April 2020, a broad range of IHEs made similar decisions:

> Students aren't the only ones feeling anxious. The closing of physical classrooms has forced the majority of instructors who've never taught anything but a face-to-face course to do so under less-than-ideal circumstances, to say the least. In the shift to remote instruction, many professors are themselves using entirely new tools and pedagogical techniques—almost certainly with varying degrees of success. ... Numerous colleges and universities are allowing instructors to opt out of collecting student ratings of their teaching for the winter and spring terms, while others have said they will continue to collect the evaluations during this time but won't consider them in assessing faculty performance.
>
> (Lederman, 2020)

Changes to Tenure Clocks and Reappointment Calendars

For probationary, tenure-track faculty, teaching evaluations represented only one point of concern through this period. Campus closures deeply affected the ability of faculty to engage in research, performances, scholarship, or creative production—activities that have a major impact on tenure, promotion, and merit decisions at many institutions, particularly research-intensive ones. As early as March 2020 and continuing through the spring, hundreds of campuses announced one- and even two-year extensions on tenure clocks, either automatically awarded or as an option faculty could select. (For more on changes in this area, including tenure clock extensions, see Butler, 2021.)

SUPPORTING STUDENT ACADEMIC SUCCESS

Just as faculty required additional support and policy adjustments due to the impact of the pandemic, so, too, did students. Ensuring students' academic continuity required more than moving classes online. IHEs quickly recognized that they needed to provide academic and other supports to keep students enrolled and making satisfactory academic progress. Many students struggled with multiple simultaneous concerns: the health impact of COVID-19 for themselves and family members; the need to assist with childcare or eldercare; worries over housing when residential campuses closed; a worsening economy that affected both personal and family budgets. Moreover, with campuses closed, they often lacked the social networks that helped them navigate college life.

For years before the pandemic, higher education leaders had increasingly come to recognize the interrelationship between academic and student affairs as they sought to increase college access and completion rates. With campus closures, student affairs leaders worked quickly to pivot student support services such as advising, tutoring, mentoring, and supplemental instruction to online modalities. At an institutional level, those already engaged in some level of online support services found the transition smoother than institutions that had not previously engaged in any type of online support services. Here too, this transition proved harder for students from low socio-economic backgrounds, students of color, English language learners and students with disabilities who often lacked access to needed technology and might bear heavy work and family responsibilities (Salazar et al., 2020). Student affairs staff members worked creatively and tirelessly to find new ways to provide the services that students needed to remain enrolled.

Advising and Early Alerts

Advisors needed to quickly pivot to (primarily) online and phone advising appointments. Many reported that the conversations with students shifted from a focus on academic planning and registration to discussions about personal matters and life scenarios that were playing out as a result of the COVID-19 pandemic. Advisors also found themselves having to answer questions about the value proposition of online education. Many students wondered if "online" meant inherently inferior. If so, was college worth the expense?

Student service leaders quickly discovered the need to provide advisors with training, not just for advising remotely, but also on how to appropriately refer students to other resources, such as physical and mental health resources, as well as technology resources like computer labs and free community WiFi access. Some institutions also created student support landing pages geared at providing a virtual "one-stop shop" for student support needs. The criticality of advisors' roles to student success became clearer during the COVID-19 pandemic as they helped students navigate enrollment decisions, new grading systems, and changing semester start dates. Furthermore, those institutions with pre-existing intrusive advising models whereby students had an assigned and dedicated advisor prior to the pandemic made their transition smoother because students already had a relationship with an advocate to assist with their advising and support service needs. Many institutions found that the availability of online advising appointments made students more likely to contact advisors. (For more on advising strategies used through this period, see Salazar, Pellegrino, & Leasor, 2020.)

Institutions that utilized early alert systems saw alarming shifts in not only the volume but the type of alerts being submitted. At the University of Michigan-Flint, Student Success Center staff saw a 63% increase in the volume of alerts, most noting a concern for the student's ability to transition to an online modality. Some institutions implemented special early alert flags that notified advisors, for example, when a student had gone some number of consecutive days without logging into an online course so that academic support staff could reach out to the student, determine needs, and connect the student with the appropriate resource.

Even with a change in meeting modalities, academic advisors needed to assure academic progress. Surveys and interviews with advisors yield one strong message: a sustained need for outreach and communication. Students needed to hear continuously that they were not alone and that there were resources available to assist with any barriers that they encountered. These efforts were critical to ensuring student retention. Some institutions had faculty call every student to ensure they had the proper resources to begin their online course and to ascertain other needs. Other institutions used a wide variety of modalities to reach students, switching back and forth between phone, email, and text to ensure messages were received.

Tutoring

Colleges and universities have long used tutoring and supplemental instruction as a student success strategy. Like everything else during this time, however, these two learning modalities needed to be handled remotely. Because in-person tutoring was not an option, virtual online tutoring was utilized. This allowed for both a tutoring experience and a tutoring relationship to occur. Asynchronous tutoring delays both the pace of study and the process of academic decision-making. In addition to moving such supports as writing centers and tutoring offices to online appointments, some campuses also scaled or implemented the use of such external options as Tutor.com, at substantial cost but with the goal of assuring student success during a turbulent time.

Supplemental Instruction

Institutions grapple with courses that have high drop, fail, and withdrawal rates, particularly in "gateway" courses that form the general education core at most IHEs. For many, a solution is the use of supplemental instruction for these particularly problematic courses. Supplemental instruction (SI) uses a trained peer educator who has already successfully taken the course to serve as a tutor-mentor for a small group of students currently enrolled in the course. Historically, SI has taken place face-to-face. The expediency with which SI could be shifted to online was of the utmost importance at the onset of the pivot to online education because the data were clear that without SI students were much more likely to fail these courses. Some institutions, like Wichita State, trained and deployed SI virtually within a week, losing almost no time during the rapid transition to remote learning (Noel-Elkins, 2020). Others worked hard to catch up, but many abandoned SI and similar programs for the remainder of the term.

Peer-to-Peer Mentoring

In recent years peer mentoring programs have been highlighted as high-impact practices. These peer-to-peer connections are shown to increase a students' sense of belonging and improve persistence and retention. At the Borough of Manhattan Community College, their "Inspires and Motivates People to Achieve in College Together" (IMPACT) peer mentoring program moved to virtual peer-to-peer mentoring half-way through the semester as a result of state shut-down orders (BMCC, 2020). One peer mentor for the program said the mid-semester shift proved beneficial because a level of rapport between students had already become established. The arrangement ultimately proved helpful for the mentors and mentees, alike, by helping them retain social connections.

Disability Services

To assure academic continuity for students, campuses also needed to address accessibility issues. IHEs worked to continue to provide accommodations and remote services. Through platforms such as Accommodate, faculty and students could have online access to service information in cases of need for individualized approaches. For hybrid instruction, deaf students might need new supports such as clear masks for faculty in order to be able to read lips. Campus IT teams also worked quickly with faculty to assure that they understood the need for accessible online materials, such as scanned documents that were legible to voice readers, colors that translated meaning even in cases of color blindness, or description of pictures and graphs for visually impaired students. While accessibility guidelines for faculty teaching online already existed, these materials were often unfamiliar to faculty who were accustomed to teaching in-person.

COMMENCEMENT AND SUMMER

By late April and May, still shell-shocked from the extraordinary experience of the pandemic, many breathed a sigh of relief that for the most part their campuses and students were in the process of completing the spring term. Yet, with no end to the pandemic in sight, campus communities turned their attention to what spring commencement and beyond might look like.

Commencement

Commencement ceremonies are a revered tradition which bring forth symbolic, human and political aspects of an institution's mission and history. For graduating students, the ritual marks an important achievement in their lives and those of family, friends, and loved ones who have been part of their journey in numerous ways. Many individuals are involved in the planning and execution of commencement ceremonies and the planning for these events begins many months before—sometimes as early as the prior academic year. Contracts for materials and services for commencement ceremonies, likewise, are generally finalized and financial commitments are made long before the end of the academic year. The outbreak of the pandemic beginning in late March and quickly escalating through April put commencement planners in a terrible bind. The unknowns of pandemic-related restrictions and the human toll of the disease, even as commencement dates began to draw near, meant that decisions about the long-planned-for event needed to happen very quickly and with no historical precedent to draw on.

For many institutions, the decision was whether to continue toward a scheduled commencement ceremony or, if not, what to do instead. Creating an alternative plan required a good deal of educated guesswork about what pandemic restrictions would look like in three to five weeks, an amount of time which was uncomfortably long with respect to how fast information and policies had been changing over the prior several weeks. Most institutions pulled the plug on their existing commencement plans. However, a key symbolic tradition in higher education institutions is to send students off with great pomp and circumstance upon completion of program requirements to mark their achievements and to welcome them into the community of alumni. The resources institutions had available to them, their size, and the beliefs of institutional leaders about the veracity and efficacy of pandemic restrictions all affected final decisions.

Given the health concerns about large gatherings, many IHEs opted to transition to fully online commencement ceremonies as a safety measure. The rapid transition to remote work and online teaching gave many individuals greater familiarity with using videoconferencing software. This gave institutions an easily deployed and scalable solution to create programming for online commencement ceremonies. In fact, it allowed for a level of flexibility in programming for the ceremonies that would be difficult to replicate for in-person events, such as inviting multiple celebrity alumni to provide recorded messages to the 2020 graduates or inviting graduates themselves to create content to be shared via a commencement website. Both of these were strategies that creative events planners implemented at commencement ceremonies that term at some IHEs. Nonetheless, institutions that opted for online commencement ceremonies often faced the anger and disappointment of the students and parents who felt cheated by the decisions, requiring compassionate communication and outreach by institutional leaders about the decisions (see Chapter 2 regarding communications strategies).

A very small number of institutions did elect to hold their commencement ceremonies in person. This was feasible at smaller institutions with large outdoor venues available to them, as these could accommodate commencement ceremonies in a socially distanced manner. William Paterson University, a regional comprehensive HSI/MSI in northern New Jersey that serves a high percentage of first-generation students, created an alternative option by following a virtual commencement held in May 2020 with a series of in-person, CDC-compliant events in August of that year. These smaller commencements, held outdoors and with limited participants, satisfied the students' desires to have their names called out in front of family members, walk across a stage and feel a sense of pomp and circumstance at the end of their educational journeys.

Summer Programming

As with commencement, planning for academic programs in coming semesters begins many months in advance. Summer semesters are particularly logistics-intensive because they involve not only the teaching of some fraction of the institutions' course offerings, but also many supplementary programs—some that the institutions themselves provide such as new student orientation programs, and some by external entities that make use of the facilities and services of the institution for a fee. Discontinuing these programs would create revenue losses at a time when many institutional budgets were already feeling the strain of the pandemic. However, modifying them to be in line with unknown-at-the-time pandemic restrictions could cost more than the revenue generated or could create a legal health and safety exposure for the institution, outweighing the benefits of continuing with such programs (see Chapter 13 on contingency and budgetary planning considerations through this period). After a spring term in which institutions either themselves transitioned to online teaching or watched most other institutions do so successfully, making the decision to teach online for the summer semester became widespread. Institutions announced such plans on a varied timeline, between mid-April and well into May. The announcements by the chancellor of the California State University System and Paul Quinn College that they would continue remote learning into the fall semester gave cover to other institutional leaders as they planned for summer and fall.

By the end of the spring semester, IHEs across the US had gained greater confidence in their ability to deliver courses online and had worked through many of the challenges, such as ensuring that students and faculty had access to computers and WiFi. Importantly, for the summer semester, leaders worked to ensure that decisions to teach online were announced with enough time that faculty had a more reasonable window of time in which to plan their courses and students knew going into the term what to expect. Not that such news was met with unanimous approval, but early decision-making reduced the level of panic and uncertainty that campuses had experienced with the March shutdowns. This alone represented a dramatic shift in a period of just over two months.

Many institutions also made use of this period either to recruit new students—by offering, for example, a free online course that could be used for institutional credit toward degree enrollment in the coming fall—or to support continuing students by permitting them to make up missed work and to get back on track after a rough spring at reduced or waived course fees. These types of aid proved critical to keeping students on track to complete their degrees as COVID-19 continued to rage across the US and the resulting economic downturn worsened.

LESSONS LEARNED

Perhaps the most important feature of the experience of ensuring academic continuity came from the rapidity of the pivot to remote learning. While painful given the crisis that prompted it, for many IHEs it was their first experience delivering online instruction. Although experts on remote learning preferred the term "emergency remote instruction" rather than online learning, given the hastiness of the shift, many faculty developed new skills that, albeit stressfully acquired, they would carry into the future. Even for IHEs that prided themselves on personalized, face-to-face classroom instruction, the need to develop and expand online instructional capabilities became imperative.

The remarkable pace and responsiveness which higher education demonstrated during the early stages of the pandemic was a testament to campus communities pulling together, in large and seemingly small ways, to ensure that students could complete their terms and that institutions could accomplish their academic mission to the greatest extent possible. Innumerable everyday heroes worked at their keyboards and webcams keeping institutions "open" despite empty campus grounds. Given the crisis nature of the situation, faculty and students both afforded each other a level of grace, as expectations of each other changed for the remainder of the term. Again and again, institutional leaders praised faculty and student services staff for their willingness to put students' welfare first. Stories of faculty and staff driving to students' homes to deliver laptops, course materials, and mobile hotspots populated the higher education press. Ideally, this praise carried over into higher levels of trust and collaboration between campus leaders and faculty and staff.

Yet the spring 2020 term revealed significant equity challenges too. Perhaps most importantly, leaders came to recognize the inconsistent access by both students and employees to computers, WiFi, and adequate workspaces. This proved true not only for those living in rural areas with limited broadband networks, but also in low-wealth urban and suburban communities. When the Federal government released CARES Funds (see Chapter 13), many institutions devoted large sums to providing loaner laptops and hotspots to students, faculty, and staff who needed them.

Across the US, IHEs devoted tremendous energy in ensuring that students could remain enrolled even as campuses shut down. The COVID-19 pandemic alone did not create the economic stressors that made college-going difficult for many, but the worsening economy and health conditions in the first half of 2020 significantly added to challenges that many students already faced—in some cases pushing them from an already precarious situation to one that made continued enrollment impossible. No longer could academic leaders consider these non-academic stressors as solely the province of Student Affairs professionals when they directly threatened students' academic continuity.

In many ways, the experiences of faculty and staff mirrored that of students. Confronted with the disruption of instruction and work life, faculty and staff, too, had to develop new competencies that proved time-intensive during the learning process. For some faculty whose professional identity centered on their mastery of their disciplines, feeling uncertain and uncomfortable delivering instruction in unfamiliar online environments was now a regular occurrence. They formed support groups on social media to ask for advice and to connect with others facing similar travails. A key role for academic leaders, particularly chairs and deans, was to provide understanding and reassurance. The need for empathic leadership amidst the global crisis became a paramount competency at all levels. Making and communicating decisions early provided a level of stability for both groups that eased the stress of the unknown. The ability to be decisive and let others know information that impacted them was key.

Higher education communities—possibly more so than other professional sectors—have long institutional memories. Leadership decisions made early in the pandemic response timeline that took into account the competing needs and concerns of multiple segments of the community, and communicated these decisions frequently, clearly, and compassionately, were less likely to meet with resistance. Leaders who instead elevated the needs of one campus constituency at the expense of other groups undermined the potential for long-term trust and collaboration with their stakeholders. To be clear, leaders had no menu of easy answers, but they could reassure campus constituencies that they took seriously the duty to *balance* the needs of all groups.

REFERENCES

Borough of Manhattan Community College. (2020, June 22). The power of peer mentoring moves to a virtual format. *CUNY Newswire*. Retrieved from https://www1.cuny.edu/mu/forum/2020/06/22/the-power-of-peer-mentoring-moves-to-a-virtual-format/

Butler, T. (2021, January 19). Tenure clock extensions aren't enough to help support researchers and their work during the pandemic (Opinion). *Inside Higher Ed*. Retrieved from https://www.insidehighered.com/advice/2021/01/19/tenure-clock-extensions-arent-enough-help-support-researchers-and-their-work

Chronicle of Higher Education. (2020). On the verge of burnout: COVID-19's impact on faculty well-being and career plans. *Research Brief*. Retrieved from https://connect.chronicle.com/rs/931-EKA-218/images/Covid%26FacultyCareerPaths_Fidelity_ResearchBrief_v3%20%281%29.pdf

Council for Higher Education Accreditation (CHEA). (2020, April). Survey of CHEA- and USDE-Recognized accrediting organizations: Meeting the challenge of COVID-19. Retrieved from https://www.chea.org/sites/default/files/other-content/2020_April_Accreditor_Survey_Results_Final.pdf

Executive Committee of Tenure for the Common Good. (2020, April 30). COVID-19 shows how precarious the positions of contingent faculty actually are. *Inside Higher Education*. Retrieved from https://www.insidehighered.com/views/2020/04/30/covid-19-shows-how-precarious-positions-contingent-faculty-actually-are-opinion

Flaherty, C. (2020, May 11). *Online proctoring is surging during COVID-19*. Retrieved from https://www.insidehighered.com/news/2020/05/11/online-proctoring-surging-during-covid-19

Higher Learning Commission (HLC). (2020, March). Temporary emergency policy related to COVID-19. Retrieved from https://www.hlcommission.org/Policies/covid-19-temporary-emergency-policy.html?highlight=WyJ0ZW1wb3JhcnkiLCJlbWVyZ2VuY3kiLCJ0ZW1wb3JhcnkgZW1lcmdlbmN5Il0=

Higher Learning Commission (HLC). (n.d.). FAQs and additional resources regarding COVID-19. Retrieved from https://www.hlcommission.org/covid-19/faqs-and-additional-resources.html

Jankowski, N. A. (2020, August). *Assessment during a crisis: Responding to a global pandemic*. Retrieved from https://www.learningoutcomesassessment.org/wp-content/uploads/2020/08/2020-COVID-Survey.pdf

June, A. W. (2015, November 8). The invisible labor of minority professors. *The Chronicle of Higher Education*. Retrieved from https://www.chronicle.com/article/the-invisible-labor-of-minority-professors/

Lederman, D. (2020, April 8). Many colleges are abandoning or downgrading student evaluations during coronavirus crisis. Will that stick? *Inside Higher Ed*. Retrieved from https://www.insidehighered.com/digital-learning/article/2020/04/08/many-colleges-are-abandoning-or-downgrading-student-evaluations

McMurtrie, B. (2021). The pandemic Is dragging on: Professors are burning out. In *Burnt Out and Overburdened* (pp. 12–17). Essay, Chronicle of Higher Education. Retrieved from https://www.chronicle.com/article/the-pandemic-is-dragging-on-professors-are-burning-out

Mojica, E.-R. E., & Upmacis, R. K. (2021. December 22). Challenges encountered and students' reactions to practices utilized in a general chemistry laboratory course during the COVID-19 pandemic. *Journal of Chemical Education*. Retrieved from https://pubs.acs.org/doi/10.1021/acs.jchemed.1c00838

National Academies of Sciences, Engineering, and Medicine. (NASEM). (2021). *The Impact of COVID-19 on the Careers of Women in Academic Sciences, Engineering, and Medicine*. Washington, DC: The National Academies Press. Retrieved from https://doi.org/10.17226/26061

National Council of State Boards of Nursing. (2020, June 22). Changes in education requirements for nursing programs during COVID-19. Retrieved from https://www.ncsbn.org/State_COVID-19_Response.pdf

Noel-Elkins, A. V. (2020. September). Supplemental instruction in a time of covid-19: Challenges and solutions. *eSource for College Transitions*, 18(1), 9. Retrieved from https://issuu.com/nrcpubs/docs/esource_18.1/s/11045782

Pettit, E. (2020, May 26). Being a woman in academe has its challenges: A global pandemic? not helping. *The Chronicle of Higher Education*. Retrieved from https://www.chronicle.com/article/being-a-woman-in-academe-has-its-challenges-a-global-pandemic-not-helping

PVCC (2020, March 27). Message from Chancellor DuBois - VCCS emergency grading policy. Retrieved from https://www.pvcc.edu/message-chancellor-dubois-vccs-emergency-grading-policy

Retta, M. (2020, April) How colleges are grading students during Coronavirus. *The Coronavirus Crisis*. Retrieved from https://www.npr.org/2020/04/10/830622398/how-colleges-are-grading-students-during-coronavirus

Salazar, A. L., Pellegrino, L., & Leasor, L. (2020, September 16). How colleges adapted advising and other supports during COVID-19 shutdowns. *CCRC*. Retrieved from https://ccrc.tc.columbia.edu/easyblog/colleges-adapted-advising-covid-supports.html

Smalley, A. (2021, March 22). *Higher Education Responses to Coronavirus (COVID-19)*. National Conference of State Legislators. Retrieved from https://www.ncsl.org/research/education/higher-education-responses-to-coronavirus-covid-19.aspx

State of California. (2020, March 30). *Executive Order N 39-20*. Retrieved from https://www.gov.ca.gov/wp-content/uploads/2020/03/3.30.20-EO-N-39-20.pdf

UC Davis Academic Senate. (2020). Academic policies and guidelines for changes in campus operating status, Spring Quarter 2020. Retrieved from https://academic-senate.ucdavis.edu/academic-policies-operating-status#spring2020

United States Department of Education (USDE). (2020, March 15). Memo Re. Information for accrediting agencies regarding temporary flexibilities provided to Coronavirus impacted institutions or accrediting agencies. Retrieved from https://www2.ed.gov/about/offices/list/ope/20-007covid19accreditorsfromomb317s.pdf

Weissman, S. (2020, December 17). Female faculty continue to face stubborn wage gap and underrepresentation in tenured positions. *Diverse*. Retrieved from https://www.diverseeducation.com/home/article/15108382/female-faculty-continue-to-face-stubborn-wage-gap-and-underrepresentation-in-tenured-positions

Chapter 5
Equity and Resilience in Academic Research

Elizabeth Orwin and Nicholas S. Wigginton

OVERVIEW OF ACADEMIC RESEARCH OPERATIONS

Research is one of the essential missions of the US higher education system. Academic research produces knowledge across a range of disciplines, from biomedical science to the humanities and arts. Research also serves as a key component in the training of thousands of undergraduate, graduate, and professional students across the country every year. According to the National Science Foundation, National Center for Science and Engineering Statistics (2019), academic institutions spent $74 billion on research in FY18 and performed nearly half of the nation's fundamental scientific research. Academic research takes place at many academic institutions—not just those that are research-intensive. According to the Carnegie Classification of Institutions of Higher Education (2018), there are 266 doctoral universities with "very high" or "high" research activity (so-called R1 and R2 universities, respectively); however, the National Science Foundation Higher Education Research and Development Survey (2019) identifies over 600 US institutions that reported research expenditures of at least $1 million in FY18. Additionally, increasingly community colleges, liberal arts colleges, and vocational schools integrate research into teaching, use it as a basis for workforce development, leverage research to build partnerships with other institutions, or are simply seeking to grow their research portfolios as part of a strategy to recruit students and faculty.

Most research-intensive universities have an administrator who serves as the senior or chief research officer responsible for broad oversight of research activities, support offices, and compliance functions. This role is often a Vice President/Provost for Research (VPR) or Vice Chancellor for Research (VCR) and reports to either the President, Chancellor, or Chief Academic Officer (CAO). Based on Droegemeier et al.'s (2017) survey of 78 senior research officers at research-intensive universities, these administrative roles are often held by senior faculty members and include oversight of many of the operational and programmatic functions of the university related to research. These include institutional review boards (IRBs), grant support offices, technology transfer, various compliance functions, and oftentimes interdisciplinary research centers or institutes (Droegemeier et al., 2017).

In addition to the senior research officer, many other faculty and staff administrators and/or committees contribute to the overall management and oversight of the research enterprise. These positions include some combination of department chairs, deans, associate deans/chairs for research, assistant/associate vice presidents/provosts, and directors of research centers/institutes and major support units. At less research-intensive institutions, there is not typically a senior research officer or central research office. Instead, research oversight and decision-making are generally delegated to individual faculty members for their programs or supported as part of the range of responsibilities within the office of the CAO. Some of these institutions have associate dean positions to coordinate hiring of students and summer programming.

Many institutions convene regular meetings of a subset of research leadership to ensure communication across campus and sharing of the needs and challenges of the campus community. Such coordination becomes especially important at large, decentralized institutions. Since research goals stretch across so many functions of the university, there are also critical roles and collaborations involving other parts of the institution, including government relations, finance, academic affairs, development, and communications.

The campus shutdown in early 2020 due to the COVID-19 pandemic caused the closure of most of in-person research activities. Some fields and individual projects were more easily adaptable to this disruption, particularly those that did not rely on in-person activities, such as computational- or digital-based scholarship. For fields or projects that relied on specialized equipment or facilities, significant travel, living subjects (plant or animal), or human participants, campus closures meant an unprecedented level of disruption. At R1 institutions and associated academic medical centers, research is such a critical part of the overall campus existence that the disruption to research had a significant impact on the finances and operations of the institution itself. As described in an early overview from leadership at six R1 institutions, resuming research activities in summer of 2020 through a phased approach—as knowledge about the pandemic rapidly evolved—was a critical priority for research-intensive universities (Wigginton, et al., 2020).

IMPACT ON RESEARCH OPERATIONS

Initial Research Disruptions

In March 2020, institutions began rapidly canceling or suspending in-person activities such as classes, athletics, and, eventually, in-person research. As an

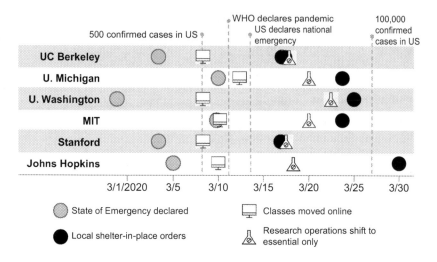

Figure 5.1 Relative timing of closure of non-essential research operations, shelter-in-place orders, classes moving online, and state disaster declarations for six R1 institutions in March 2020.
(Graphic assistance from J. Brassard, U. Michigan)

example of the rapid timing and interplay with other campus operations and government orders, Figure 5.1 shows the relative timing of six R1 institutions' closure of non-essential research operations and how that compared to shelter-in-place orders, classes moving online, and local or regional disaster declarations. Local or state public health orders prohibiting non-essential activities drove the timing of these impacts and creation of specific campus guidance on research. States and regions varied in whether they deemed research activities as essential and determined how they might be distinct from other essential operations to support education activities on campuses. The State of Washington, for example, permitted non-essential biomedical research to continue during stay-at-home orders, whereas the orders from many other states required that most on-site activities shut down.

Regardless of when or how quickly institutions ramped down, the continuity of research operations throughout the shutdown required the continuance of many essential activities. Without federal leadership, the definition of "essential" fell to local governments and, in some cases, to individual institutions. Most institutions defined "essential" as related to one or more of activities required to maintain highly specialized equipment or materials (e.g., sensitive cell lines, animal colonies), research that could affect patient health (e.g., clinical trials or potentially life-saving experimental treatments), or research directly related to addressing the COVID-19 pandemic.

Of the latter category, academic research played a key role in the early understanding, treatment, and mitigation of COVID-19. Without the exemption to allow essential researchers access to facilities during the initial shutdown of campuses, many advances would not have been possible. Some solutions came from researchers who had historically worked on infectious diseases and public health, but others also emerged from researchers who rapidly pivoted to use their expertise to help address the pandemic [e.g., sterilization of N95 masks by engineers as a response to personal protective equipment (PPE) shortages (MacKenzie, 2020)].

Ramping Up on-site Research

Over the late spring and summer of 2020, many institutions across the country developed plans to support the gradual ramp up of non-essential in-person research activity. These plans mostly proceeded in a piecemeal fashion across the country and varied widely due to a lack of strong federal guidance for institutions, as well as external factors, including orders from public health agencies, the status of community disease transmission, and other local government mandates. Internal factors that informed reopening plans for research included the institution's tolerance for risk, input from faculty governance, and reopening plans for other parts of campus including teaching, athletics, and housing.

Most institutions laid out a phased approach to ramping up research activities. These phased approaches aligned with public health guidelines, which also recommended a phased approach to reopening other sectors of society should conditions continue to decline and operations needed to be pulled back again. Most of the phased plans began with the gradual addition of researchers to campus, with significant health screening mandates and limits on the density of people in on-campus spaces by room or building. At the University of Michigan, the ramping-up process began with a pilot wave to help identify issues and challenges and to prepare for a broader reopening. This pilot wave involved six schools and colleges on the Ann Arbor campus, each of which opened multiple facilities in one or two buildings each. Lessons learned from this first phase helped refine guidelines for the next wave of ramping up. Institutions often included explicit reference to the state of the infection in their communities – for example, Columbia University's first phase required stabilization of the virus spread, and it specified that to enter the second phase infection rates must be relatively low and stable.

Universities worked closely with public health officials and state and local officials to align reopening guidelines with governmental guidance. Some institutions faced difficulties in communicating with state and local government agencies regarding the nature of research activities at universities. For example, in California, state and county guidance for reopening included research activities in biotech and other industries, but specifically excluded universities. Ten schools in southern California worked together to help government officials better understand that the research and education functions of a university are fundamentally different, and that research activities at a university could be compared to research activities at companies. In addition, state, county, and city guidance sometimes contradicted each other, delaying research ramp-up activities in some places.

Given the diversity of research activities on campuses, many institutions provided specific guidance for particular kinds of research activities or facilities. Such policies addressed lab-based research (wet and dry labs), human subjects work, studios, machine shops and makerspaces, off-site field research, social, behavioral and professional school research, community-based research, animal work, and visual and performing arts. For human subjects work specifically, many institutions involved their institutional review boards in approving plans to restart projects that had been paused and provided specific templates for plans in this area (Lumeng et al., 2020).

Senior administrators designed most institutional research reopening plans implicitly or explicitly with the health and safety of the community as their top priority. As such, institutions implemented a number of public health control measures to ensure that returning to in-person research work was safe. Such plans included a combination of mandatory face coverings, rigorous cleaning procedures, symptom screening, contact tracing, testing requirements, physical modifications to spaces, social distancing rules, limited building access, and controls on the density of people in any given space at a time. Institutions varied on how they implemented phased reopening plans, in the same region or state. The University of California, San Diego (UCSD), for example, began with 25% occupancy rules, then ramped to 50% and eventually 100%, whereas the University of California, Davis, began with 33% occupancy rules, then ramped to 66% before arriving at 100%. The California State System began with 35% occupancy then increased to 50%, 75%, and eventually 100%. Some schools specified separating people into cohorts, scheduling those cohorts in shifts, and limiting the contact between cohorts to minimize the chance of spreading the disease and facilitate contact tracing.

Most institutions' plans for ramping up research allowed exceptions for personnel concerned about returning to in-person work—especially individuals who were deemed high-risk due to existing medical conditions or susceptibility to COVID-19. Many institutions also accommodated the wishes of faculty, staff, or trainees who requested to stay home for any reason. UCSD's guidelines prohibited anyone pressuring undergraduate and graduate students or postdoctoral scholars to return to in-person activities during the earliest, highest-risk phases. In some cases, institutional policy prohibited altogether certain classes of students (e.g., undergraduates) from returning to work out of an abundance of caution.

FINANCIAL IMPLICATIONS

During the first days of the research shutdown, very few institutions recognized the severity of the disruption and the potential financial implications. As the weeks progressed, it became clear that not only would it take months before the first stages of reopening could take place, but that research activities would be significantly reduced for months to follow. Therefore, the financial implications of the shutdown on research expenditures went from mostly an afterthought to a major crisis in the span of a few weeks.

The primary issue driving the initial concern was that graduate students, postdocs, and research faculty relying on external funding for salary support would be unable to draw salary from federal grants if the performance of in-person work was not permissible. Such a limitation made thousands of workers vulnerable across the US, including many who were in their early career or in positions with less job security. To address this concern, the federal government issued guidance authorized by the Office of Management and Budget (OMB) that provided flexibility and administrative relief from specific legal requirements and responsibilities that are conditions of receiving federal funding. The initial memorandum was issued in early March 2020 and extended multiple times through September 2020 (see, for example, OMB, 2020).

In the earliest days of the shutdown and subsequent ramp-up, in-person activities ground to a halt (essential research, defined above, being an exception) as a control measure to mitigate the spread of the virus. Many universities instituted spending freezes to account for the uncertain financial impact that COVID-19 would have on operating budgets, which also limited spending on research activities, even those that could be done safely or remotely (with exceptions only rarely being granted to those working on essential activities). Such freezes included restrictions on internal spending of resources that research-intensive institutions historically fund themselves (e.g., seed funding programs, equipment, fellowships). Some institutions did invest in new seed funding programs for research related to COVID-19 despite the considerable budgetary implications of the shutdown. As an example, Johns Hopkins University rapidly launched a $6.4M COVID-19 Research Response Program in March 2020 that supported multiple early scientific discoveries related to addressing the pandemic, which led to $59M in external funding (Messersmith, Stoddart-Osumah, Lennon, and Wirtz, 2021). Such institutional support—along with rapid funding programs from federal agencies, private foundations, and other organizations—led to significant national investment in research related to COVID-19. Many states and federal agencies also used funding received from the $2.2T Coronavirus Aid, Relief, and Economic Security (CARES) Act, passed in late March 2020, to fund research on COVID-19.

As the length of the shutdown wore on, and it became clear that the ramp-up would be protracted over months (or longer), institutions also began worrying about how declines in research activity would affect revenue generated from funded research, in terms of actual research expenditures and the related indirect cost recovery associated with most federal grants. As a result, there was also an active push from institutions and membership organizations, such as the Association of American Universities, for additional research relief in the form of the Research Investment to Spark the Economy (RISE) Act to address a so-called "salary gap" on grants that were still drawing down salary support but were unable to complete the actual research. Although this effort ultimately was unsuccessful, several federal agencies including the National Institutes of Health (NIH) offered supplemental funding for research most affected by COVID-19 shutdowns.

IMPACT ON RESEARCHERS

Given the personal impact of COVID-19's disruption of both institutional and social structures, it is not surprising that the effects for members of the research community mirrored that of other academics. In many ways, COVID-19 exacerbated existing inequities across the research enterprise (Kromydas, 2017) and introduced new ones. Research inequities were not simply caused by the lack of access to research facilities and materials due to the research shutdown, but also from the side-effects of the pandemic's closure of other sectors of society, including schools, daycares, elderly care facilities, and travel. There were additional burdens of other modified campus operations including teaching and increased service requirements.

Equity Insights

The limitation on time available for research due to new or increased demands proved one of the COVID-19 pandemic's primary and inequitable impacts on researchers' activities. A survey of over 4,500 researchers during the first months of the pandemic highlighted the disparate impacts COVID-19 was having on the research community (Myers et al., 2020). In particular, it showed clearly that the pandemic was having a tremendous impact on women (due to caregiving and remote school responsibilities disproportionately falling on them). Subsequent studies also demonstrated the reduced productivity of women during COVID-19 as measured by publications or social media activity, which were primarily attributed to disproportionately reduced time for research (Anderson et al., 2020; Kim & Patterson, 2020). As outlined in a related opinion article, these interruptions to research productivity—combined with economic disparities and increased teaching and service expectations—will clearly be a significant long-term impediment to career advancement for women, with intersectional identities increasing this likelihood (Malisch et al., 2020).

Researchers from multiple other vulnerable groups also felt the effects of COVID-19. Those who lacked access to high-speed internet or other resources required to work from home were unable to pivot quickly to remote work arrangements. At the same time, those with disabilities or health conditions found themselves unable to return to in-person activities early, which impacted their ability to perform research. Individuals with co-morbidities had the additional burden of balancing health and economic risks with the need to conduct in-person research. Researchers from underrepresented groups, including ethnic and racial minorities, often experienced exacerbated impacts given preexisting systemic discrimination and bias. For example, these researchers already experience disproportionate requests for service—particularly DEI work—which left them even more time constrained early in the pandemic when other issues (e.g., childcare, eldercare, teaching, supporting student mental health) required immediate and time-intensive attention. Additionally, early financial restrictions on internal spending disproportionately affected researchers receiving internal sources of support, including programs meant to diversify the workforce or compensate for some of their additional service burden.

Some institutions implemented steps to mitigate some of these disparities, including stopping tenure and promotion clocks (for early career faculty), subsidizing childcare, or reducing teaching loads; however, some of these interventions could also inadvertently create inequities. A report from the National Alliance for Inclusive & Diverse STEM Faculty, for example, highlighted how tenure clock extensions alone were insufficient and might be applied inequitably without clear safeguards in place (Gonzales & Griffin, 2020). Nevertheless, justifiable concern existed about whether the progress, albeit limited, from years of DEI programs across the research community would be undone. Given the long-term financial impacts of the pandemic on institutions, these effects on the next generation of researchers might be felt for years to come.

The careers of early career researchers were significantly impacted. Many graduate students missed a critical time in their PhD training to complete research, network or present at conferences, or receive training in new methodologies. The shutdowns from COVID-19 also essentially eliminated a full cycle of the academic job market, which had multiple effects on senior PhD students and postdocs hoping to secure positions for the coming year. Not only would the loss of that cycle reduce future employment opportunities and make subsequent cycles even more competitive, but significant uncertainty was also created regarding job security given inability to remain fully funded for another year in the same research group or program. This uncertainty led to the loss of many early career researchers from the research community as they sought more secure or stable employment opportunities.

Travel and visa restrictions associated with COVID-19 also had a significant impact on researchers, both domestic researchers with international research activities as well as international researchers trying to work in the United States, and indeed on research collaborations overall. (See Chapter 3 for a discussion of the pandemic's impact on international programs.) Institutions that have large numbers of international doctoral students were likely to be particularly affected; a survey from the Council of Graduate Schools showed that first-time international graduate student enrollment decreased 39% from fall 2019 to fall 2020 (Zhou & Gao, 2021). A dramatically smaller pool of doctoral students nationally may severely hinder the research enterprise over time. Similarly, those researchers whose research required travel, and particularly international travel, experienced significant professional effects due to the global impact of the pandemic. For example, travel restrictions could result in the loss of entire seasons of data collection or observational periods for long-term studies by researchers who work in certain field sites abroad or domestically. Some research activities were able to continue virtually after an initial interruption, such as conferences or qualitative interviews, but it was not possible to replace all the functions of travel—for performing research or sparking new collaborations—with online alternatives.

In the early stages of the research ramp-up, decisions about which researchers could return to in-person work, and when, also may have inadvertently exacerbated issues of equity and access. Most institutions stated explicitly that those who could work from home should continue to do so, reserving limited capacity for in-person activities to those who needed to be on-site. In many cases, institutions gave individual faculty members responsible for leading a lab or research group the authority to prioritize who could access on-site facilities within their own groups, often giving priority to deadline-driven research and scholarship. Such triage likely created inequities within research groups with potentially long-term implications for researchers who were not permitted to return to on-site activities even when they wished to do so.

Researchers at different types of institutions were affected in varying ways. For example, faculty overseeing research projects at primarily undergraduate institutions lost most of the people in their research groups for the summer of 2020 and the academic year 2020–2021, resulting in essentially a lost year of research. This loss was particularly challenging for faculty with experimental research in the early stages of their careers. Institutions that relied more heavily on doctoral students and postdoctoral positions were able to absorb more of the impact and return to research quickly, though initially at a reduced capacity. Conversely, having trainees bear the greatest health risk in returning to campus to perform research while most faculty continued to work remotely, even with proper mitigation strategies in place, highlights the disparities in the research training model. Most notably, this model has an overreliance on trainees as a core component of the research workforce in the US, particularly in the laboratory sciences and medical research.

RESEARCH LEADERSHIP AND DECISION-MAKING ON CAMPUSES

The initial decisions to shut down all non-essential research activities were made in concert with decisions tied to other institutional closures. In the early stages of the pandemic, most institutions delegated the development and implementation of policies and plans specific to reduced research operations to the senior research officer, who worked in close collaboration with other senior leadership. Given that most institutions developed these plans in just a matter of days, there was very little time for deliberative decision-making (such as deep engagement with faculty governance or the broader research community). The urgency and uncertainty of the pandemic in those early stages required quick decisions to ensure the safety of community members.

During the time that research operations were mostly shut down (beginning in March 2020) to when non-essential research began ramping up (around June 2020), decision-making again became more collaborative and inclusive of additional campus stakeholders. Various pandemic response teams comprised of members of faculty governance or research leaders across campus (e.g., associate deans for research, center directors, department chairs) helped represent the research community's needs and interests and advocated for the ways in which the research community could assist in the pandemic. At the University of Illinois, Urbana-Champaign, for example, researchers quickly developed and deployed COVID-19 testing strategies for the university and eventually surrounding communities (Citizen Access, 2022). These groups, whether formal or informal, worked tirelessly to aid institutions in developing plans and guiding principles for reopening. In addition to senior administrators, campus response teams included or were at least informed by relevant research expertise on campus. These experts spanned disciplines from public health to engineering and contributed significantly to campus response plans. Institutions also set up review committees that often consisted of these same groups to rapidly approve COVID-19 research projects that could continue as essential while other on-site activities were still prohibited.

Many institutions articulated guiding principles for decision-making during the stages of preparing to ramp up non-essential research planning. The priority put on health and safety helped to explain why institutions were proceeding cautiously despite significant pushback from some faculty who wanted to return to their in-person research immediately with limited restrictions. These principles also stressed a need to adhere to public health directives from local, state, and national entities. Some guiding principles statements also mentioned that decisions would be led by available evidence, which was changing rapidly in 2020 as our collective understanding of COVID-19 evolved. Other topics denoted in these statements included maintaining research excellence, providing a transparent and consistent process for determining permissible levels of activity, ensuring equitable outcomes for all, and reviewing and updating approaches regularly as information changed. Other principles included working to ensure timely and effective decisions, and, when possible, allowing for flexibility within the necessary parameters for different kinds of research activities.

Reopening research safely in the summer of 2020 allowed institutions to pilot and test reopening plans that would later be implemented in the fall of 2020 for broader campus operations, including the anticipated reintroduction of large populations of undergraduate students to campus. The decisions and processes put in place for research activities, and the generally safe outcomes from those decisions, helped guide decision-making for improved outcomes later across all campus operations despite many institutions still operating at reduced capacity for the entire 2020–2021 academic year.

Although emergency response planning at major research institutions includes some research operations, the focus is generally on critical safety or compliance functions (e.g., laboratory and personnel safety, animal care). Planning is not always focused on subsequent or downstream effects that most other research activities will experience, such as maintaining long-running experiments, preserving rare materials or equipment, or being unable to access research and scholarship physical spaces for prolonged periods of time. Emergency plans are also typically focused on short timeframes, from a brief interruption (such as a storm or power outage) to a more acute emergency or crisis (e.g., natural disaster, security risk). Many of these emergency plans are required components of accreditation for performing certain types of research on campus. In 2017, the National Academy of Sciences released a report highlighting the critical importance of strengthening the disaster resilience of the biomedical research enterprise, for instance, but that study, too, focused on examples of more acute disasters (e.g., hurricanes, earthquakes) to highlight vulnerabilities (National Academies of Sciences, Engineering, and Medicine, 2017). The fact that research operations ground to a halt for months in spring 2020 due to a global respiratory pandemic represented an unprecedented level of crisis that caught nearly everyone off guard, from institutions to funding agencies.

LESSONS LEARNED

There are numerous lessons from having experienced the early, and subsequent, days of the pandemic. The following presents six areas where insights are provided, across a range of considerations. These include: (1) emergency planning for research must evolve; (2) people are at the center of the research enterprise; (3) the new normal presents new opportunities for equity; (4) institutions must double down on diversity, equity and inclusion efforts in research; (5) research incentives need deep rethinking; and (6) research can significantly inform campus operations.

Emergency Planning for Research Must Evolve

Though not alone, research-focused institutions found themselves unprepared for a disruption as extensive as that caused by COVID-19. Future planning to improve research resilience needs to include faculty, staff, students, participants, and other stakeholders. Although ramp-up plans were carried out in a more inclusive manner than the initial shutdown mandates, many institutions still experienced challenges in working with stakeholders—especially faculty governance and local public health authorities. The lack of federal leadership in providing guidance to the research community resulted in a piecemeal approach for research operations across the country, with institutions responding in dramatically different fashions.

This lack of preparedness affected not only the scientific workforce, but also the ability of researchers to help find solutions to ongoing challenges created by the crisis itself. With COVID-19, had it not been for institutions finding creative solutions for researchers to continue working, we would have been even further behind in the national response to the pandemic. Building resilience across the research enterprise should therefore become a top priority nationally. Although one size does not fit all, higher education membership organizations can help facilitate resiliency planning and accountability for institutions to develop and maintain plans. Critically, these research resiliency plans should be developed in concert with better preparedness across other key missions of higher education, including teaching, economic development, and workforce development. Research represents a critical sector of the US economy. Maintaining the research pipeline is crucial for economic and national security at the macroscale, and at the university level, it comprises a significant budgetary component of large academic research institutions.

People are at the Center of the Research Enterprise

The COVID-19 pandemic highlighted the fact that the research enterprise is, first and foremost, composed of people. The pandemic immediately introduced new vulnerabilities to many groups within the research community, threatening not only their livelihoods and career advancement, but also institutional commitments to the performance of research. The pandemic provided another example of how the system has evolved to a state of over-reliance on trainees with poor job security to keep research programs running, and these people suffered enormous losses during the shutdown. The federal government's allowance to continue paying trainees and soft money researchers on grants was instrumental in helping, yet was only a temporary first step. Moving forward, the federal government and institutions must consider how to invest more directly in people—making their work less tied to individual research grants—to sustain a functional research infrastructure.

The New Normal Presents New Opportunities for Equity

Despite the deep inequities introduced or exacerbated by COVID-19, the disruption caused by the pandemic did provide some opportunities for enhancing equity in the research enterprise. The shutdown allowed some people who normally would be unable to travel to conferences or to give seminars (e.g., due to childcare responsibilities, health conditions, or institutional travel budgets) to participate remotely. It also leveled the playing field in terms of normalizing flexible work arrangements that some groups (women, in particular) had been seeking prior to the pandemic to accommodate disproportionate home care and childcare responsibilities. Overall, more flexibility in the research community could aid in efforts to retain diverse members of the research workforce. Institutions must critically examine how simply returning to the way things were done before COVID-19 may not be possible or ideal in the future.

Institutions Must Double Down on Diversity, Equity and Inclusion Efforts in Research

COVID-19 revealed that numerous advances around diversity, equity, and inclusion (DEI) were not as irreversible and structural as many would have hoped. The early phase of the pandemic shone a harsh light on, and in many cases exacerbated, systemic equity issues that have persisted for decades. Our most vulnerable researchers by career stage, gender, race, and ethnicity stand to be deeply impacted by COVID-19 for years to come. True structural changes in training, recruitment, retention, and promotion will help all members of the academic research enterprise, not just those who are the most privileged, withstand future disruptions. We also need further research on the topics around diversity, equity, and inclusion themselves to learn new ways to mitigate biases, understand what creates unintended consequences, and assess those actions that do lead to sustained successes. Until that happens, the academic research enterprise will continue to be susceptible to simply reverting to historical inequitable structures in the face of future disruptions.

Research Incentives Need Deep Rethinking

The disparate impact on research productivity by field, type of research, and type of institution highlights the need to rethink current research incentives. Institutions must recognize that easy assessment tools such as number of publications or grant dollars have significant caveats. Assessment for promotion and tenure, national research awards, and other honorifics need to consider the inequities within research structures, including the resources and time certain researchers have to perform their research activities. Attempts to help faculty by granting optional extensions on tenure clocks, for example, further exacerbated the inequities by allowing faculty who could complete research work remotely to remain on track while others (for example, with equipment needs or significant childcare responsibilities) continued to fall behind. The proving grounds of promotion and tenure were not designed to consider these nuances or inequities but must do so in the future or risk further alienating and pushing out researchers from vulnerable groups.

Research Can Significantly Inform Campus Operations

Across the country, researchers at academic institutions helped provide their expertise to inform decision-making at all levels of society—from the federal government to local municipalities, including decision-making about campus operations during the pandemic. Large research institutions brought expertise related to epidemiology, finance, behavioral sciences, and engineering, among other fields, that informed how campuses reopened facilities and reintroduced people back to campus in a safe way. Moving forward, research expertise can and should continue to inform campus operations beyond the pandemic response—from transportation services to communications to disaster planning.

REFERENCES

Anderson, J. P., Nielsen, M. W., Simone, N. L., Lewiss, R. E., & Jagsi, R. (2020). Meta-Research: COVID-19 medical papers have fewer women first authors than expected. *eLife* 9, e58807 Retrieved from https://doi.org/10.7554/eLife.58807

Carnegie Classification of Institutions of Higher Education (2018). *Indiana University Center for Postsecondary Research (n.d.)*. Bloomington, IN: Indiana University. Retrieved from https://carnegieclassifications.acenet.edu/

Citizen Access (2022). The race to test for Covid-19 at the University of Illinois. Retrieved from http://www.cu-citizenaccesso.org//2022/01/the-race-to-test-for-covid-19-at-the-university-of-illinois/

Droegemeier, K. K. Snyder, L. A., Knoedler, A. Taylor, W., Litwiller, B., Whitacre, C., Gobstein, H., Keller, C., Hinds, T. L., & Dwyer, N. (2017). The roles of chief research officers at American research universities: A current profile and challenges for the future. *Journal of Research Administration* 48(1), 26–64.

Gonzales, L. D., & Griffin, K. A. (2020). *Supporting Faculty and Their Careers During and After COVID-19*. Washington, DC: Aspire Alliance.

Kim, E., & Patterson, S. (2020). The pandemic and gender inequality in academia. *SSRN*. Retrieved from https://doi.org/10.2139/ssrn.3666587

Kromydas, T. Rethinking higher education and its relationship with social inequalities: past knowledge, present state and future potential. *Palgrave Commun* 3, 1 (2017). Retrieved from https://doi.org/10.1057/s41599-017-0001-8

Lumeng, J. C., Chavous, T. M., Lok, A. S., Sen, S., Wigginton, N. S., & Cunningham, R. M. (2020). Opinion: A risk–benefit framework for human research during the COVID-19 pandemic. *Proceedings of the National Academy of Sciences*, 117 (45) 27749–27753. Retrieved from https://doi.org/10.1073/pnas.2020507117

Mackenzie, D. (2020, June). Reuse of N95 masks. *Engineering* (Beijing, China). Retrieved from https://www.ncbi.nlm.nih.gov/pmc/articles/PMC7153525/

Malisch, J. L., Harris, B. N., Sherrer, S. M., Lewis, K. A., Shepherd, S. L., McCarthy, P. C., Spott, J. L., Karam, E. P., Moustaid-Moussa, N., Calarco, J. M., Ramalingam, L., Talley, A. E., Cañas-Carrell, J. E., Ardon-Dryer, K., Weiser, D. A., Bernal, X. E., & Deitloff, J. (2020). Opinion: In the wake of COVID-19, academia needs new solutions to ensure gender equity. *Proceedings of the National Academy of Sciences*, 117 (27) 15378–15381. Retrieved from https://doi.org/10.1073/pnas.2010636117

Messersmith, J., Stoddart-Osumah, C., Lennon, M., & Wirtz, D. (2021). Emergency seed funding for COVID-19 research: Lessons from Johns Hopkins University, *Journal of Clinical Investigation*, 131(1), e145615. Retrieved from https://doi.org/10.1172/JCI145615

Myers, K. R., Tham, W. Y., Yin, Y., Cohodes, N., Thursby, J. G., Thursby, M. C., Schiffer, P., Walsh, J. T., Lakhani, K. R., & Wang, D. (2020). Unequal effects of the COVID-19 pandemic on scientists. *Nature Human Behavior* 4, 880–883. Retrieved from https://doi.org/10.1038/s41562-020-0921-y

National Academies of Sciences, Engineering, and Medicine. (2017). *Strengthening the Disaster Resilience of the Academic Biomedical Research Community: Protecting the Nation's Investment*. Washington, DC: The National Academies Press. Retrieved from https://doi.org/10.17226/24827

National Center for Science and Engineering Statistics (2019). *Higher education research and development survey: Fiscal year 2018*. Alexandria, VA: National Science Foundation.

National Science Foundation, National Center for Science and Engineering Statistics. (2019). *National Patterns of R&D Resources: 2017–18 Data Update*. NSF 20-307. Alexandria, VA: National Science Foundation. Available at https://ncses.nsf.gov/pubs/nsf20307

Office of Management and Budget (OMB). (2020, March 19). *Memorandum to the heads of executive departments and agencies*. Retrieved from https://www.whitehouse.gov/wp-content/uploads/2020/03/M-20-17.pdf

Wigginton, N. S., Cunningham, R. M., Katz, R. H., Lidstrom, M. E., Moler, K. A., Wirtz, D., & Zuber, M. T. (2020). Moving academic research forward during Covid-19. *Science*, 368(6496), 1190–1192. Retrieved from https://doi.org/10.1126/science.abc5599

Zhou, E., & Gao, J. (2021). *International graduate applications & enrollment: Fall 2020*. Washington, DC: Council of Graduate Schools.

Part II
Community and Operations

Chapter 6

Student Services, Housing, and Dining

Kristi N. Hottenstein

For all sectors of higher education, from large community colleges to small residential liberal arts colleges, from regional publics to research-intensive universities, a range of supports are needed beyond academic affairs to assure student success and engagement. Many of these areas—from bookstores to dining halls—also provide key auxiliary revenues to help institutions balance budgets and offset instructional costs. When the COVID-19 pandemic hit, residence and dining halls, health and counseling centers, and student support services scrambled to deliver the support students needed while responding to shifting public health policies and new safety protocols.

HOUSING

Along with the move to online education detailed in Chapter 4 on Academic Continuity, swift changes to campus housing occupied the forefront of institutional responses to the COVID-19 pandemic. Decisions varied across regions and sectors, but most campuses closed residence halls and some sent students home as early as the first week of March 2020. The differences in decision patterns regarding moving students out of housing varied by institutional type, and perhaps more importantly, by the percentage of the institution's budget that depended on revenues from room and board. Some institutions, particularly smaller private institutions with significant budgetary consequences for refunding housing payments, allowed students to remain in the residence halls longer, holding on to hope (and revenue). Institutional peer pressure was another contributing factor to housing decisions through this period: when it became clear that most peer institutions were moving people off campus and out of the residence halls as quickly as possible, many IHEs felt pressure to refund students for housing. Most institutions, despite the financial consequences, put student and staff safety above revenue loss and got out in front, not only to move students out but also to issue refunds.

> You know one of the interesting things about how this has all played out, is it is very clear that higher ed, to a degree, is kind of a big game of "follow the leader." What one institution is going to do ends up putting a lot of pressure on other institutions, either like institutions, neighboring institutions, or institutions within the same state. There was no way we were going to allow students to move out and not provide some sort of a credit refund, so we got out in front of it.
>
> —Christopher Giordano, Vice Chancellor for Student Affairs, University of Michigan-Flint.

For those colleges and universities existing within some type of system, central directives or collective decisions also impacted institutional actions around housing in spring 2020. Some "loose" systems allowed for decisions to vary from campus to campus, while others took a coordinated all-campuses approach. In North Carolina, for example, the community college system recommended suspension of all face-to-face instruction across its 58 campuses by March 23, 2020. In turn, the University of North Carolina system refunded almost $77 million to students for housing in April 2020 after shutting down campuses, and by June 2020 were rewriting housing contracts to avoid future need for such refunds (Divers, 2020). The Pennsylvania State System of Higher Education (PASSHE), on the other hand, did not issue a master directive when the pandemic hit. Institutions in the system are spread out across the state and were impacted differently by COVID "hot spots." Thus, each institution had autonomy to make its own decision regarding closures.

While student affairs and other institutional leaders knew it was in students' best interest to vacate the residence halls, how that outcome was handled had financial implications. If moving out was "mandatory," IHEs would need to refund housing for the term. However, if leaving residence halls was termed "voluntary" or "strongly encouraged," IHEs could perhaps thread a needle on refund decisions. Specific student populations also informed institutional decision-making. For example, at Saginaw Valley State University, with a large foster care population as well as many veteran students, the need to provide housing for these students drove their decision to remain open. Approximately 500 of their 2400 residential students chose to remain on campus. According to their housing operations manager, budget did play a role in the optional decision for Saginaw Valley State University. Students who chose to leave the residence halls did receive a refund although framing decisions as optional meant the university did not have to make refunds to all residential students.

The University of Michigan-Flint did not require mandatory move outs but used language that implied students needed to leave without directly saying so, by strongly encouraging students to vacate the residence halls as part of the campus's

"Stay Home, Stay Safe" initiative. They also gave deadlines for students to move out and attached refund eligibility to those deadlines. This tactic proved successful and by the deadline, only 46 of its nearly 500 residential students remained in residence.

Housing Exceptions

Housing and residence life leaders worried through this period about how to best care for those students who could not vacate the residence halls. Boston University, for example, notified their students while on spring break not to return to campus. They used strong (essentially mandatory) language but left a caveat that students could apply to remain in housing if they faced extraordinary circumstances. For many international students, students who had aged out of foster care programs, and others with vulnerable or fragile home circumstances, college or university housing was, effectively, home. Survey results from the Hope Center in April and May of 2020 indicated that 6% of college and university students reported a lack of safety where they lived (Goldrick-Rab et al., 2020).

Given the desire to reduce density as much as possible, most institutions favored opt-in rather than opt-out strategies, meaning that if students wanted or needed to stay, the IHEs required them to petition and explain why this was necessary. One practice that many institutions utilized was a scale, or rubric, to determine the need of the student to remain in housing, a process intended to ensure fairness and consistency in decision-making. Others felt that requiring explanations could exclude some vulnerable students from the support they needed on campus if they were uncomfortable revealing conditions at home or their lack of housing.

> One of the things that I made really clear to our staff is we are not sending anyone into an environment where they could be put into some kind of danger, or where there would be a danger to their health, safety, or emotional health. If someone volunteered the information that 'I can't return home for X,' we didn't ask for any kind of proof or anything like that, we just said, "Stay."
> —Christopher Giordano, Vice Chancellor for Student Affairs, University of Michigan-Flint.

Housing Consolidation for Security and Cost Measures

For many IHEs, once most students went home, it made sense to consolidate remaining students into one (or more) residence halls. Decisions on which halls to close, and into which to consolidate students depended largely on social distancing capabilities, as well as other space considerations, such as the ability to isolate and quarantine students or the ability to provide them with food service. Consolidation helped to save on utility costs, and, in some cases, allowed for unused residence hall space to be converted into housing for COVID-19 patients or for essential front-line workers (see Chapter 9 on Facilities).

Communication

Communication to residential students regarding decisions about housing and move-out was critical during the early stages of the pandemic. National, state, and local public health mandates all needed to be digested and weighed, as did information from professional associations related to housing and residence life. In addition, these communications needed to be coordinated with the daily information being distributed from other parts of the institution (see Chapter 2 for additional details about communications). Information from the Centers for Disease Control and Prevention (CDC), the states, and both state and national higher education associations and professional bodies framed decisions and communications. Further, regular meetings with peer group institutions helped to inform decisions on many campuses. Institutional leaders wanted to understand what their colleagues and other IHEs were doing both nationally and regionally, and then translate that information into local decisions. Housing directors and student affairs divisions had to weigh the various levels of recommendations (and later mandates) and to communicate them in an effective way to students. Clear, consistent, and frequent messaging for stakeholders on a variety of platforms, all within a short window, proved critical. In some residence halls, staff went door to door to try to gather information on who had vacated residences, since many students had left voluntarily and without notice after classes moved to remote instruction.

Those IHEs largely serving a local population had an easier time creating plans to move students out of the residence halls, as the majority of their students could just drive home or have someone pick them up as opposed to flying. Those with larger national or international populations faced huge challenges assisting students in securing travel as regions began to shut down. Since many institutions made the decision to shutter campus during or around spring break, while many students were away and while some short-term study abroad programs were still running, access to or storage of students' belongings became another logistical hurdle. Institutions with space for students to store larger belongings were at an advantage, as some students could not move out completely from their campus rooms on institutions' timelines if they lived a significant distance away. Housing and residence life staff worked to catalog items students left behind or requested to store and then, where appropriate, began outreach to determine when students could come and pick up their belongings.

Challenges for Residence Life

For those students who remained on campus, leaders needed to determine how best to continue on-campus services, including food, hall programming, and support for those who needed to quarantine. One challenge for housing and residence life leaders was motivating and calming the remaining on-campus staff, including resident assistants (RAs) who were themselves students with many wanting to go home. This reliance on student-workers threatened to leave residence halls that did remain open very short-staffed. Questions from parents about RAs' safety and protocols flooded the inboxes of housing directors, who grappled with how to address the contractual relationships with these student-workers.

Campuses also had to develop protocols for resident students who were exposed to those with COVID-19, symptomatic, or in need of testing. They created reporting and self-reporting procedures, with different protocols and responses depending upon if a student self-reported, was referred, had had a test, and if the test proved positive. Housing and residence life leaders and staff had to determine policies regarding quarantine and self-isolation, as well as make decisions on how to get food, medication, toiletries, and other essential items to quarantined students.

Students who remained on campus needed social connections for their well-being. Yet the social distancing requirements, designed to reduce exposure, made the creation of such opportunities a challenge for housing directors and Student Life offices. Some institutions tried to create topical programs to address COVID-19 related needs and concerns, including programming on health and wellness, along with more practical sessions like how to cook healthy food in the residence halls. Despite efforts, many institutions experienced extremely low participation rates given fears of exposure. IHEs used virtual outreach through platforms such as Zoom, to communicate with remaining residential students.

Housing directors also needed to develop new training for RAs and desk workers around shifting residence protocols, programming, and cleaning and safety guidelines. They shared up-to-date information with housing staff regarding how they needed to carry out their duties within evolving public health guidelines. Housing and residence life leaders also needed to make sure that their staff were protected, which involved ensuring that they had whatever personal protective equipment (PPE) they needed, such as masks and gloves, and that they knew and practiced strategies to keep them safe.

To get a sense of the many changes taking place almost simultaneously around housing, Figure 6.1 reflects the decision-making and information timeline followed in March–June 2020 by the University of Michigan-Flint Office of Housing and Residence Life to ensure timely and adequate communication to its residential students.

Housing related timeline of decisions and related communications by the University of Michigan-Flint Office of Housing and Residence Life from March to June 2020.

- March 18, 2020: Notification to Residential Students:
    - Move-out of residence halls by March 22
    - Eligible students receive flat-rate room refund ($900 per resident
    - Eligible students receive pro-rata meal plan refund (up to $483)
    - Total Refund for Room: $234,094
    - Total Refund for Board: $39,434
- March 20, 2020: Follow-up communication to residential students about move-out process
- March 22, 2020:
    - Move-out process completed; First Street Residence Hall closed
    - Remaining students housed in Riverfront Residence Hall; 47 students in total (mostly international)
- March 23, 2020:
    - Michigan "Stay Home, Stay Safe" announced
    - Housing actions include: incorporating public health safety measures into operations; implementing "no guest" policy; transitioning to online food ordering (Food Service delivers meals to Riverfront); Department of Public Safety begins daily grocery shuttle to Wal-Mart; housing staff transitioned to remote work
- March 31, 2020:
    - Follow-up communication to residential students that board refund was processed
- April 3, 2020:
    - With support from the Mott Foundation ($100K grant), First Street Residence Hall opens for *Healing Heroes Housing* (housing for healthcare workers)
    - Averages approximately 20 healthcare workers per week @ $20/night
- April 27, 2020:
    - Per Executive Order, face coverings are required within public spaces in both residence halls
- May 2020:
    - Housing 18 students for Spring term
    - Estimated housing budget shortfall for FY20 to be $57,000
    - Installed plexiglass barrier at the front desk of both residence halls
- Fall 2020 Planning:
    - Prepared room assignment model per public health guidelines and set residence occupancy rates
    - COVID-19 modeling reduces total occupancy to 317 with an anticipated budget deficit of $682,254
- Reviewing the following with EOC Committee:
- Occupancy limits in common areas (e.g., hallways, stairwells, elevators, etc.);
- Self-isolation and quarantine locations and protocols;
- Physical distancing guidelines per public health recommendations;
- Daily cleaning guidelines per public health recommendations;
- Use of face coverings within each residence hall (in public spaces);
- Hybrid on-site and remote staffing structure.

Figure 6.1 Housing related timeline of decisions and related communications by the University of Michigan-Flint Office of Housing and Residence Life from March to June 2020.

STUDENT SERVICES, HOUSING, AND DINING

STUDENT HEALTH AND COUNSELING SERVICES

With rapid changes occurring, demand for health and counseling services reached unprecedented levels. The following sections present information on both these types of services, along with campus faith ministries.

Health Centers

At IHEs that offered health services, leaders of campus health centers played a key role in early and ongoing responses to the global pandemic in spring 2020. One of the first challenges they faced was the need to establish student health services related to the novel coronavirus, including testing, quarantine recommendations, and contact tracing in collaboration with local health agencies. Campus health leaders focused on developing reporting forms, apps, and screening procedures, and worked with state and local government agencies on protocols and strategies for contract tracing. Residential campuses needed to quickly operationalize daily monitoring plans of quarantined and ill students. They needed to ensure adequate supplies for example, PPE were available for staff and develop cleaning and care protocols to support quarantined students. Campus health practitioners and centers that had been set up to provide in-person care had to quickly pivot to offer telehealth appointments for students due to government mandates or campus closures. They also had to immediately explore options for mass testing, in many cases making use of such campus spaces as gymnasiums or stadiums to create testing sites that permitted social distancing while also working to assure HIPAA compliance and privacy guidelines in such extraordinary venues. Residential institutions that did not offer on-campus health services directed students to private healthcare but still had to have options available to serve students who were unable to travel home or off-campus due to COVID-19 exposure or diagnosis.

Some IHEs, particularly those in rural areas, struggled to get assistance and guidance from local health departments and had to rely on professional associations for guidance. Bridgette Winslow, Dean of the Institute for Pre-Health and Wellness Studies at Defiance College, a small private college in Defiance, Ohio, for example, shared:

> Location matters. Being in a rural location during a pandemic has its benefits, but local health departments were not ready, not prepared. They didn't have the resources for testing. We've had to get our guidance from the Association of Independent Colleges and Universities of Ohio.

Where smaller or more isolated institutions had challenges in getting public health guidance, others, particularly those with research capacities, were at the forefront of providing it by engaging in researching and developing COVID testing protocols for their local and state communities. The University of Michigan, for example, examined ways to scale up COVID-19 testing in the state and worked with the University's Institute for Health Policy and Innovation to provide considerations for policymakers (Anupindi et al., 2020). As Rebecca Cunningham, University of Michigan Vice President for Research, noted, "the generation of scientific knowledge across the University of Michigan will play a critical role as we work together to find solutions to this pandemic" (Researching a global pandemic, n.d.). Partnering with the private sector was also helpful for institutions located near biotechnology centers, such as the testing partnership announced between the University of California, San Francisco and the CZ Biohub in California's Bay Area in March 2020 (Hatmaker, 2020).

Counseling for a Mental Health Epidemic

The complete upheaval for students of their living and learning environments, coupled with the prevailing unease related to the escalating pandemic, took a toll on student mental health. Surveys and research on college student mental health in spring 2020 revealed how significantly the uncertainty and isolation of the pandemic environment created anxiety. College student mental health had already been at the forefront of concern for many higher education leaders before the pandemic hit, but early research indicated that the COVID-19 pandemic exacerbated mental health concerns in student populations. One study reported that 71% of student participants experienced increased stress and anxiety as a result of COVID-19 (Son et al., 2020). Contributing stressors noted in this survey ranged from fear for personal and family members' health to difficulty concentrating on coursework. Data from the CDC released in August 2020 reported that one in four students aged 18 to 24 years had seriously considered suicide in the last 30 days (Czeisler et al., 2020).

As the pandemic advanced, college counseling centers became more critical than ever in supporting student mental wellness. In the wake of the campus closures and stay-at-home orders, many counseling centers moved to virtual engagement such as telehealth screening and virtual counseling services. For some campuses, telehealth was an expansion of pre-existing virtual services, but for others, this was a completely new modality of operation. According to a survey conducted by the Association for University and College Counseling Center Directors (AUCCCD) in May 2020, prior to the pandemic 52% of college counseling center directors had reported no use of tele-counseling (LeViness et al., 2020). Tele-counseling was certainly not a new concept. In 2015, the Higher Education Mental Health Alliance (HEMHA) committed to advancing tele-counseling and have since produced resources like the HEMHA Guide to College Counseling at a Distance to assist colleges and universities with establishing tele-counseling services (Higher Education Mental Health Alliance, 2018). Though a recognized practice in the field, tele-counseling was unfamiliar to many institutions when the pandemic thrust campus counseling centers into this realm.

Varying state lockdown orders and licensure limitations for mental health counselors only compounded the problem of how to deliver services. Some universities successfully made the transition on their own to virtual mental health services while others used third-party services. In April 2020, for example, Johns Hopkins University partnered with TimelyMD, a telehealth service for physical and mental health. Some campuses also offered virtual wellness programming such as mindfulness, yoga, lectures, and guest speakers to aid students in maintaining mental wellness during the pandemic. Many faculty, particularly in psychology and psychiatry departments, shifted their research focuses to explore student mental health during the pandemic. Departments utilized their websites to provide additional resources for students, such as the page dedicated to COVID-19 resources established by the University of Michigan Department of Psychiatry (*Michigan psychiatry resources for COVID-19*, 2021). Student Affairs professionals acknowledged early on just how much they were asking of students—and the stress this was causing—and put plans in place to help with student physical and mental health.

> We wanted to ensure we were able to continue to provide counseling services through Counseling and Psychological Services. Initially we allowed in-person or virtual meetings, and we were able to identify a secure platform so we could have virtual meetings and counseling sessions, as well as some in-person sessions. Then, we got to a point where there was no more in-person and all counseling moved to online. Our other focus was a broader pursuit of wellness, not just mental health, but overall wellness. We made sure we continued to communicate with students on how they could maintain some kind of physical health during this. Our recreation center had all kinds of videos with different workouts that you could do or on nutrition, making sure that students are attending to those needs, as well. Wellness things that you could do on your own, such as recommendations for self-care or care for others. That was another piece of this, trying to think outside yourself: how can I help others who might be in need? There is some intrinsic value in helping others that might not have that sense of purpose through all of this. So doing what we could through social media, through online, through direct messaging, through referral services and resources, and through direct service is how we tried to get at some of this wellness piece for students.
> —Chris Giordano, Vice Chancellor for Student Affairs, University of Michigan-Flint.

KRISTI N. HOTTENSTEIN

Campus Ministries—the Intersection of Faith and Education

Nearly 1,000 of the 5,300 colleges and universities in the United States are religiously affiliated. These institutions self-identify as associated with a particular religion or denomination, with their institutional mission and culture generally very grounded and connected to the tenets of this faith. Such institutions tend to have strong campus ministry programs.

When the pandemic impacted all aspects of college life, campus ministries were no exception. A series of interviews on Atlanta's National Public Radio (NPR) in August 2020 highlighted how campus ministries adapted, and struggled, during the pandemic (Scott, 2020). In one of these interviews, Elliot Karp, the CEO of Hillels of Georgia, a state-wide organization focused on inspiring Jewish life on campuses, discussed the challenges the pandemic presented for the start of the Fall 2020 semester. This term coincides with the Jewish high holidays and is usually an opportunity to welcome new Jewish students to campus, but for 2020, these organizations faced a very different series of events due to the pandemic. From the need for plexiglass to protect participants during the blowing of the ram's horn during Rosh Hashanah to moving traditional Shabbat dinner gatherings to "Shabbat in a box" taken and then eaten in dorm rooms, Karp underscored that the COVID-19 pandemic had been particularly difficult for campus faith centers. Sharing some strategies to keep students engaged, Karp noted that while traditional meetings and meals were no longer possible, he had found success in enticing students to participate in virtual events by mailing them gift cards for meals and then inviting them to bring that meal to their computer for a virtual dinner. He also emphasized maintaining personal contact with students and training staff on addressing mental health concerns.

In another interview, Dema Mohammad Salih, president of the Muslim Student Organization at the University of Georgia, expressed similar sentiments to Karp's. In the hope that the foundations of the Muslim Student Association would stay strong during the pandemic, she shared that they had been offering weekly lectures via Zoom. Discussing the traditional Friday prayer, in which the group would usually have hosted 60 to 80 people, she noted that recently there had only been a handful of people in attendance. Salih said going to Friday prayer helps her practice her faith but that this practice now looked very different; instead of standing shoulder to shoulder with members of the faith, the group now maintained social distancing:

> We did put a sign up ... and we ensured that each person was 6 feet apart from each other, and everyone had to wear their mask, of course. We checked the temperature for each person and limited the number to 20.
>
> (Scott, 2020)

Like campus counseling services, campus ministries were both more significant than ever in providing a sense of connection, belonging, and support, and simultaneously cut off from their normal means for doing so. Excluded from their physical gathering places, campus ministries joined their colleagues in an increasingly crowded virtual space to try to connect with the students they served (Robles, 2020).

A Close-up Lens on Leadership

> At Alma College in Michigan, the COVID-19 pandemic was an opportunity to reaffirm leadership structures and reporting lines, as well as campus ministry strategies and priorities. The campus chaplain, Rev. Andrew Pomerville, reported directly to the college's CEO. This structural relationship proved a critical leadership decision when it came to campus ministries during the pandemic, providing the faith center direct access to the CEO and strengthening the credibility of the chaplain and his work during this difficult time. This Presbyterian-affiliated institution moved its interfaith activities online. Rev. Pomerville provided everyday reflections for 100 days for a variety of faiths via Facebook. This outreach, he observed, brought the Alma community together and engaged alumni and others. When asked if there was an advantage to engaging alumni during these particularly difficult times with campus ministries, the answer was a resounding, "yes." When the pandemic hit, Alma College had been in the middle of a fundraising campaign for significant chapel renovations.
>
> > I was nervous about fundraising for the chapel during a pandemic. I thought, given what people are going through, I doubt they will be thinking about being philanthropic. I was wrong. It was the opposite. We raised $2.1M for chapel renovations. My only worry now is how changing (renovating) such an iconic piece of campus during such a time of uncertainty will impact our community.
> >
> > Rev. Andrew Pomerville, Campus Chaplain, Alma College

DINING AND FOOD PANTRIES

Similar to mental health services, reliable access to sufficient and nutritious food was a serious problem for college-age students even prior to the onset of the COVID-19 pandemic. In 2019, the Hope Center found that 48% of two-year college students and 41% of four-year college students reported food insecurity. Not surprisingly, food insecurity is tied to low socioeconomic status, and has a disproportionate impact on students of color and first-generation students (Goldrik-Rab et al., 2019). In April and May of 2020, the Hope Lab commissioned an additional study to look at the impact of COVID-19 on basic need insecurities with disheartening results. Three out of five college students reported basic needs insecurities, and the gap between Black and White students in terms of basic needs securities was 19 points (Goldrik-Rab et al., 2020).

As the pandemic unfolded, campus food pantries across the country saw increased traffic, even with significantly fewer students on campus (Vespoli, 2020). One takeaway for student affairs professionals was to try to meet students where they are, even when many students were uncomfortable traveling to campus or did not have the means to do so due to COVID-compounded economic concerns. The City University of New York (CUNY) system, for example, allowed its students or staff members to go to any of the system's 18 open food pantries rather than require them to go to the food pantry at the university where they were enrolled or employed.

As residential students began to move home, and many colleges and universities moved to refund housing and dining fees, the volume of students eating on campuses quickly diminished. This shift left food service providers with large amounts of food that had been pre-purchased in bulk or frozen. Rather than let such food go to waste, some universities and food service providers pivoted to providing food to some of their communities' neediest members. At the University of Rhode Island, for example, dining services transitioned to providing meals to senior citizens within the community (Nunes, 2020). Other campuses, with students in proximity, remained open for "grab-and-go" options for students. Saginaw Valley State University dining, for example, continued to provide takeaway options for students after state mandates required the closure of campus cafeterias.

STUDENT ACTIVITIES AND ORGANIZATIONS

Student affairs professionals made outreach to and engagement of students a key focus through this period. This simultaneously kept staff motivated to deal with the pandemic's student impact and aware of the criticality of their work. Boston University, for example, opted to allocate supplemental funding for student activities to encourage student engagement through increased programming, especially events centered around inclusion and belonging. As Kenneth Elmore, Associate Provost and Dean of Students at Boston University, shared, "I don't like to manage from behind. I go to a lot of events and keep telling the students, 'You're doing something historic and you don't even know it yet.'" Similar to other campuses, Boston University moved their summer 2020 orientation programs online and encouraged virtual student engagement programs. They figured out ways to have student government elections and senior breakfasts online using both synchronous and asynchronous methods. "Many of the events were like a TV show with a continuous web presence," reported Elmore.

Student Groups

For students experiencing isolation and stress through the early pandemic, the function of student centers and clubs as gathering spaces proved more important than ever. As Chris Giordano, Vice Chancellor for Student Affairs at the University of Michigan-Flint, shared, before the pandemic, spaces like the campus's Center for Gender Studies or the Veterans Center allowed students to congregate in community with each other. No longer possible with COVID-19 restrictions,

> So, what we've tried to do is we've tried to create those spaces virtually. We have regularly scheduled times where we have these virtual gatherings where people can come together and they can just connect with each other and feel that sense of belonging, feel less isolated, and those kinds of things.

Like many IHEs, University of Michigan-Flint worked actively to try to create such opportunities for students to engage in peer-to-peer interaction, with a careful eye to ensuring inclusion, equity, and belonging—not just in the immediate moment but with a view of what would follow. As Giordano shared,

> There are certain populations that are going to be hit harder by this by nature of some of the disparities that already exist within our society and culture. We've been monitoring as best we can, to make sure there is no anti-Asian treatment that's happening within our community, any blaming for the virus. We are trying to guard against some of that bias. That's really important also that the community sees that DEI continues to be a value for us, and we've engaged students in that. One of the things we are going to be doing, so this is a little broader than the affinity groups, is we are going to meet with identified student leaders, student government, other presidents of student organizations, where we want to create a social compact for how we want to return to campus. We want them to really be the drivers in writing this social compact. What are the expectations for returning to a post-COVID environment? Because it's not going to be the same and we all have to agree that there are things that are not going to be convenient or comfortable that we are going to have to do. We want them involved in how we are going to manage this.

Recreation Centers

While most campus recreation centers and swimming pools quickly closed, some campuses kept these spaces open despite increased costs generated by new sanitation and cleaning protocols. The National Intramural and Recreational Sports Association (NIRSA) provided guidelines and resources to help guide campuses through this period. Lacking specific guidelines for campus rec centers in spring 2020, campus leaders needed to establish protocols for use of locker rooms, for masking, for towel services or cleaning of machines to keep such spaces open. Campuses that wished to provide access to such facilities needed to figure out what equipment they needed to shut down, what level of service they could provide, what occupancy limits they needed to set, and what the implications would be for staffing.

LESSONS LEARNED

The pandemic pushed IHEs to transition student services online as campuses shut down across the US in spring 2020, a decision that many might never have otherwise pursued. Although most expected that this change in delivery mode would prove temporary, both students and student affairs professionals grew in their comfort level with online services. Many quickly began to see that it offered some students, particularly working adults and commuter students, a level of flexibility and accessibility that on-campus services lacked and spoke enthusiastically of maintaining at least some online options after a return to "normal."

Although awareness had grown for the decade preceding the COVID-19 outbreak of the epidemic of student homelessness, basic needs insecurity (such as food), and mental illness, the crisis also rendered more visible these ongoing and underlying issues as student mental health and economic insecurity increased nationally. As it became clear that the COVID-19 pandemic would continue to impact operations beyond initial lockdown periods, increasing concerns for student mental and physical well-being provided the impetus for institutions to view these aspects of support as major contributors to student success and to put additional resources into addressing them. Additional federal funding through the CARES Act (See Chapter 13) provided emergency aid funding for students, as did institutional fundraising at many IHEs, but addressing these systemic issues became a priority for campuses as part of their student success and retention efforts.

The pandemic taught campus leaders that crisis management is not an optional element of higher education leadership and encouraged many campuses to reexamine their leadership structures. Since departmental autonomy varies greatly across IHEs, the rapid decision-making processes surrounding student services, housing, and dining through this period led some leaders to reconsider how teams interacted, how decisions impacting diverse units could be reached and communicated, and what cross-unit connections were necessary to develop in support of student engagement and success.

> **A Close-up Lens on Leadership**
>
> Kenneth Elmore, Associate Provost and Dean of Students at Boston University, had been in the office every day since the campus closed in March 2020 when he was interviewed for this chapter. As he explained, "I wanted to make sure I wasn't asking my staff or my students to do anything I wouldn't do." In fact, a key piece of advice that he offered leaders for future crises is to pay careful attention to staff, especially the younger ones, through such periods. When asked what he would have done differently in retrospect, he shared: I would have started a number of things sooner. I would have started parent engagement earlier. Some leaders also cited a need to have engaged faculty earlier to ensure buy-in and done a better job at addressing the "whys" behind decisions. Dean Elmore added that, in hindsight, he would have engaged campus partners like enrollment management and auxiliary services earlier and that he wishes he would have called a retreat with multiple campus stakeholders. Acknowledging the different lenses that different units approach their work, he noted that student affairs professionals often view things first through a student advocacy lens, while auxiliary services first view things through a business or finance lens: "If I had known we were going to be in a lifeboat together, I would have created a retreat beforehand to get to know people better."

REFERENCES

Anupindi, R., Schroeder, L., Dewar, R., Rajaram, S., & Edkins, E. (2020). Institute for Healthcare Policy and Innovation brief: COVID-19 testing scale-up: Key issues and considerations for Michigan policymakers. University of Michigan (October). Retrieved from https://ihpi.umich.edu

Czeisler, M.É., Lane, R.I., Petrosky, E., et al. (2020). Mental Health, Substance Use, and Suicidal Ideation During the COVID-19 Pandemic — United States, June 24–30. *MMWR Morbitity and Mortality Weekly Report* 69:1049–1057. Retrieved from http://dx.doi.org/10.15585/mmwr.mm6932a1externalicon

Divers, N. (2020, July 13). No housing refunds put UNC System students in tough spot. The James G. Martin Center for Academic Renewal. Retrieved from https://www.jamesgmartin.center/2020/07/no-housing-refunds-put-unc-system-students-in-tough-spot/

Goldrik-Rab, S., Baker-Smith, C., Coca, V., Looker, E., & Williams, T. (2019, April). College and university basic needs insecurity: A national ... National #Real College Survey. Retrieved from https://hope4college.com/wp-content/uploads/2019/04/HOPE_realcollege_National_report_digital.pdf

Goldrick-Rab, S., Coca, V., Kienzl, G., Welton, C. R., Dahl, S., & Magnelia, S. (2020). #REALCOLLEGE during the pandemic - hope center. Hope4College.Com. Retrieved from https://hope4college.com/wp-content/uploads/2020/06/Hopecenter_RealCollegeDuringthePandemic.pdf

Hatmaker, T. (2020, March 19). Chan Zuckerberg Biohub and UCSF will boost Bay Area COVID-19 tests by 1,000 per day. *TechCrunch*. Retrieved from https://techcrunch.com/2020/03/19/bay-area-coronavirus-testing-chan-zuckerberg-initiative-cz-biohub-ucsf-gavin-newsom/

Higher Education Mental Health Alliance. (2018). College counseling from a distance: Deciding whether and when to engage in Telemental Health Services. HEMHA Guide. Retrieved from https://www.sprc.org/printpdf/7659

LeViness, P., Gorman, K., Braun, L., Koenig, L., & Bershad, C. (2020, May 31). The Association for University and college ... - AUCCCD. 2019 AUCCCD Survey. Retrieved from https://www.aucccd.org/assets/documents/Survey/2019%20AUCCCD%20Survey-2020-05-31-PUBLIC.pdf

Nunes, R. (2020, April 20). Uri dining services delivers meals for RI seniors: Coronavirus. *Yahoo! News*. Retrieved from https://news.yahoo.com/uri-dining-services-delivers-meals-212954414.html

Researching a global pandemic. The University of Michigan Office of Research (UMOR) aims to catalyze, support and safeguard U-M research. (n.d.). Retrieved from https://research.umich.edu/covid-19

Robles, K. C. (2020, October 20). *Covid-19 has forced campus ministry to enter a new era of digital spirituality. It's going O.K. America: The Jesuit Review*. Retrieved from https://www.americamagazine.org/faith/2020/10/20/covid-19-campus-ministry-digital-spirituality

Scott, R. (2020, August 27). How college campus ministries are finding faith amid the covid-19 pandemic. 90.1 FM WABE. Retrieved from https://www.wabe.org/episode/how-college-campus-ministries-are-finding-faith-amid-the-covid-19-pandemic/

Son, C., Hegde, S., Smith, A., Wang, X., & Sasangohar, F. (2020). Effects of COVID-19 on college students' mental health in the United States: Interview survey study. *Journal of Medical Internet Research* (2020) 22(9). Retrieved from https://www.jmir.org/2020/9/e21279

University of Michigan Psychiatry. (2021, February 23). Michigan psychiatry resources for covid-19: Psychiatry: Michigan medicine. *Psychiatry*. Retrieved from https://medicine.umich.edu/dept/psychiatry/michigan-psychiatry-resources-covid-19

Vespoli, L. (2020, November 12). College food pantries have grown exponentially in recent years, an attempt to address rising food insecurity: What happens when campus is closed? The Counter. Retrieved from https://thecounter.org/college-food-pantries-rising-food-insecurity-covid-19-coronavirus/

Chapter 7
Athletics

Ann T. S. Taylor and Rhonda Phillips

INTRODUCTION

For institutions of higher education (IHE) with athletic programs, sports can serve as a nexus of campus operations. Athletics influences admissions, student life, alumni relations, and operations. It also creates connections among institutions and helps to shape institutional identity. The impact of the COVID-19 pandemic on athletic operations offers opportunities to better understand mission, leadership models, and the interconnections and complexity of higher education communities. The symbolic aspect alone along with the building of collective identity, team spirit, and bonding with alumni and donors are crucial aspects of the college experience shaped by athletics on many campuses. Additionally, athletic programs can help maintain and foster alumni connections well after graduation. Collegiate athletics, in myriad ways across operations, strategy, and leadership dimensions, both mirrors and shows new dimensions of the impact of the COVID-19 pandemic on institutions.

This chapter focuses on impacts of and responses to COVID-19 related to athletic sports associated with the National Collegiate Athletics Association (NCAA) and its member colleges and universities. It leaves for other researchers to explore the impact of COVID-19 responses on related activities such as bands, cheer squads, intramural sports, and social activities (such as tailgating), as well as connections with other intercollegiate organizations such as the National Association of Intercollegiate Athletics (NAIA) and the National Junior Colleges Athletic Association (NJCAA).

THE CONTEXT: DIVISION I SPORTS

The NCAA is a member-led organization that uses committee structures to propose rules and regulations for collegiate athletics. NCAA employees interpret and enforce these agreed-upon standards. NCAA member schools are categorized into three divisions by level of competition and resources. These divisions were created by the NCAA in 1973 to "align like-minded campuses in the areas of philosophy, competition and opportunity" (NCAA, 2016, p. 1). As of spring 2020, there were 350 schools in Division I, with a median undergraduate enrollment of 8,960. In Division I institutions, which award athletic scholarships, student athletes represent one out of every 23 undergraduates (NCAA, 2016).

Revenues from athletics generate substantial revenues on NCAA campuses. For example, across all three divisions of NCAA institutions, over $18 billion was spent on athletics in 2018. Of that amount, IHEs spent approximately $3.5 billion on financial aid for student-athletes, with the same amount of approximately $3.5 billion to coaches' compensation. On the other side of the balance sheet, athletics generated $10.3 billion of revenue for their schools in 2018 (NCAA, 2021a).

At Division I schools, athletics budgets can be quite significant, especially for those with television network contracts for either football or basketball. For example, both Purdue University and the University of Arizona have athletics budgets of over $100 million annually, much of this generated by contracts or revenues through football and men's basketball (media contracts, ticket sales, donor contributions and alcohol sales at games). It is "big business" at such schools to have Division I sports that generate revenues from ticket sales along with media contracts for broadcasting games to larger audiences. Purdue University generates around $1.6 million for each home game; a loss of six or so games in a season therefore constitutes a large financial loss (Carmin, 2020).

THE IMPACT OF COVID-19 ON COLLEGE ATHLETICS

On NCAA member campuses, athletics provided the perfect storm for disruptions related to COVID-19. Initial responses of IHEs were marked by creative pivoting to serve athletes, institutions, and their communities. At many institutions, care for student-athletes dominated institutional approaches initially because this group traveled often or were the subjects of much scrutiny at the onset of the pandemic. Given their close relationships with student-athletes, coaches, athletic trainers, and other support staff played key roles. They were often the first to communicate with and console their team members as competitions were canceled and institutions ceased on-campus operations.

The timing of campus pivots and the extent of COVID-related restrictions that were initially implemented varied significantly by region of the country. Institutions were taking guidance from their local and state health agencies before the NCAA made decisions that could be applied across college sports more uniformly. Even then, some institutions continued to use tighter restrictions if their local guidelines required it. The range of physical contact in each athletic activity, the relationships among institutions, and the budgetary considerations of related decisions mirrored the complicated, interconnected problems raised by the

COVID-19 pandemic across campuses nationwide. Tensions among health considerations, institutional competition, finances, and politics revealed the importance of rapid decision-making as well as strategic and creative leadership in the face of existential challenges.

Health and Safety Impacts

Throughout spring and summer 2020, constantly changing information about the pandemic and college campus responses made for an uncertain environment and led to frequent changes in plans. The NCAA March Madness Men's Basketball tournament demonstrated this uncertainty. On March 10, 2020, the Ivy League canceled its basketball championships due to concerns about COVID-19. On March 12, 2020, Duke University withdrew their teams from conference championship tournaments (Duke Today, 2020). On March 12, 2020, the NCAA decided that teams would play the March Madness Basketball tournaments in nearly empty venues. Conferences across the country followed suit and changed their championship spectator policies to limit the number of attendees. However, the next day, March 13, 2020, the NCAA canceled all post-season championship tournaments. To the shock of spectators, St. John's and Creighton Universities, for example, canceled their game at half time; Michigan and Rutgers' basketball teams were pulled off the courts about 15 minutes before their scheduled noon tipoff time. While there was recognition that the health and safety needs outweighed the financial losses, these abrupt cancellations created a shock wave of realization of the severity of the pandemic. This also meant, for some student-athletes, that they had already played the last game of their collegiate careers.

For athletes especially, the impact of COVID-19 was as much about mental health as physical health. The impact of canceled competitions along with decreased access to training during virtual learning as well as the connection between physical activity and mental health prompted concern for student-athletes' psychological state. The NCAA provided guidance about supporting student mental health (NCAA, 2020a), and coaches and training staff became front-line mental health support for students. As one athletics director explained,

> I think that the morale impact was huge and I think that's something that needed to be managed. We can manage testing—that's administration. A morale issue was a nuanced issue, and we had to do that every day. For example, we had coaches who had just moved here in January of 2020 with their families to a part of the country where they don't know anyone, and now they're wondering if they're going to get furloughed. ... The student-athletes had to be managed during this because they weren't doing what they always do, and we needed to make sure that they were OK. So, the morale issue became my focus.
> —Drew Marrochello, Director of Athletics, Boston University

Creating Institutional Standards in Unknown Territory

Institutions looked for guidance in setting institutional standards for resumption of both campus athletic activities and competitive play. Until May of 2020, athletics directors at institutions consulted with one another, with their conference leaders, and with leaders at their own institutions to determine the best course of action for play, safety, or withdrawal. When the NCAA's Guidelines for Resocialization of Collegiate Sports (NCAA, 2020b) emerged, they served as a basis for standards at many institutions, though many others had already put into place guidelines that were more stringent and, due to local guidance or requirements, these would remain.

The NCAA guidelines were based upon the gating criteria from the Federal Opening Up America Again guidelines, including downward trajectories in influenza-like illnesses and documented COVID-19 cases, hospital capacity, institutional and community plans for preventing, monitoring and responding to illness, and availability of personal protective equipment, testing and tracing. The plan included three phases, each consisting of 14 days with continued declines in illness and cases in the area or implementation of stringent COVID-19 testing, contact tracing, isolation and quarantine strategies. In the first phase, teams could meet virtually with gatherings of no more than 10 people; non-essential travel was minimized; and gyms and common areas were closed unless strict distancing and sanitation protocols were implemented. In phase two, gatherings of fewer than 50 people could occur and non-essential travel could resume. Virtual meetings replaced in-person gatherings, and physical distancing and other strategies to protect vulnerable populations continued. In the third phase, gyms and common areas could reopen and full team meetings could resume, but the NCAA recommended avoiding crowded environments.

The net effect of these three phases was an increased pre-season time. Whereas, normally, students come to campus, have a physical, and start practice the next day, they now needed more than a month of acclimatization and small group work before they could operate as a large group. Football teams would now be back on campus in June instead of early August, as in previous years. All three divisions allowed extended pre-season housing and meal service for athletes.

Despite these precautions and the fact that many schools tested every incoming athlete for COVID-19, there was tremendous variation in the approaches to testing and even in the attitudes toward exposure to COVID-19. The extent of asymptomatic cases among incoming athletes created concern about reopening colleges. Within a short time of being on campus, almost 10% of Clemson's team and supporting personnel tested positive for COVID-19 (with the majority being football players). Other colleges reported outbreaks as well. While many of those who tested positive were asymptomatic, the spread of an airborne respiratory virus was difficult to contain in group settings, especially during intense training. In fact, the

US Centers for Disease Control (CDC) only began calling for mask-wearing in early April as evidence emerged that COVID-19 was primarily spread through respiration. Additionally, some student-athletes did not comply with the guideline to avoid crowded situations, which led to outbreaks on teams. For example, when the Louisiana State University team socialized at a drinking establishment, this resulted in the quarantine of a quarter of the team in early June 2020. Institutions could do everything to try to keep their own students safe within their own setting, but had little control of the conditions during competitions with other schools.

The return-to-competition plans in the resocialization guidelines divided sports into three tiers, based upon the level of contact among players and between teams, and on whether the sport is played indoors or outdoors. For example, wrestling was in the highest risk category as there was direct contact between opponents, and it is an indoor sport. On the other end of the spectrum, golf and tennis are played outdoors and have minimal contact among teammates and between competitors. These tiers determined the level of testing required for pre-season, in-season, and pre-competition days. For high-risk sports, the NCAA required antigen testing three times a week; only participation in campus surveillance testing and access to symptomatic testing were mandated for the lowest risk sports.

A Close-up Lens on Leadership

Mike Bobkinski (2020), Vice President and Director of Intercollegiate Athletics at Purdue University, offered the following insights on initial responses and reactions to the onset of the pandemic in the summer of 2020.

> There is a standard rhythm and structure with time and place for things to happen in athletics. All this goes out the door with a loss of sense of structure and direction and initially an absence of control, placing us all in a reactive state, and creating anxiety and uncertainty. We have to put people first and try to meet needs to get through. We've learned a lot through this process of having to connect in different ways. Four things became more apparent to focus on from the beginning: (1) relationships and connections are so important. For example, recruitment quickly became something very different from how it was conducted in the past, with personal conversations becoming even more important; (2) focus on facts and where truth is; (3) engage in realistic optimism and make adjustments and adaptions to impact control; and (4) communicate regularly and in a very open and transparent way, people want to be informed and know what will happen to the extent possible.

Financial Impacts

The appearance of the pandemic across the US by mid-March 2020 had a dramatic and almost immediate impact on institutional athletic budgets through the cancellations of events. March Madness, for instance, not only generates large sums of funding and influences revenue-sharing for NCAA member institutions, but is also the main source of revenue for the NCAA administrative body. The NCAA distributed $225 million to schools in June 2020, less than half of the originally forecasted $660 million (NCAA, 2020c). This loss of funding severely hampered operations both at the NCAA and at its member schools. The NCAA furloughed employees, imposed hiring freezes, and moved its operations online, which reduced travel and venue expenses. At Division I schools, however, facilities proved a relatively fixed cost, and there were also substantial investments in personnel. In addition to coaches, trainers, referees and umpires, there are people involved in game day operations, marketing, recruiting, academic support services, and facilities maintenance. While some are seasonal and/or game day employees, many were year-round employees. This fiscal reality put institutions in the difficult position of furloughing or re-assigning employees to other duties, since they could no longer perform their normal responsibilities.

Other institutions adopted cost-savings measures. The University of Michigan athletic program anticipated a $25.1 million deficit, due to a 50% decrease in attendance and a slight increase ($0.8 million) in scholarships for extended eligibility of spring athletes. In response, it imposed salary reductions based on yearly salaries: 5% for coaches earning between $50 and $100,000, 7.5% for those making between $100 and $150,000, and 10% for the head basketball and football coaches (VanHaaren, 2020).

Other schools cut or furloughed entire programs. Initially, Bowling Green State University, for example, eliminated its baseball program, but under pressure by alumni and friends of the program, the institution's leaders reinstated it (Bowling Green State University Athletics, 2020). Akron University, which had previously generated Olympic medal-winning cross country runners, eliminated its men's cross country program as well as its men's golf and women's tennis (Dellenger and Forde, 2020). Altogether, as of June 27, 2020, 56 institutions cut, dropped or suspended 208 programs with no timetable for return and IHEs, looking ahead to the next academic year, continued to cut sports programs (Bryant, 2021). While many of these schools were junior colleges or California State University system campuses that had moved to online only course offerings, other schools selectively closed "high density, high contact" sports such as football, as did, for example, Florida Tech (Florida Tech Panthers, 2020). Brown University leveraged the crisis to eliminate eleven varsity athletics programs, a delayed response to a 2018–2019 study that recommended downsizing the number of sports offered. Brown's actions reflected the institutional risk of using the health crisis as a reason to cut athletics, in their case it led to backlash from students who had come to the university with the intention of participating in collegiate sports (Anderson, 2020; Pagones, 2020).

Although the COVID-19 crisis had the clearest and most dramatic impact on Division I institutions, it also affected those with Division II and III status. The conferences and divisions worked together to find ways to save money. Division III allowed for shortened seasons and reduced the championship structure (Villanueva, 2020). Many conferences adopted schedules with no overnight stays or air travel, reducing both costs and potential virus exposure through travel.

In addition to lost revenue, institutions had to find personnel and resources to implement COVID-19 testing requirements. Large Division 1 schools could often rely upon their affiliated medical schools or research centers to provide these services. In some cases, testing sites could be staffed by personnel who were repurposed from other institutional roles rather than furloughed. For smaller and leaner Division II and III schools, the testing requirements posed a barrier to athletic contests (Scoggins, 2020). The development of faster and cheaper testing methods, such as the $5 Abbott BinaxNow antigen test, allowed more schools to participate in athletic contests (Dellenger, 2020a).

Admissions and Eligibility Effects

The NCAA also altered its policies regarding eligibility and scholarship funding. They allowed athletes in spring 2020 sports an additional season of competition to maintain eligibility (NCAA, 2020d) and instated use of the Student Assistance Fund for scholarships to foster increased flexibility in the 2020–2021 season. Normally, the NCAA imposes caps on the roster length and the total amount of scholarship money a school could provide for a team. With potentially five years' worth of students on the team, and institutions already feeling a budget crunch, the NCAA's Division 1 council voted to give schools flexibility on the amount of financial aid they gave "super seniors" whose last season of eligibility would have been in 2019–2020 had the pandemic not impacted their ability to play.

Baseball experienced the most profound effect of these cumulative actions. The decision by Major League Baseball (MLB) to reduce the number of players drafted left fewer slots for the should-be-graduating seniors interested in continuing their baseball careers. The impact of the MLB's decision trickled down: as more players on the collegiate team reduced the playing time per player and further restricted scholarship slots for incoming freshmen. Conversely, an additional college season was not necessarily a viable option for everyone, as some seniors had committed to graduate school programs or jobs. The uncertainty of the time made it more challenging both to keep student-athletes and to recruit for the next season.

Recruiting

The recruiting process itself was also dramatically altered by the shutdown of high school and collegiate programs in spring 2020. IHEs found themselves unable to conduct traditional scouting activities for spring sports, as high school sports canceled their seasons and travel restrictions between states made travel challenging or impossible. In addition, the NCAA instituted a "dead period" that extended to July 31 for Division I (NCAA, 2020d). During the "dead period," coaches could not have any in-person contact with recruits and/or their parents, although they could communicate via phone, email, or social media (NCSA, n.d.). While travel restrictions would have hindered recruiting activities during this time regardless, the NCAA's guidelines created uniformity in the process across the country. During this quiet period, a college coach could not have face-to-face contact with college-bound student-athletes or their parents off the college campus and could not watch student-athletes compete or visit their high school (NCAA, 2020e). While intended to protect the health of the scouts, coaches, and prospective players, shifting the time frame so dramatically impacted sports that played during the dead or quiet period, since scouts and coaches did not have the opportunity to observe prospects in the field or on the court. This challenge was addressed for basketball by extending recruiting into the fall of the senior year (NCAA, 2020f), but this restriction would affect the next several entering classes of athletes (Kope, 2021).

Institutional Image

Especially for Division I schools, much of their institutional image is formed and shared through athletic programs. Indeed, many students select schools for the branding and image that is associated with major athletic programming (Finch and Clopton, 2017). Athletics is by nature a group activity, defined by in-person interaction for training and competitions. The collective spirit of rooting for a team is binding and builds a sense of community between the athletes, fans, and others. One of the challenges of addressing COVID-19 and its potential impact on team and institutional image was that the behavior of an individual or a small subset of players could lead to infections on teams and/or negative publicity. Some leaders addressed this head-on with their student athletes. For example, in a meeting with athletes, Ball State President Geoff Mearns used the analogy of a pilots' association needing to be able to state that 100%, not 80% or 90%, of its pilots do not fly while drunk. The analogy then for team mitigation practices to work, everyone must follow the guidelines fully, otherwise it puts all at risk.

Lack of compliance with COVID-19 mitigation practices had the potential to generate negative publicity for institutions. At most institutions, athletes underwent more frequent COVID-19 testing than the general student body (Kelderman, 2020), amplifying conversations about differential treatment of athletes. Outbreaks on teams not only led to canceled events, but often generated negative media coverage. Some student-athletes did not comply with the guideline to avoid crowded situations, which led to outbreaks on teams. The Louisiana State University team socialized at a drinking establishment, leading to a quarter of the team being quarantined in early June. Concern about whether college athletes could comply with required mitigation practices was discussed in national-level newspapers and magazines such as *USA Today* (Wolken, 2020) and Sports Illustrated (Dellenger, 2020b).

In many instances, the NCAA gave conferences flexibility in determining whether to operate competition seasons, then determined whether enough teams were participating to merit holding a national championship. This was most evident for the fall 2020 football season. As a high-risk activity for COVID transmission due to direct contact among players, there was justified concern about outbreaks on teams. At that point in time, access to tests was a major barrier for most institutions, leading Division II and III schools to cancel football seasons. However, Division I, especially the Power Five conferences (Athletic Coast, Big Ten, Big 12, Pac-12, and Southeastern Conferences), are known for their elite football programs and were eager to play as hundreds of millions of dollars in television broadcasting rights were at stake with the loss of media contracts (Smith and Ourand, 2008). Initially, these conferences agreed to cut non-conference games to reduce interstate travel and outside contact, but as the pandemic worsened in August, there were outbreaks on teams and concerns arose about cardiac complications in athletes (Dellenger, 2020c). This led to emergency discussions, with the Big Ten and then the Pac-12 choosing to postpone fall sports; after negotiating stringent medical protocols, however, they resumed play in October (Big Ten Conference, 2020). Initially, the Group of Five conferences (American Athletic Conference, Conference USA, Mid-American Conference, Mountain West Conference, and the Sun Belt Conference) planned to postpone conference play until the spring semester, but later decided to play a shortened season.

For conferences that did play, there were often reduced numbers of spectators, or none at all. Spectators provide a major source of income, as well as contributing to the home court advantage. To compensate for the empty stands, some schools sold cardboard cutouts. For the Final 4, the NCAA sold cutouts to benefit social services agencies in the area (NCAA, 2021b).

LESSONS LEARNED

IHEs often highlight athletics as an opportunity for students to learn leadership and teamwork skills, and this characteristic rang very true during the pandemic.

The COVID-19 pandemic called on athletic directors, coaches, trainers, and student-athletes to be adaptable and creative, to develop new practices, to collaborate among institutions in ways that still retained institutional autonomy and local control, to navigate political situations, to address equity issues, and to communicate clearly in a manner that built morale. Without a playbook for leading during a crisis as all-encompassing as the COVID-19 pandemic, many institutions used their influenza and SARS preparedness plans to guide campus operations. Athletic directors and coaches had to demonstrate creativity and flexibility, being able to pivot quickly to workable or more feasible approaches to large-scale challenges. This has required adaptive thinking and problem-solving with no time for long periods of planning and design or the kind of vetting typical of many processes in the academy during non-crisis times.

Like other units within IHEs, the pandemic forced athletics departments to repurpose staff in order to execute institutional COVID operations, such as reconfiguring classrooms and living spaces, as well as conducting COVID-19 testing and contact tracing (Winkelmann and Games, 2020). Some institutions deployed their athletic staff in interesting ways. For instance, at Ball State University, a Division I institution, athletics staff served the larger community, including organizing food pantries and delivering food and supplies to shut-ins (Guskey, 2020). In general, COVID-19 underscored the importance of relationships and collaboration in the world of college athletics.

Athletics also became a leader in developing and implementing COVID-19 testing protocols. Given the physical proximity of players in some sports and the need to keep the team, coaches, and support staff safe, campuses developed regular testing and monitoring protocols that continued when campuses reopened. As early adopters, athletics programs helped to lead other units across campus to implement such protocols.

Collaboration across institutions soared during this time as major decisions were often made in conjunction with other colleges and within divisions. Working together yielded better results across aspects such as securing access to testing. Yet negotiating differences in institutional, or even individual, attitudes towards COVID-19 became challenging in some cases. Athletics Director Marrochello from Boston University commented,

> Each school was different and at one point I was compelled to say, "I really don't care what they're doing at [other institution] and I don't care what your friends are doing; these are the conditions to play here." Ultimately what we had to say to them was "don't play if you don't want to play; it's completely OK. You can be an active dissenter, and you will certainly keep your scholarship—but you're not going to do what you want to do, because these are the policies and protocols that we are following".

By establishing guidelines for when and how institutions could continue athletic play, the NCAA served an important leadership role for college athletics nationally in mid-2020 and the planning phases for the following academic year. In a sense, given their regulatory role, the NCAA helped move national college athletics beyond institutional boundaries and differences by ensuring that all divisions had a uniform starting place for their protocols.

> **Equity Insight**
>
> Division I athletics mirrored the inequitable impact of exposure to COVID-19 seen in other sectors across the country. For example, in 2018 Black men represented 2.4% of undergraduate students enrolled at the 65 universities in the "Power Five" athletic conferences (i.e., ACC, Big 10, Big 12, Pac 12, and SEC), yet they comprised 55% of football teams and 56% of men's basketball teams on those campuses (Harper, 2018). Thus, participation in these two contact sports placed Black undergraduate men at disproportionately higher risk of COVID-19 infection compared to the general student population.
>
> Equity concerns, particularly over athletes' amateur status and the role of minoritized student-athletes, is nothing new. For years, players and analysts have claimed that IHEs exploit these students to raise revenues and reputations while doing too little to ensure that they graduate. The COVID-19 pandemic heightened these concerns as players experienced divergent institutional responses and protocols and responded to more visible inequities.
>
> Collegiate athletic revenue is primarily generated from football and men's basketball, especially in the Power 5 conferences: the ACC, Big Ten, Big 12, Pac 12 and SEC. These championships are the most successful NCAA conferences, measured in terms of athletic revenue (every football champion since 1989 and every men's basketball championship since 1991 except the University of Connecticut and Villanova University). An economic analysis of this trend found that the distribution of monies from these sports effectively transfers resources away from students who are more likely to be Black and more likely to come from poor neighborhoods towards students who are more likely to be white and come from higher income neighborhoods (Garthwaite et al., 2020). At the same time, Black male athletes in the Power 5 are less likely to graduate than either student athletes overall or Black undergraduate males overall (Harper, 2018).

A group of players from the Pac-12, one of the Power 5 conferences, began a campaign called #WeAreUnited (Butler et al., 2020). They were protesting having to play college sports during a global pandemic in a system that failed to include enforcement of health and safety standards, in order to provide income to the NCAA and their home institutions, and for the entertainment of national audiences. Instead, they requested the ability to opt out of playing during the 2020–2021 season but to retain scholarship eligibility and healthcare coverage in the future for COVID-related long-term illnesses, as well as pushing for more equal sharing of the revenues generated through their performances.

Player demands conflicted with institutional desires to restart sports with the largest audiences and income potential in order to fund athletic operations and to fulfill their Title IX requirements of providing equal access to women's sports (which generate fewer revenue dollars). These tensions, along with demands that institutions address racial inequities within collegiate athletics, proved daunting for both athletic directors and the NCAA, but eventually contributed to NCAA- and university-level policy changes (such as requiring a minimum graduation rate for eligibility in conference and national championships), direct financial support for athletes, a move toward student-athletes being able to use their name, image, and likeness to earn income and as well as revisions of how students who graduate from college are treated in the NFL, NBA and MLB drafts.

REFERENCES

Anderson, G. (2020, June 1). A winning plan and a major letdown. *Inside Higher ED*. Retrieved February 28, 2022 from https://www.insidehighered.com/news/2020/06/01/brown-university-cuts-11-varsity-sports

Big Ten Conference. (2020, September 16). *The big ten conference adopts stringent medical protocols; football season to resume October 23–24, 2020*. The Big Ten Conference Adopts Stringent Medical Protocols; Football Season to Resume October 23–24, 2020. Retrieved February 23, 2022, from https://bigten.org/news/2020/9/16/the-big-ten-conference-adopts-stringent-medical-protocols-football-season-to-resume-october-23-24-2020.aspx

Bobkinski, M. (2020, June 24). Personal communication. Telephone interview.

Bowling Green State University Athletics. (2020, June 2). *BGSU reinstates baseball program*. Bowling Green State University Athletics. Retrieved February 23, 2022, from https://bgsufalcons.com/news/2020/6/2/bgsu-reinstates-baseball-program.aspx

Butler, T., Curhan, J., Daltoso, V., Drayden, J., Grant, J., Guidry E., Hausman, M., Hobbs, D., Holland, J., Jones, T., Shear, C., Tyron, J. (2020, August 2). *College Football Player Opt-Out Movement*. Retrieved February 23, 2022, from https://cdn.theathletic.com/app/uploads/2020/08/02165240/Press-Release-WeAreUnited-Opt-Out-8_2_2020-2-1.pdf

Bryant, J. (2021, May 7). *Covid-19 ERA dropped & suspended sports*. Mat Talk Almanac. Retrieved February 23, 2022, from http://almanac.mattalkonline.com/covid-19-era-dropped-sports/

Carmin, M. (2020, April 11). Forecast for Purdue Athletics Budget: Short term manageable;long term hinges on football season. *Journal and Courier*. Retrieved January 17, 2022, from https://www.jconline.com/story/sports/2020/04/11/forecast-for-purdue-athletics-budget-short-term-manageable-long-term-hinges-on-football-season/5129479002/

Dellenger, R. (2020a, September 2). *Inside the Testing Advancements Key to College Sports*. Sports Illustrated. Retrieved February 23, 2022, from https://www.si.com/college/2020/09/02/coronavirus-covid-testing-college-football

Dellenger, R. (2020b, June 20). *At Least 30 LSU Players Quarantined Due to Covid-19 Outbreak*. Sports Illustrated. Retrieved February 23, 2022, from https://www.si.com/college/2020/06/20/lsu-football-players-quarantined-coronavirus

Dellenger, R. (2020c, August 9). *Cardiac Inflammation Next Covid-19 Hurdle for College Leaders*. Sports Illustrated. Retrieved February 23, 2022, from https://www.si.com/college/2020/08/09/ncaa-cardiac-inflamation-coronavirus-myocarditis-concerns

Dellenger, R., and Forde, R. (2020, June 11). *The Crippling Impact of Schools Cutting NCAA Sports Teams. Sports Illustrated*. Retrieved February 23, 2022, from https://www.si.com/college/2020/06/11/college-sports-program-cuts-ncaa-olympics

Duke Today (2020) Duke suspends athletic competitions. *Duke Today*. (2020, March 12). Retrieved February 23, 2022, from https://today.duke.edu/2020/03/duke-suspends-athletic-competitions

Finch, Bryan, and Clopton, Aaron W. Examining the role of Athletics in the Development of University Image among College Students. *Journal of Contemporary Athletics* (2017) 11(3): 1370143. Retrieved from https://search.proquest.com/openview/6b0aefeabd6c77b224a103273942bd73/1

Florida Tech Panthers. (2020, May 11). *Covid-19 forces Florida Tech staff and program reductions*. Retrieved February 23, 2022, from https://floridatechsports.com/news/2020/5/11/general-covid-19-forces-florida-tech-staff-and-program-reductions.aspx

Garthwaite, C., Keener, J., Notowidigdo, M., & Ozminkowski, N. (2020). Who profits from amateurism? Rent-sharing in modern college sports. *National Bureau of Economic Research Working Paper*. Retrieved from https://doi.org/10.3386/w27734

Guskey, J. (2020, March 22). *How Ball State Athletics is Stepping Up for Those Affected by Coronavirus Concerns*. The Indianapolis Star. Retrieved February 23, 2022, from https://www.indystar.com/story/sports/college/ball-state/2020/03/22/coronavirus-concerns-lead-ball-state-athletics-response-COVID-19/2879487001/

Harper, S. R. (2018). *Black Male Student-Athletes and Racial Inequities in NCAA Division I College Sports:* 2018 edition. Los Angeles: University of Southern California, Race and Equity Center.

Kelderman, E. (2020, September 17). *'A Scene Out of Gladiator': Big Ten Football Players Get Daily Coronavirus Tests, but Other Students Don't*. Retrieved February 23, 2022, from https://www.chronicle.com/article/a-scene-out-of-gladiator-big-ten-football-players-get-daily-coronavirus-tests-but-other-students-dont

Kope, J. (2021, April 16). *What does coronavirus mean for my recruiting?* NCSA Athletic Recruiting Blog. Retrieved February 23, 2022, from https://www.ncsasports.org/blog/2020/03/17/what-does-coronavirus-mean-for-my-recruiting

NCAA. (2016, January 7). *Our three divisions*. NCAA.org. Retrieved January 17, 2022, from https://www.ncaa.org/sports/2016/1/7/about-resources-media-center-ncaa-101-our-three-divisions.aspx

NCAA. (2020a, March 20. *Covid-19 and mental health*. NCAA.org. Retrieved January 17, 2022, from https://www.ncaa.org/sports/2020/3/20/covid-19-and-mental-health.aspx

NCAA. (2020b, May 1). *Core principles of resocialization of collegiate sport*. NCAA.org. Retrieved January 17, 2022, from https://www.ncaa.org/sports/2020/5/1/core-principles-of-resocialization-of-collegiate-sport.aspx

NCAA. (2020c, March 26). *NCAA presidents set revised financial distribution to support college athletes*. NCAA.org. Retrieved January 17, 2022, from https://www.ncaa.org/news/2020/3/26/ncaa-presidents-set-revised-financial-distribution-to-support-college-athletes.aspx

NCAA. (2020d, March 30). *Division I Council extends eligibility for student-athletes impacted by COVID-19*. NCAA.com. Retrieved February 23, 2022, from https://www.ncaa.com/news/ncaa/article/2020-03-30/division-i-council-extends-eligibility-student-athletes-impacted-COVID

NCAA. (2020e, June 10). *Division II extends quiet period through July 31*. NCAA.org. Retrieved February 23, 2022, from http://www.ncaa.org/about/resources/media-center/news/division-ii-extends-quiet-period-through-july-31

NCAA (2020f, June 16). *Fall recruiting calendar proposed in men's basketball*. NCAA.org. Retrieved February 23, 2022, from http://www.ncaa.org/about/resources/media-center/news/fall-recruiting-calendar-proposed-men-s-basketball

NCAA. (2021a, November). *s.* NCAA.org. Retrieved February 23, 2022, from https://www.ncaa.org/sports/2019/11/12/finances-of-intercollegiate-athletics-database.aspx

NCAA. (2021b, March 4). *NCAA unveils New Final Four Fan Cutout program*. NCAA.org. Retrieved February 23, 2022, from https://www.ncaa.org/about/resources/media-center/news/ncaa-unveils-new-final-four-fan-cutout-program

NCSA. (n.d.). *Dead-period*. NCSA Sports. Retrieved February 23, 2022, from https://www.ncsasports.org/ncaa-eligibility-center/recruiting-rules/dead-period

Pagones, S. (2020, June 29). *Brown University student-athletes fight for reinstatement of Varsity Sports*. Yahoo! Finance. Retrieved February 23, 2022, from https://finance.yahoo.com/news/brown-university-student-athletes-fight-115736771.html

Scoggins, C. (2020, October 27). *NCAA decision on testing rules could impact whether schools restart sports*. Star Tribune. Retrieved February 23, 2022, from https://www.startribune.com/ncaa-decision-on-testing-rules-will-impact-if-d-ii-d-iii-minnesota-schools-restart-sports/572876261

Smith, M., & Ourand, J. (2008, August 25). *ESPN pays $2.25B for SEC rights*. Sports Business Journal. Retrieved February 23, 2022, from https://www.sportsbusinessjournal.com/Journal/Issues/2008/08/25/This-Weeks-News/ESPN-Pays-$225B-For-SEC-Rights.aspx

VanHaaren, T. (2020, June 30). *Michigan coaches Jim Harbaugh, Juwan Howard to take 10% pay cut amid revenue losses*. ESPN. Retrieved January 17, 2022, from https://www.espn.com/college-sports/story/_/id/29385308/michigan-coaches-jim-harbaugh-juwan-howard-take-10-pay-cut-amid-revenue-losses

Villanueva, J. (2020, June 16). *DIII strategic planning and finance committee endorses nearly $2 million a year in budget cuts*. NCAA.org. Retrieved February 23, 2022, from http://www.ncaa.org/about/resources/media-center/news/diii-strategic-planning-and-finance-committee-endorses-nearly-2-million-year-budget-cuts

Winkelmann, Z. K., & Games, K. E. (2020). Athletic trainers' job tasks and status during the COVID-19 pandemic: A preliminary analysis. *Journal of Athletic Training, 56*(1), 20–30. Retrieved from https://doi.org/10.4085/1062-6050-0275.20

Wolken, D. (2020, September 15). *Opinion: College football celebrates covid-19 outbreaks, ridicules cautious approach*. USA Today. Retrieved February 23, 2022, from https://www.usatoday.com/story/sports/college/columnist/dan-wolken/2020/09/15/college-football-celebrates-covid-19-outbreaks-lsu-texas-tech/5809446002/

Chapter 8

Information Technology Leadership

Juanita M. Cole

RISING TO THE CHALLENGE

Things were going well during my fellowship year with the American Council on Education (ACE) until, eight months in, the unimaginable occurred. Just as the spread of the novel coronavirus sent the usually predictable world of college and universities into crisis mode, the normal course of the ACE Fellows Program was disrupted for all of us. After months spent shadowing a university president at a large public research university, I returned quickly to my home institution. Despite the crisis, I felt a sense of hopeful anticipation at the opportunities that arose through this period to leverage the knowledge and skills I had recently acquired. One of those opportunities included representing my home institution on a COVID-19 task force in a consortium of regional universities. This task force provided me the opportunity to interact weekly with vice presidents and chief executives from 17 diverse institutions representing every sector in higher education.

We conducted much of our work via teleconferences, with our leadership teams making broad and collective decisions and relishing the opportunity to share common problems. Our COVID-19 task force provided, in fact, an emblematic tale of how higher education leaders rising to an unforeseen challenge could work together effectively as a community to navigate a unique set of circumstances in uncertain times. Regardless of the institution type, the immediate and common theme for each of our campuses was the conversion of the organization to the online environment for working, learning, and teaching. Each institution relied heavily on the expertise and guidance of their Information Technology (IT) personnel to accomplish this task.

When a Chief Information Officer (CIO) on the task force asked the question, "How can the teaching and learning process be transformed or improved in some way?", our planning focus experienced a level change. I noted that responses differed among the institutions depending on whether or not a CIO was present on their respective teams. As it became increasingly evident that the spring 2020 academic term—and possibly beyond—would change dramatically, every element of the university was brought into question. Drawing upon observations and discussions from this work, I could see that the role of the CIO in higher education was in the process of changing.

In today's institutions of higher education, CIOs are expected to participate not just in the development of technology and information systems, but also in helping build the institution's fundamental strategy. IT leadership is an integral strategic partner in supporting the institutional mission of colleges and universities. While IHEs varied in their experience with distance education, the degree to which each institution in our group could easily switch to remote work and instruction arguably depended upon the flexibility of their network infrastructure and upon the positioning of the CIO in the organizational leadership hierarchy. The global coronavirus pandemic demonstrated that IT leadership is more than bits and bytes and blinking lights.

Network Systems and Infrastructure

As colleges and universities quickly closed campuses at the onset of COVID-19, they needed to support employees working from home and students and faculty shifting to distance learning. At most IHEs, teams from Human Resources (HR), Academic Affairs, Legal, Student Affairs, among other campus units, worked together to address a necessary rush to remote work, teaching, and learning. Primary among the challenges institutions faced through this period was technology. Converting an entire campus workforce overnight was a heavy lift for any IT team. However, at institutions where the modernization of the network systems and infrastructure had already occurred, the load was lightened. From upgrading computing power and storage to accelerating cloud and Virtual Private Network (VPN) adoption, modernization extended the ability of some colleges and universities to work, teach, and communicate with and support users virtually anywhere. At these institutions, CIOs and IT directors reported that from a technological standpoint the switch was accomplished rather painlessly, yet the pandemic introduced new challenges.

> Everything we needed. ... we had in terms of infrastructure. What we had to do was scale. Scale A LOT to cover the whole community. We focused on maximizing our efforts. Compared to others in the consortium, we were way ahead of the curve before, and now we are in a position to define what the curve looks like.
> —IT Director of a large Mid-Atlantic community college

Timing was definitely on our side. In 2016, we had made the decision to replace portions of our 22-year-old existing enterprise resource planning (ERP) applications with a new technology system for human capital and financial management services with a leading provider of enterprise cloud applications for finance and human resources. Modernization of the system made it easy for our staff to work remotely. There were few, if any, disruptions to our business processes in the functional areas of human capital, management, payroll, and financial management. The change was definitely needed. The president supported it after I conducted an internal analysis of the university's systems and an external review of industry best standards for modern technology ERP applications. Because we have this new system, the university is leveraging technology to gain more efficiency. Freeing people to do the work of student success that only people can do is one of the major benefits of this change. Cloud-based systems enabled us to work smarter and focus on student achievement.

—VP and CIO of a regional comprehensive university

Less well-prepared institutions were left scrambling to catch up as quickly as possible to update their systems and establish proper requirements. Learning Management Systems (LMS) were already in place across many institutions due to course modality changes or support systems that had evolved in IHEs over the two decades preceding the pandemic. An LMS is software designed specifically to create, distribute, and manage the online delivery of educational content, hosted as a stand-alone product on the institution's server or accessed as a cloud-based platform that is hosted by the software firm. Often referred to as technology that can improve learning—making it faster, more productive, more cost-effective, and trackable—the most basic LMS contains a core functional platform that enables institutions to upload learning content, deliver lessons to students, serve notifications, and share data with authorized users. The institutional LMS most often operates inside of a web browser, behind a secure login. The intention of such systems is to provide all students and instructors easy access to courses on the go, and to allow administrators and leaders the ability to monitor student progress and to make improvements. However, variations in the system's full functionality for the administration, documentation, tracking, reporting, automation, and delivery of educational courses varied greatly pre-pandemic and impacted the transition to the online environment. Additionally, even at IHEs that had implemented LMSs prior to the pandemic, the level of faculty usage and familiarity varied considerably.

To implement fully remote work and learning capabilities and to ensure system access that was reliable and secure, IT teams worked overtime to support the increased demand and to monitor system usage and activity. IT personnel had to recognize the different needs of institutional operations and administrative staff, as they were unlikely to be mobile workers using desktop devices linked to the internal network, which meant creating secure and remote access for laptops. As an IT manager from one small private liberal arts college explained, remote work before the pandemic at their institution had been limited to a few employees and used mainly for email and other non-operational systems. Given the college's mission and brand which centered on their residential identity with faculty and students engaging onsite, distance learning represented a very minimal feature. To make the switch to remote work and learning, IT personnel at this college divided the organization into distinct groups with differing requirements and dealt with the needs of each to support the mass exodus. These groups consisted of students, teaching faculty, administration, and operations. The assessment of each group determined the level of access required to the network system.

In the switch to fully remote teaching and learning, colleges and universities could not operate without significant student engagement. Faculty required virtual conferencing facilities, and the administration teams needed network access. Table 8.1 further illustrates the issues and requirements CIOs and IT managers contemplated during the early pandemic in meeting these needs.

It was crucial for colleges and universities to have the right technical infrastructure to secure access to the services and information to support remote workers. Additionally, many colleges embraced technologies like cloud computing, Microsoft Teams, Zoom, and Google to give staff, faculty, and students access to each other and to allow them to conduct their business activities both in the office and remotely. These tools offered mechanisms for collaboration and information sharing both within and between IHEs.

Table 8.1 Issues for Consideration by CIOs and IT Managers and System Requirements for Remote Work

- Access controls
- Bandwidth
- Budgeting cost and long-term investment in technology
- Sensitive data that cannot leave internal servers
- Multi-Factor-Authentication
- Network Capacity
- Secure procedures for performing business processes remotely
- Systems Integration
- Technology access at home (e.g. laptops, internet connection, dedicated workspace)
- Videoconferencing solution(s) to encourage face-to-face interaction
- Virtual Private Networks (VPNs) access
- Work schedule policies and expectations communicated by management

Security Concerns

As more work and learning occurred remotely, ensuring network and data security became increasingly important. Security raises continual strategic questions for CIOs and is often at the top of the list of concerns in the field of IT in general. In the pivot to remote operations, many CIOs scaled up their VPN and Virtual Desktop Infrastructure (VDI) capabilities to enable secure access to the network; however, some security practices were never employed at home because those IHEs without existing campus security networks lacked the oversight of protections. The shift to remote work and instruction due to COVID-19 shone a bright light on concerns about security and privacy. These were concerns about which institutions of higher learning had been working to educate their users prior to the pandemic (Cole and Schaffer, 2019).

A key leadership competency is the ability to communicate with the right cadence. CIOs reported that, during the COVID-19 pandemic, it was essential to launch a cyber awareness campaign and to reeducate employees and students to think before clicking on email links from suspicious sources and to avoid connecting to unknown WiFi accounts, placing users at risk of having their devices penetrated by bad actors.

Effective IT leaders understood the importance of looking ahead and of creating policies that would keep their organizations safe. The responsibility of developing reasonable and actionable university IT security policies is a key element of the CIO's campus role. For example, IT managers set limits on operating systems, memory, storage, and processing while encouraging online access to network resources. Like other businesses, colleges and universities participate globally in financial matters via their IT infrastructure connectivity to the Internet—which makes them equally vulnerable to information security breaches. IHEs are targets for three common reasons: identity theft, espionage, and notoriety. Thus, campus IT managers were especially proactive against the variety of threats in this pandemic environment.

> Due to the frequency of security breaches in higher education systems, we can easily become anesthetized to them. The various security reports regarding the rise of data breaches in higher ed foretell a potentially systemic challenge that must be addressed aggressively. Although many industries suffer similar breaches, colleges and universities must address the problem to maintain their integrity. They must apply more than just the latest technology to defend the university's data and information systems if they are to adequately protect the information and data entrusted to them.
> —CIO of a Historically Black College and University

With the shift to remote learning, early on CIOs focused on the phenomenon of "Zoombombing" (uninvited guests intruding in a videoconference) and provided tips about configuring Zoom to reduce vulnerability. CIOs showed concern that staff using institutional laptops at home might download inappropriate software or share account information with family members. While some CIOs stressed the need for enhanced or supplemented multi-factor authentication procedures where possible, others started to think about robust training efforts for students, staff, and faculty. CIOs kept their foot on the accelerator of cybersecurity vigilance, particularly during the pandemic with more individuals working and learning at home.

MUDDYING THE WATERS: ACCESS AND CONNECTIVITY

Equity Insight: Digital Equity in Higher Education

The CEO of Google, Sundar Pichai, said, "It matters that we drive technology as an equalizing force, enabler for everyone" (Bohn, 2015). Digital equity means embedding fairness in the development and implementation of digital systems (City of Casey, 2021). It is to recognize that individuals, groups, and communities are situated differently in relation to access, affordability, and the skills needed for digital platforms and systems. The COVID-19 pandemic highlighted long-standing barriers to digital access for historically underserved and underrepresented groups. A research study found that 25% of students in a large public research university did not have the adequate technology needed to participate in online learning, with higher rates among Black, Indigenous, Latino, and small-town or rural students (Jaggers et al., 2021; Wood, 2021). Discovering that students had limited access to reliable internet led many senior administrators in colleges and universities to repurpose nearby parking lots and other outdoor public spaces, including WiFi and hotspots. As time went on, CIOs implemented solutions to provide technology directly to students through device loaner programs and overhaul infrastructure.

Although many college students have access to information communication technology, lingering disparities remain. These disparities stretch further than the technology and broadband access gap for students and affect students' self-efficacy in remote learning environments. Nearly 20% of students reported struggling with learning how to use education technology efficiently, and 15% of undergraduate students at public research universities lacked familiarity with the technical tools necessary for online learning (Wood, 2021). These disparities exist both at the individual and

> at the institutional level, which may exacerbate inequalities in academic achievement.
>
> Digital equity as a framework rallies higher education leaders to ensure that all students have access to and ownership of the tools that best support them as learners (Holland, 2021). Faculty and administrators should provide opportunities for students to develop the skills and competencies required to take advantage of these digital resources. The end goal, of course, is for students (regardless of background and ability) to develop a deep understanding of not simply using technology tools—but using them to engage with learning experiences that are targeted, authentic, relevant, socially connected, and growth-oriented. The conversation CIOs and IT managers need to engage in is not about the problems of the Digital Divide; it is about the promise of Digital Equity. How can senior leaders ensure that institutions help students learn about, with, and beyond today's technology and not make educational divides worse in the process?

The era of remote instruction brought on by the COVID-19 crisis exacerbated many challenges that institutions and their students already faced, but perhaps none as widespread as the "digital divide"—the gap between those with reliable internet access and those without. While some IHEs attempted to meet these needs for the short-term emergency, the increasingly apparent gap in access to technology and WiFi across the US indicated that a sustainable, longer-term solution was critical to make remote learning possible for everyone. With online instruction launched and remote work in place for staff and faculty, CIOs faced another set of challenges: teaching effectiveness, access, and connectivity.

Supporting Teaching Effectiveness

Teaching effectiveness was another point of concern for CIOs, as it was for faculty and academic leaders through this period. With assistance from instructional designers, academic technology specialists, as well as teaching and learning centers, CIOs strategically worked to address distance learning demands. COVID-19 forced most faculty to deliver their in-person curricula in a meaningful way at a distance using technology tools some had never used before. Both large-scale and peer training efforts provided necessary skills and functionalities. For example, several faculty members from a consortium of universities located in the Mid-Atlantic states turned to more digitally experienced peers at their own colleges and elsewhere. They sought advice from their colleges' technology partners, newly crowdsourced resource lists, sessions being offered through disciplinary associations and the ACE Engage platform, and from experts sharing their tips in higher education resources such as *Inside Higher Ed*. The willingness of so many instructors to acknowledge their need for help and to seek it out was a heartening phenomenon.

It became increasingly clear, however, that many IHEs needed a more systematic approach to promoting alternative pedagogies and teaching modes. CIOs partnered closely with faculty and academic leadership to facilitate both synchronous and asynchronous instruction options. Some institutions favored the latter in an effort to ease bandwidth for the institution and to reduce schedule misalignments for students. Additionally, CIOs assessed their capabilities to improve the accessibility of online tools to support learning outcomes for students with disabilities, while providing needed training for faculty on universal learning design principles and practices.

The question of teaching effectiveness in the online environment raised many questions and concerns through this period, particularly for those institutions with more limited experience in the delivery of distance education. In one study of course delivery through the early pandemic, the authors concluded that the instructional achievement of online learning in this period was debatable because it removed the opportunity for a face-to-face relationship among learners, and between learners and instructors (Joshi et al., 2020). Likewise, another study asserted the importance for institutions to differentiate adequately planned online learning experiences from courses presented online as response to crisis (Hodges and Fowler, 2020). These researchers argue that it is more accurate to refer to online education during the early pandemic as "emergency remote teaching" given the inexperience of many faculty and IHEs in providing remote instruction and the crisis environment.

Student Technology Access and Equity

> Michael, a college sophomore at a Hispanic-Serving Institution (HSI) in a large metropolitan city, settles down in the library lounge on campus about every weekday to complete his homework for class—relying on the library's computers and internet connection. With a broken computer and a slow connection to the internet at home, he depends on the campus' technology to keep pace with his academics. With the library now closed due to the coronavirus, Michael will face even more challenges keeping pace with schoolwork.
> —Observation Field Note by author, April 12, 2020

When college and university presidents and chancellors decided to send students home and shift to remote learning to prevent the spread of COVID-19, problems with access and connectivity emerged almost immediately. The shift to online instruction required CIOs and IT managers to take a central role in ensuring students could continue to access their course materials. It further illuminated the deep digital divide that persists among populations in lower-income areas, in urban communities where internet service is costly, and in rural areas with poor broadband infrastructure. Both IT and academic leaders needed to formulate strategies based on institutional missions, as well as the context of their students' lives.

One CIO shared that their institution received complaints within two weeks after the shift to online from those students who lacked personal computers or laptops, as well as those without WiFi access. Many institutions across the country began loaning laptops to students in need during March–April 2020, or even removing desktops from unused computer labs for students to take home. Additionally, CIOs established WiFi hotspots on campus, often in parking lots, to enable students to connect from their cars; in some rural areas, some colleges (and K-12 school districts) brought WiFi closer to students by parking buses with hotspots in different communities. Some IT leaders considered ways to ease bandwidth through asynchronous instruction options. Later, many IHEs used the institutional portion of the CARES Act to provide laptops and mobile hotspots for those who needed them. (For more on the CARES Act, see Chapter 13.)

Examining the capabilities to improve the accessibility of their online tools, CIOs sought solutions to support learning outcomes for all students. IT leaders coordinated efforts to scale training and pass along necessary tool skills and functionalities. For faculty members who resisted remote instruction, CIOs reframed the situation by reminding faculty of the institutional mission and their shared commitment to student success. Without dismissing faculty concerns, successful leaders sought to reframe the perceived problem and move people forward by acknowledging their concerns while also pointing to the negative impact of educational disruption for students (Bolman and Gallos, 2011).

The pressure to address access and connectivity sparked creativity and collaboration both internally in IT offices, as well as between IT and academic units. For example, at one university, the CIO partnered with the Center for Teaching and Learning and with engineering and computer science faculty to ensure that all courses could be completed with a smartphone. At tribal colleges, higher education leaders created tracking logs which identified the dates, times, and locations of various businesses with WiFi access on or in proximity to area reservations. Some CIOs partnered with businesses and other nonprofit organizations to supply students with computers or to provide internet access.

Yet even with all of these efforts, there remained some IHEs for which an online model was unrealistic. When Berea College in Kentucky, with a historical mission to serve rural Appalachia, made the decision to shut down the remainder of Spring 2020 semester, they knew that many of their students were returning to homes with no WiFi access, so they established ways for them to complete their work for the term by mail or other means.

Not only was it IHEs serving rural areas that faced challenges in the transition to remote learning. A large community college district in a national technology center discovered that many of its urban students lacked access to laptops and WiFi, too. Trinity Washington University, an urban campus in Washington, DC, with a majority of low-income students, opted to keep its doors open to provide access to technology for their students who would not otherwise have it (Fischer, 2020). Campus by campus, such contextually distinct dilemmas about equity and access to technology drove many leadership decisions through this period.

> We are not shifting to online instruction. Half of our students' family income falls below the federal poverty line. That means that when they leave campus and go home, they will not have all the amenities that we expect for middle-class students. We know that more than 10% of our students do not have decent internet access where they live. Online education is easier said than done. Context matters.
>
> —Director of Technology and Operations of a Private Liberal Arts College

STRATEGIC LEADERSHIP LESSONS AND THE ROAD AHEAD

It is important to understand the complex leadership required to guide campuses successfully during times of crisis and significant change. The COVID-19 pandemic is one of the most significant and unpredictable global public health crises in recent times, which impacted the decision-making of CIOs and IT managers in higher education. Bolman and Deal's (2017) Four-Frame model provides one means to analyze IT and academic leaders' decision-making and organizational contexts through this period within Political, Structural, Human Resource, and Symbolic lenses. Bolman and Deal argue the Four-Frames provide leaders with detailed descriptions of organizational mindsets and associated leadership actions that lead to improved organizational understandings (Holmes & Scull, 2019).

As described earlier in the chapter, the focus of many IT managers in the pivot to remote working, teaching, and learning very much aligns with the structural frame in terms of setting measurable goals, clarifying tasks, responsibilities and reporting lines, developing metrics and deadlines, and creating systems and procedures. Through the lens of the Structural frame, effective IT managers acted as architects who understood how to set plans and processes during the crisis. They often saw their primary role as a coach and performance monitor. In contrast, ineffective leaders in this frame were perceived by their employees to be micromanagers who relied too heavily on a top-down command-and-control style of leadership.

The traditional models of hierarchical leadership might have been adequate when faced solely with technical problems, but when confronted with the complexities and uncertainties of the COVID-19 pandemic (e.g., multi-layered and multicultural in nature), leaders often needed to incorporate all four leadership frames for effective decision-making. A shared and distributed approach, which included attention to symbolic, human resources, and political lenses proved imperative in many cases for effectively leading a campus through the abrupt pivot to remote teaching and learning. CIOs and IT managers serving institutions that operated from a shared leadership model (Kezar and Holcombe, 2017) benefitted from a greater degree of agility, innovation, and faculty support in the crisis. Moving forward in response to the crisis, CIOs often adopted a distributed leadership style and erased cross-organizational boundaries in favor of creative opportunities to handle an emergency and meet universities' needs (Fernandez and Shaw, 2020). Capitalizing on the importance of leaders throughout the college or university (e.g, program coordinators, rank-and-file faculty members and long-term serving staff), not just those in positions of authority; CIO's created an infrastructure so that the institution benefitted from the leadership of multiple people.

The Changing Role of the Chief Information Officer

There has been a major shift in the role of the CIO on campuses across the country—predating the COVID-19 pandemic but accelerated by it—that has been driven by continuous improvement and transformation goals. According to Huer (2018), 67% of higher education institutions have a CIO, and those numbers were growing before the pandemic. This is a drastic change from two decades ago when the responsibilities, skill sets, and leadership of information managers focused primarily on computer hardware and programming. Arguably, the CIO role has changed in four major ways: strategic planning, outsourcing, balancing mobility, and reporting structure.

Strategic Planning

Today the CIO must think and act strategically about the entire academic enterprise. As demonstrated earlier in the chapter, CIOs have needed to evolve to meet shifting educational needs, address a wide range of user requirements, and keep pace with changes in technology. As one CIO described, the procurement of technology is a small aspect of their responsibilities. In fact, a survey of the higher education landscape revealed that much of the purchase of technology to support the academic mission has migrated to other leadership divisions in the organization. CIOs in higher education spend up to 27% of their time in a business strategist role and would like to see more of their functional duties lifted to focus even more on strategy (Noonan, 2016). Increasingly, the CIO's role is about understanding how IT and the larger institution align, or how they *should* align.

Before I could evaluate or introduce solutions to address the COVID-19 crisis on my campus, I first had to understand the weaknesses, strengths, threats, and opportunities of the different colleges and administrative departments. I built relationships and demonstrated appropriate leader behaviors —compassion and flexibility to match the context of crisis management. Moving forward, I used that knowledge and relationship to inform my technology decisions.
—CIO at a Mideastern regional public university

Outsourcing

The responsibilities of this role have also expanded to include the need to delegate and outsource, which is why those CIOs who embraced a distributed leadership approach were much more successful than those who did not. For instance, managing the complexities of interactive whiteboards, assuring effective data analytics platforms, and handling security and privacy concerns proved heavy lifts during the pandemic. Additionally, CIOs needed to manage interdepartmental and institution-wide relationships and to contribute to strategic planning. Under this pressure, even CIOs with large teams and robust skills found it increasingly necessary to delegate and to strategize around staffing, workflows, and project management.

Mobility and Agility

The COVID-19 crisis also provided CIOs an opportunity to assess mobility and agility. While mobile-first approaches are all the rage, the fast-track development of mobility can hinder institutional efficiency if not done properly. Too often applications are built with agility rather than longevity in mind. They are created quickly to address an immediate and pressing institutional or educational need. However, these rapidly developed applications may not integrate well with other systems or applications, or may have weak user experiences that result in poor student or educator engagement. Yet mobility is important. Not only do students and educators expect mobility, but it can also yield positive effects for everything from student advising and recruitment to registration and grade tracking. Agile development of short-lived piecemeal solutions, however, is neither a cost-effective nor an efficient way to connect students, educators, and administrators. Today's higher education CIOs must help universities to embrace a holistic view of technology, marrying the convenience of mobility to the comprehensive and long-term needs of both students and their institutions.

Reporting Structure

The reporting structure within most institutions of higher education also changed from years past. Pomerantz (2018) observed a striking variation in

CIOs' reporting relationships depending on the type of institution. A greater percentage of CIOs at doctoral institutions report to the provost (41%) than at any other type of institution. In contrast, a greater percentage of CIOs at bachelor's and associate's institutions report to the president or chancellor (44% and 45%, respectively). These findings indicate that at doctoral institutions, the CIO role is tightly integrated into the institution's academic mission, whereas at master's, bachelor's, and associate's institutions, the role is more closely aligned with the operational and business side of the institution. Those who served on the president's cabinet reported a strategic advantage through the early pandemic that is likely to impact how institutions align technology with leadership and decision-making moving forward.

Opportunities in Times of Trouble

Fernandez and Shaw (2020) argue that it is a time for academic leaders to demonstrate enough courage to disrupt long-standing patterns of behavior, challenge opinions and organizational norms, and re-envision the status quo. CIOs proved they could successfully navigate the transition to remote work and learning with flexibility, understanding, and compassion. Looking beyond the early pandemic period, it was clear that, once the immediate crisis was over, academic leaders would face a dilemma as they rebuilt. What would be the long-term status for makeshift online course offerings rolled out in an emergency to get through the semester? Would they be refined and sustained in a new reshaped reality or discarded like a used band-aid? Academic leaders with the adaptive capacity (Heifetz and Laurie, 2001) to take advantage of strategic opportunities as they arose might now be able to redefine organizational responsibilities by disruptive innovation and employ digital technologies to alter or eliminate inefficient legacy practices. Perhaps the digital resources produced in response to the crisis could be employed to assist disadvantaged students, those with physical or learning disabilities, or to create vocational course design for non-traditional students returning to education once the crisis subsides.

The Road Ahead

The VP and CIO at the University of Maryland addressed the above questions by describing IT's role in creating a more inclusive, respectful, and supportive environment. The COVID-19 crisis revealed the university's shortcomings in meeting everyone's IT needs regardless of income or disability. Figure 8.1 depicts key transformation phases CIOs highlighted that updated IT Departments.

As technology expands institutions' ability to understand factors leading to recruitment, retention, academic choices, graduation, and more, the role of the CIO is likely to continue to grow.

INFORMATION TECHNOLOGY LEADERSHIP

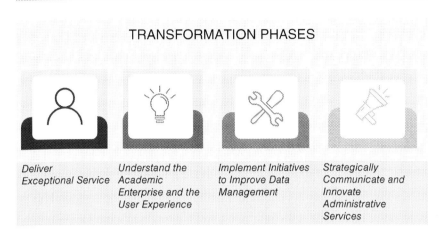

Figure 8.1 IT Transformation Phases

LESSONS LEARNED

When asked what they would have done differently given the chance, the CIOs and IT managers interviewed for this book openly shared the following list of recommendations:

1. Work with executive leadership to establish policies accommodating remote work and instruction that is equitable.
2. Ensure that institutional disaster recovery and business continuity planning actually model a pandemic.
3. Stress test systems for gaps and solutions, and reduce enterprise complexity and friction.
4. Invest more in disaster recovery, continuity planning, and better collaboration tools.
5. Develop more complete policies and practices for remote work.
6. Focus on the digital experience including means to address common tasks for staff, faculty, and students.

Another major lesson many leaders would take away from the early pandemic is the power of collaboration and compassion, as modeled by the work of the consortium in which I participated. Many colleges and universities collaborated and shared best practices throughout spring 2020. Numerous CIOs and other administrators were proactive in getting students technological tools, though not all educational institutions had the resources to do so. When academic institutions allowed themselves to be inspired by those who placed concern for community above competition and stood in solidarity with others in higher education, they helped to create a better digital work and learning environment for all.

135

In conclusion, the pandemic forced colleges and universities to rapidly scale their use of technologies—such as videoconferencing software, learning management systems, and data analytics tools—to continue to serve students and to deliver on their core educational mission. Additionally, colleges and universities rethought strategies to meet students' needs and how to prepare faculty and staff to conduct business more efficiently to overcome the challenges brought on by the pandemic. Remote learning and delivery capability, for the institution, the faculty, and the students, was pushed front and center for executive leadership and external governing bodies to observe. This extreme visibility of an often-invisible IT function afforded many CIOs the opportunity to engage in and lead conversations around how challenges were going to be solved. CIOs also became key players in their institutions' emergency responses, addressed concerns about pandemic management and return to campus planning, as well as developed ideas about how technology would help the institution adapt to new modalities of learning and work. The challenge for CIOs, now and in the foreseeable future, lies in helping institutions transform themselves into responsive organizations that can meet student needs while simultaneously doing more with less.

REFERENCES

Bohn, D. (2015, May 29). Chasing the next billion with Sundar Pichai: Inside the mind of the man behind Google's most important products. *The Verge*. Retrieved from https://www.theverge.com/a/sundars-google/sundar-pichai-interview-google-io-2015

Bolman, L. G. and Deal, T. E. (2017). *Reframing Organizations: Artistry, Choice, and Leadership*, 6th ed. San Francisco, CA: Jossey-Bass.

Bolman, L. G. and Gallos, J. V. (2011). *Reframing Academic Leadership*. Jossey-Bass, An Imprint of Wiley.

City of Casey. (2021). Casey Digital Equity Framework 2021–2025. Retrieved from https://hdp-au-prod-app-csy-conversations-files.s3.ap-southeast-2.amazonaws.com/1216/3330/9883/DelosDelta-Digital_Equity_Framework_Accessible.pdf

Cole, J. and Schaffer, J. (2019, November 13–14). Preparing for disruption to information technology infrastructure in professional military education [Conference session]. *2019 National Defense University, College of Information and Cyberspace, Annual Cyber Beacon Proceedings*, Washington, DC, United States.

Fernandez, A.A. and Shaw, G.P. (2020), Academic leadership in a time of crisis: The Coronavirus and COVID-19. *Journal of Leadership Studies*, 14: 39–45. Retrieved from https://doi.org/10.1002/jls.21684

Fischer, K. (2020, March 11). *Chronicle.com*. Retrieved from https://www.chronicle.com/article/when-coronavirus-closes-colleges-some-students-lose-hot-meals-health-care-and-a-place-to-sleep/

Heifetz, R. A. and Laurie, D. L. (2001). The work of leadership. *Harvard Business Review*, 79(11), 131–141.

Hodges, C. B. and Fowler, D. J. (2020). The COVID-19 crisis and faculty members in higher education: from emergency remote teaching to better teaching through reflection. *International Journal of Multidisciplinary Perspectives in Higher Education*, 5(1), 118 122.

Huer, J. B. (2018). *Higher Education Technology Leadership: A Delphi Study*. Lamar University-Beaumont, TX. Dissertation Abstracts International, Ann Arbor, MI, Retrieved from https://csumb.idm.oclc.org/login?url=https://www.proquest.com/dissertations-theses/higher-education-technology-leadership-delphi/docview/2149672642/se-2?accountid=10355

Holland, B. (2021, November 30). Why digital equity is about so much more than access. *EdSurge*. Retrieved from https://www.edsurge.com/news/2021-11-30-why-digital-equity-is-about-so-much-more-than-access-and-infrastructure

Holmes, W. T. and Scull, W. R. (2019). Reframing organizations through leadership communications: The four-frames of leadership viewed through motivating language. *Development and Learning in Organizations: An International Journal*, Retrieved from https://doi.org/10.1108/DLO-09-2018-0107

Jaggars, S. S., Motz, B. A., Rivera, M. D., Heckler, A., Quick, J.D., Hance, E. A., and Karwischa, C. (2021). *The Digital Divide Among College Students: Lessons Learned From the COVID-19 Emergency Transition*. Minneapolis, MN: Midwestern Higher Education Compact

Joshi, O., Chapagain, B., Kharel, G., Poudyal, N. C., Murray, B. D., and Mehmood, S. R. (2020). Benefits and challenges of online instruction in agriculture and natural resource education, *Interactive Learning Environments*, DOI:10.1080/10494820.2020.1725896

Kezar, A. and Holcombe, E. M. (2017). *Shared Leadership in Higher Education: Important Lessons from Research and Practice*. Washington, DC: American Council on Education.

Noonan, A. (2016, March 1). How the CIO's role has changed in Higher Ed., *Ed Tech Magazine*. Retrieved from https://edtechmagazine.com/higher/article/2016/03/how-cios-role-has-changed-higher-ed

Pomerantz, J. (2018, April 5). C-Level Reporting Lines. *EDUCAUSE Review*. Retrieved from https://er.educause.edu/blogs/2018/4/c-level-reporting-lines

Wood, S. (2021, November 10). How Colleges Are Bridging the Digital Divide. *Yahoo! News* Retrieved from https://news.yahoo.com/colleges-bridging-digital-divide-151607571.html

Chapter 9

Operations Facilities and Auxiliaries

Kristi N. Hottenstein and Rachael A. Kipp

At the beginning of the COVID-19 pandemic, it quickly became apparent that personnel working in facilities and auxiliary units would be central to the initial planning stages since the very first steps campuses faced involved closing down buildings or minimizing on-campus population density. Faced with the reality that some students simply did not have homes to return to, many campuses had to maintain core operations and allowed limited numbers of students to remain on campus. After the initial shutdown and transition to remote operations on campuses, the next phase of pandemic response involved maintaining basic on-campus operations as well as supporting those offices and personnel needed for remote learning. In addition to providing support during remote operations, facilities personnel took on a central role in the planning for reopening campuses for fall 2020.

INITIAL RAMP-DOWN: TIMING AND LOGISTICS

While colleges and universities nationwide engaged in varying strategies and decision-making processes for the initial planning around campus closures and moving to remote learning, eventually almost all institutions closed for the remaining portion of the spring 2020 term and for summer sessions. Whether this was the result of a "follow the leader" mentality or of the need to abide by widespread stay-at-home orders, nearly all institutions shifted to remote operations within a very short time period. While the situation remained fluid and uncertain into summer, campus leaders had to plan and to inform faculty, staff, and students of the most likely course of operations well in advance of when academic semesters were to begin. Thus, they were obliged to finalize and act upon plans before all pertinent data were available.

Planning Principles

Many physical plant leaders turned to professional associations like the Society for College and University Planning (SCUP) and Association of Physical Plant

Administrators (APPA) for advice and emerging best practices. Amidst the COVID-19 pandemic, these organizations and many others like them began offering webinars and other resources related to COVID-19 planning to assist colleges and universities with their facilities and operations plans. Nicholas Santilli, Senior Director of Learning Strategy at SCUP, noted how the needs of the membership shifted in notable ways as the pandemic unfolded. As he explained,

> [Our] membership did not need theoretical presentations on how higher education was going to be forever changed. Instead, our members needed real-time advice regarding how to keep campus operations moving forward in the crisis moment with an eye toward recovery planning once a pivot regarding campus operations was complete. Initially, our corporate members needed information on how campuses intended to respond to the campus closures. What were campuses doing to shift online, support remote work by their faculty, staff, and students, and create safe physical spaces? Our on-campus members needed [physical] space. The shift to online dominated their day-to-day experiences. … Our corporate members were interested in how institutions were making decisions regarding campus construction projects, repurposing physical space, and anticipating how institutions would need to be prepared for on campus activities in the fall term.—Nicholas Santilli, SCUP

Lander Medlin, Executive Vice President for the APPA, offered similar sentiments

> Our members needed targeted information that applied to their specific facilities' circumstances and how COVID-19 was impacting their world. Because they cover so many major areas of responsibility (planning, design, and construction; operations and maintenance; energy and utilities; and general administration and finance), their operations touch every aspect of campus life.

Such associations and consultants seemed to understand the immediacy and responded with an intense focus on the practical needs of physical plant directors and managers. They also served as repositories and information-sharing sources for those working in these fields within institutions. Since campuses were operating at reduced density during remote operations, many were able to implement new guidelines, practices and procedures necessitated by COVID-19 in advance of their potential need (when campuses would be repopulated).

Institutional Emergency Operation Plans and Procedures

Facilities and operations divisions found themselves dusting off prior emergency operations plans (EOPs) and considering options for their institutions.

The imperative to shut down campus operations at a quick pace and for an unknown period added to the complexity of operational decision-making. Moreover, differences in institutional missions, student demographics and needs, as well as the need to negotiate procedures with faculty, staff, and stakeholders, shaped individual IHE plans and strategies (Farris & McCreight, 2014).

Very little consistency exists across higher education in how emergency programs are organized and maintained, and many programs, particularly in small and underfunded institutions, are not robustly resourced. One study from 2010 found that 75% of universities had emergency management offices staffed with only one employee (Farris & McCreight, 2014). As a result, institutional preparation in the face of COVID-19 varied considerably both across individual IHEs and across sectors. Those that did not have emergency plans were at a great disadvantage as they figured out how to organize their resources for decision-making and action related to the pandemic, but even for those with emergency plans few had envisioned a global pandemic as a possible scenario.

As a case study, we can examine what the University of Michigan-Flint (UM-Flint) did as the pandemic unfolded. An urban public institution of just over 7,000 students in fall 2019, UM-Flint serves a predominantly undergraduate and in-person population, with approximately 75% of its enrollment at the undergraduate level and, prior to the pandemic, approximately 75% of its courses being delivered in a face-to-face modality. In 2019, 57% of its undergraduate population received federal grants, and approximately 10% of students lived on campus, including roughly 35% of the freshman class. The campus had an EOP, as well as departmental-level continuity of operations plans (COOPs) already in place prior to the pandemic.

In early March 2020, campus leaders instructed all departments to update their COOPs to plan for the possibility of both 75% and 100% remote work. Although part of the University of Michigan (UM) system, both the Flint and Dearborn campuses function autonomously. This said, the UM System campuses engaged in two-way communication about COOP planning and best practices daily through participation in the system's Ann Arbor Emergency Operations Center (EOC). UM-Flint also activated its own EOC in late March 2020.

Engaging key stakeholders became a critical early task for the EOC led by the Vice Chancellor for Business and Finance at UM Flint. Initially, it consisted of public safety, environmental health and safety, communications, housing and residence life, events and building services, the international center, and a member of the Provost office to represent the academic operations of the university. They ordered masks, sanitizer, toilet paper and other cleaning supplies before these items became scarce. In late March, climbing case numbers necessitated the move of more and more functions to remote work. The institution was positioned well for these moves because of preexisting EOP and COOP plans and the decision to activate an EOC. Additionally, daily meetings gave the response team the opportunity to debrief and retool amidst the ever-changing recommendations and orders at the national, state, and city levels.

Timing and Communications

The first phase of the pandemic response involved making swift decisions to move students off campus, including vacating as many of the residence halls as possible (Larkin, 2020). While difficult and stressful to set aside the core academic mission, the mantra "safety first" guided the first wave of responses for many institutions.

> The first stage was what I would call the ramp-down stage. That was the first moment there were issues and we realized we needed to get people off campus. The ramp-down phase lasted probably four or five weeks. Then came the maintenance stage where (almost) everybody is off campus and education is happening remotely.—Mike Hague, UM-Flint Vice Chancellor for Business and Finance, and Chair of the Campus Emergency Operations Center

During the ramp-down stage, the initial concerns focused on getting students in the residence halls safely home, either in this country or to their homes abroad (see Chapter 3). The logistics behind these processes varied considerably, depending in part on whether the decision to move to remote operations was made before, during, or after a school's spring break.

At UM-Flint, campus leadership announced the decision to move to remote learning on Wednesday, March 11, three days after students returned from their spring break. Canceling classes for two days gave faculty time to prepare and move to alternative delivery formats beginning Monday, March 16. The initial university ramp-down phase was driven by the state ordering a "stay home, stay safe" initiative on March 24, 2020. It was also guided by CDC recommendations and best practices from other UM campuses, particularly the Ann Arbor campus, whose planning team included representatives from the Office of Research and the Medical Center.

Unlike UM-Flint, some institutions were able to take advantage of their spring break to give themselves more time to plan the transition to remote learning. Institutions that began their switch to remote learning over their spring break had the advantage of working with a much smaller on-campus population. However, these institutions then faced the decision to either allow the wider population of students to return to campus to collect their belongings before they went home, with an increased risk of exposure to all involved, or to deny students access to their dormitories.

Consider two small private schools in urban locations with approximately the same number of undergraduates. University X chose not to allow their students to return to campus. That meant that those students made the transition to remote work without access to their textbooks, notes, and sometimes laptops, having only the necessities that they had packed for what they thought was their spring break. University Y, on the other hand, was able to arrange for their students to move out entirely from residence halls before the campus moved to remote work. As these two examples reveal, the situation across the country was fluid, with varying state and regional mandates, and the correct course of action was not at all clear. Under different circumstances, the move out at University Y could have been a "super-spreader event" had some percentage of students and families working to move out of residences been exposed to the virus. And even the most well-thought-out plans had the potential for disruption if city or state guidelines changed suddenly, which they often did in the early months of the pandemic.

For example, at one midsize state institution, students were initially encouraged to return and get their belongings according to a carefully planned move-out schedule only to have the state's shelter-in-place order take effect mid-move out. Even the most understanding of students expressed exasperation at the conflicting messages. The best the leadership team could do was to emphasize the need to put safety above all else in their considerations and to quickly plan the return of the belongings of students who were unable to collect them in person. Although no amount of contingency planning could have accounted for shifting guidelines at the local, state, and national levels, the differences among institutional responses led to a great deal of frustration from both students and parents. Students at University X understandably wondered why they were not allowed to claim their belongings while they observed everyone from University Y in the same state being allowed to do so.

At Boston University (BU), the decision to move to remote instruction was undertaken over spring break. BU residence halls include both double- and triple-occupancy rooms. This configuration posed a significant problem for facilities personnel tasked with packing up students' belongings for either storage or shipment, as there was no way to identify which items belonged to which roommate. BU quickly developed an app that would allow students to circle their own belongings in a picture of the room so that each roommate's belongings could be allocated correctly. As labor-intensive as this proved for the facilities staff, it allowed BU to minimize travel and exposure while also granting each student access to their own belongings.

Many institutions struggled with the messaging to encourage those students who had a place to go to leave campus, without making those who remained to feel burdensome. Since no one knew what the duration of the remote learning period would be, very few institutions initially announced that they were switching to remote operations for the remainder of the semester. Instead, most announced some sort of interim date at which they would make further decisions.

The uncertainty in March 2020 regarding the length of the campus shutdowns contributed to the reluctance of some students to comply with the request to go home. Some students tried to delay their decisions hoping that on-campus instruction would return. This meant that institutions had to resort to various creative strategies to encourage compliance, such as freezing these students' ID-enabled access to facilities.

LOGISTICS: RUNNING A PHYSICAL CAMPUS IN REMOTE MODE

As campuses settled into the work of remote instruction and work, the functions of facilities management involved the maintenance of basic on-campus operations as well as supporting those offices and personnel needed for remote learning. These maintenance functions included providing services for students who remained on campus while also ensuring the health and safety of the campus community with a reduced on-campus presence.

Reconfiguring Distribution of Essential Services

With smaller populations on campuses following the move to remote instruction, the more complex and time-consuming cleaning protocols now necessary did not prove to be too burdensome in late spring 2020. However, it soon became clear that colleges and universities also had to consider the need for additional personnel and supplies to maintain the same level of cleanliness when campuses reopened, possibly, in fall 2020. In some cases, campuses planned alternatives to pre-COVID-19 student service approaches that would make safety compliance easier. For example, some campuses created one-stop student services for students in order to cut down on the number of offices that needed to be cleaned. Before the pandemic, a student might have needed to drop off transcripts in admissions, visited the financial aid office, followed by a trip to see an advisor, and stop by the bursar's office to pay their bill. Some of these services were moved to online modalities, but if these offices were at least minimally staffed when students returned to campus, maintaining prior practices would require the cleaning of four different offices daily to serve a student in a similar pre-pandemic manner. Campuses that chose to place a representative from each of these offices all within a single area where they could maintain the appropriate social distancing cut the necessary cleaning and disinfecting significantly and avoided the need to increase cleaning staff.

Campus dining options were also reduced to account for fewer students and new safety protocols. Campuses added "grab-and-go" options and developed delivery options for people in quarantine or isolation. In most cases, this required the reconfiguration of physical spaces to provide appropriate social distancing in high-traffic areas. Although it is relatively easy to modify seating areas to accommodate social distancing, serving areas where patrons pick up their food are often quite small and not well defined in many cafeterias. A solution was to create new one-way traffic patterns to minimize contact and maximize social distancing while also tightly controlling the number of people allowed within a given area.

Securing Campus Buildings

As campus populations dwindled, it made fiscal sense to consolidate housing to decrease cleaning and utility costs. Decisions on closure and consolidation depended on such factors as social distancing capabilities, the capacity to isolate/quarantine exposed and ill students, access to modified dining services, and the ability to maintain new and stricter cleaning protocols. Once residence halls were almost entirely emptied, campuses began to lock down buildings for student and staff safety and to allow only essential staff into the buildings. While such closures caused some issues with campus access for students, on balance locking down unused buildings addressed safety concerns and reduced the need for the extensive cleaning and disinfecting protocols required in occupied areas. The approach to limiting access only to essential personnel varied depending on the type and use of each building. While it was a relatively simple matter to close off classrooms, other basic campus operations needed to continue. For example, even with research activities limited to critical activities, there could still be people needing access to laboratory buildings to maintain instrumentation and to care for animals.

Even with remote learning, both faculty and students sometimes needed access to library sources that were not available online. In at least one case, a public research university kept its main library open, although this library was eventually forced to move to a closed stack model. Neither staff nor patrons were allowed to wander the stacks after state guidelines limited gatherings to less than ten people, so users would come to a central point to request materials, which library staff would then locate and provide.

With so many buildings effectively closed or at least substantially understaffed, package and mail delivery to individual buildings quickly became problematic. Although external deliveries could be funneled to one or more collection points on campus relatively easily, delivery to the recipients had to be coordinated amongst the remaining staff. This was not an issue if the delivery contained book or office supplies, but more complicated if it contained, for example, temperature-sensitive materials for scientific research. In these situations, facilities personnel identified and assisted in the development and implementation of solutions within a short window of time.

Facilities Safety and Cleaning

Unoccupied and barely used buildings offered potential targets for theft and vandalism. Empty classrooms and labs often contain expensive equipment or possibly dangerous materials. Decreased occupancy resulted in a need for increased security while maintaining access for faculty and staff on an as-needed basis. The nature of the challenges varied depending on institution type, size and location. In some areas where state or local orders closed public facilities, there was a need to ensure that buildings were not being accessed by local displaced individuals. Safety concerns, especially in urban areas, were alleviated to some extent if the city implemented a curfew. In buildings that remained even partially in use, custodians cleaned more often, up to several times a day in the common or high traffic areas. They needed to focus on some areas more than they typically did, such as doorknobs, and needed to use new types of cleaning equipment, such as ionizers.

Equity Insight: Safeguarding Essential Staff During the Shut Down

As campuses shut down in March 2020, leaders confronted the complexity of balancing what often prove to be competing institutional and stakeholder interests and equity concerns (Harper, 2020). For example, the nature of the work performed by essential facilities employees, including maintenance and cleaning staff, often could not be performed remotely. At many IHEs, low-income and minoritized populations and women form a large segment of facilities staff. Whereas in most states, non-essential workers fell under state stay-at-home orders compelling them to work remotely, essential and frontline workers were generally exempt from this governmental regulation. "Black and Latino workers are more likely to have lost their jobs, while white and wealthier Americans are much more likely to be able to work from home and to not be deemed essential, front-line workers, who are more likely to be exposed to the virus" (Fain 2020)

For those who relied on public transportation to get to work and lived in neighborhoods with high rates of COVID-19 infections, on-campus work created additional risk of contact with infected people. At a time when accurate testing was still in development and little was known about the mechanisms of transmitting COVID-19, "safety", regardless of institutional policies, seemed especially elusive.

> Early in the pandemic, fears existed that surfaces might serve as a primary conduit of COVID-19. This meant, for instance, that IHEs undertook to increase the zealousness of their cleaning protocols. At the University of Maryland-College Park, the union representing housekeepers and other facilities workers filed a complaint with the Maryland Higher Education Labor Relations Board alleging that the university had put these workers at risk by failing to provide needed safety measures and equipment, such as N95 masks. Additionally, when UMD turned off air conditioners in residence halls to control moisture levels, housekeeping staff complained about the health results of having to clean in extreme heat. Other IHEs experienced similar complaints. Yet, early in the pandemic, IHEs struggled to locate adequate amounts of personal protective equipment (PPE), including masks. These circumstances exposed disparities in the distribution of risk—previously unknown but now associated with COVID-19—across job types and the dissimilar demographic composition of the high-risk and low-risk jobs. (See also Chapter 10.)

Institutions with strong contingency planning began procuring needed supplies early on. Obtaining cleaning supplies, hand sanitizer, toilet paper, plexiglass, and PPE became increasingly difficult as the spring wore on, even with smaller amounts needed for reduced operations. Many institutions were able to reallocate items from areas that were not functioning, such as redistributing PPE from educational and research laboratories that had been shut down within and outside their institutions. Many chemistry and pharmacy departments had the materials on hand to formulate hand sanitizer, and some institutions repurposed 3-D printers for making face shields (Redden, 2020). Although supply chain issues improved moving into summer 2020, there was concern that these challenges would return as institutions prepared to open for the fall. In order to operate safely, campuses encouraged and sometimes required employees to follow strict public health guidelines (wear masks when around other people, maintain social distancing, and wash hands frequently) while on campus. Although it was clear from the beginning that the housekeeping staff would need additional PPE, the need for proper PPE for public safety was less well understood at that time. Campus police officers needed training in new protocols to keep themselves safe, as well as anyone with whom they might come into contact. For example, if a police action required transporting someone in their vehicle, the passenger needed to wear a mask in order to protect the officers.

CONSEQUENCES OF RUNNING A PHYSICAL CAMPUS IN REMOTE MODE

Once personnel in facilities made the needed changes to move instruction and work to a remote mode and secure the campus, the changes themselves had consequences on the ways that institutions carried out the business of higher education. While some of these were foreseeable, all of them required new procedures to be implemented, sometimes based on little or rapidly changing information.

Impacts on Human Resources

Even though most campuses technically remained open and maintained essential functions, the need for much of the facilities and auxiliary staff was substantially decreased, or even eliminated. This meant either paying salaries to people who could not work while stay-at-home orders were in effect, finding an "essential" alternative to their regular job function (like having a groundskeeper work on the cleaning staff), or furloughing them (see Chapter 10, Human Resources). With the expansion of unemployment benefits provided by the CARES Act (see Chapter 13, Contingency Planning for more detail), staff below a certain salary level actually earned more money while on furlough. Some institutions offered voluntary furloughs in the hopes of preventing the involuntary sort.

Custodial staff were deemed to be essential workers throughout the crisis. However, the terms of their employment varied significantly depending on the type of institution. Custodial and maintenance services are often outsourced or unionized, which added to the complexity of managing the personnel in these areas. Many physical plant leaders had to navigate third-party contracts and union negotiations to change the scope of work, furlough, or lay off employees. Generally, unions understood the necessity of finding alternatives when there was simply no work for their members, especially as the financial toll of the pandemic response deepened across higher education institutions.

Many colleges and universities also contracted with dining and housing services from third-party vendors. These vendors lost a significant amount of money in the spring semester, and certainly needed to furlough or lay off staff. Since they were not directly employed by the institutions, the loss of these employees is not generally tallied as a part of the layoffs and furloughs occurring in higher education, but these losses certainly had an impact on the economic sectors that depend on IHEs in their community (see Chapter 10). Given the size of the impact, there were concerns about the ability of all these vendors to resume operations whenever campuses reopened.

As states began to limit the size of gatherings or to prohibit them completely, activities and conferences had to be canceled. These cancellations impacted not only planned academic conferences, but also revenue-generating weddings and other community events scheduled in campus locations. The loss of these events was devastating to the food service providers on some campuses, particularly those with smaller residential populations, as oftentimes those providers lost money on student meal plans but subsidized those losses with revenue generated from event catering. Food purchased early on for many of the canceled events ended up going to waste and event staff were laid off. Some leaders made the decision to use the food to address morale issues on campus, either by providing campus workers with free meals or by giving employees meals to go. Others chose to use these perishable resources to address food insecurities within their communities, partnering with local food services such Meals on Wheels, which saw a huge increase in demand from the start of the pandemic. Much as they did with room and board, many campuses chose to return conference and event deposits, creating major financial losses that compounded fiscal strains as institutions worked to meet costs with no revenue coming in.

Refunds for Student Housing

The leadership decision to close residence halls and send the majority of students home was one taken by hundreds of higher education institutions by mid-March (Mervosh & Swales, 2020). Institutions made and executed their move-out plans quickly, as the situation rapidly worsened. Consequently, most institutions felt obliged to issue a prorated refund for the housing and dining fees for the remainder of the semester, though this was a fluid and controversial series of decisions through the spring (Kerr, 2020). The differences in decision patterns regarding moving students out of the residence halls varied by institution type, and, perhaps more importantly, by amount of bottom-line room and board revenue provided to institutions' budgets (Cromar, 2020). Refunds represented a significant financial expense. Coupled with indicators of the likelihood that summer programming would also be canceled and the tremendous uncertainty about the upcoming fall semester, the cost of refunding housing brought some institutions to the brink of financial collapse. (See Chapter 13 for a discussion of budgetary and contingency planning.)

At UM-Flint, whose student body included a large percentage of commuters, the prorated room and board refunds resulted in a comparatively small hit to the overall budget. Only about 500 of the 7,300 students resided on campus at the start of the pandemic, and meal plans were only required for the first year. By contrast, at institutions where room and board comprised a large portion of the budget revenue, the closing of residence halls had a much greater impact both in terms of budget and on the decision-making processes regarding the shifts to remote teaching. Take, for example, a small private college that required students to reside on campus and to have a meal plan for all four years. With room and board generating upwards of $15,000 per student, or 25% to 30% of annual revenue, refunding students could be financially devastating.

Despite the cataclysmic impact of COVID-19 on campus partners, many worked hard to put students first. American Campus Communities, Inc. (ACC), for example, the largest owner, manager, and developer of student housing communities in the United States, operated over 160 student housing properties containing nearly 112,000 beds (American Campus Communities, 2020). In collaboration with its university partners, the company agreed to refund a portion of students' rent totaling over $15 million during the second quarter of 2020, resulting in a net loss of $13.3 million for the quarter (American Campus Communities, 2020).

While striving to maintain financial viability, ACC leadership adopted several principles to guide their work during the pandemic, including ensuring a healthy and academically oriented environment for residents and a compassionate approach for students and their families, many of whom faced unemployment and diminished incomes as a result of the pandemic. The company formed a Resident Hardship Program to provide relief on a case-by-case basis to those residents and families who endured financial hardship due to the COVID-19 pandemic. For the months of April 2020 through June 2020, the company granted approximately $8.6 million in rent relief to approximately 6,500 qualified residents (American Campus Communities, 2020). The guiding principles and the Hardship Program are clear examples of leaders creating guidance and programs led by mission and student-centeredness, rather than budget, while also strategically positioning a private enterprise to maintain a strong reputation and positionality for a post-pandemic future.

Alternative Uses for Vacant Residence Halls

Campuses emptied of students and non-essential workers ended up with a great deal of available housing space. Across the nation, some colleges and universities considered repurposing facilities for community COVID needs (Leckrone, 2020). Many offered their now-vacant residence halls to healthcare workers, first responders, non-critical hospital patients, and others in need (Busta, 2020). Tufts University provided housing for patients needing non-COVID-related medical attention to free up bed space at local hospitals for COVID patients (Diep, 2020). Suffolk University in Boston partnered with Pine Street Inn, a local homeless shelter, to provide additional beds to reduce congestion and increase social distancing in the homeless population (Suffolk University dorm transformed into shelter for homeless during coronavirus crisis, 2020). Sonoma State University in the California State University system secured a contract worth up to $5 million to provide the county an alternative care site for patients experiencing mild COVID symptoms or those needing to be isolated due to exposure (Silvy, 2020). In order to allow outside groups to use residence hall space, the remaining students on campus had to be moved to reduce the risk of contact and transmission. The residence halls had to be staffed with housekeeping and food services, which likely saved some employees in those areas from being furloughed or laid off.

Many institutions, especially those in areas with higher densities of COVID-positive patients, understood that it was only a matter of time before they were going to be approached to assist their communities. One strategy deployed by institutions was to get out in front of the potential "asks" in order to control the type of assistance they would ultimately provide. These institutional leaders foresaw that it would be better to offer the type of assistance they would be willing to give, rather than to be asked for assistance later that they could not, or would be unwilling to provide, and then have to deal with the implications of saying no. For example, offering space to front-line workers provided valuable assistance and good public relations, but did not generate as much risk and challenge as housing COVID-positive patients or homeless individuals.

One challenge of this approach was that housing offices at institutions that did provide support for these higher-risk populations were barraged by calls from parents and students requesting that they not be placed in residence halls for the coming 2020–2021 year, where such individuals had been housed. This concern from families became an unintended consequence to what presumably seemed like a good deed.

> We knew an ask from the community was coming and we knew that ask would likely be to assist in housing local indigent and homeless persons. This raised concerns for the safety of our students, especially given the decreased staffing structure we had moved to. We decided to proactively offer up our facilities for medical professionals, and we were very careful with the terminology. We said medical professionals, not first responders because that was a broader population. It was an identifiable group that we could target, limit, and then provide an environment that we felt we could keep reasonably safe and clean. Getting out in front of this allowed us to control the ask and we were able to establish a facility that would meet an identifiable community need with a specific population that we felt could maintain a reasonably healthy and safe environment for the duration of the time that they were there.—
> Vice President of Student Affairs at an urban serving institution

Overall, institutions willing to open their doors to assist with the pandemic received positive community responses, including donations from alumni and community foundations. These donations helped with the various unanticipated costs of the pandemic response.

Facilities Maintenance and Capital Projects

There is a certain amount of routine maintenance necessary after students move out every year. In spring 2020, assuming the institution could afford to do so, that work was carried out after the early move out. At some nearly empty campuses, the early move-out also provided an opportunity for certain capital projects to be accomplished with minimum disruption, while those in states with stay-at-home orders were completely halted. Federal, state, and even city guidelines determined procedures that needed to be implemented for construction projects to proceed. These projects, if permitted to move forward, had to be accomplished without interaction between the construction workers and the remaining students and staff on campus. Regulations required that projects that did not allow for complete separation of on-campus and off-campus groups be stopped, the exception being work that would be hazardous or dangerous to leave incomplete. For example, a half-finished roofing project was deemed acceptable to complete for safety purposes. Cash flow issues also impacted the progress of capital projects, with some projects that were still in early stages needing to be postponed indefinitely until institutions could reassess their financial position.

PLANNING FOR THE EVENTUAL RETURN TO CAMPUS

As spring and summer 2020 wore on, and it became clear that the crisis was not abating, a return to "normal" operations looked increasingly unlikely. The question became: how much of the college experience could be safely recreated under COVID-19 conditions? When the pandemic first had its impact on higher education in March 2020, almost all institutions shifted to remote operations during a very short period of time. However, to prevent further chaos and financial losses, and while the situation remained fluid and uncertain, many campus leaders made early decisions about summer and fall semesters to allow faculty, staff, and students to plan for the most likely course of operations well in advance. Thus, they were obliged to finalize and act on plans long before all pertinent data were available.

For campuses that planned to reopen in the fall, there was a substantial amount of work needed to prepare. Movement and traffic patterns within and around campus needed to be considered. In order to maintain social distancing, furniture needed to be removed, paths marked, plexiglass shields installed at the front of classrooms and in any offices that offered face-to-face services, hand sanitizer stations posted, and so on. Because most campuses consist of a collection of buildings of varying ages and conditions, facilities planners needed to establish individual plans for each building. This process was incredibly labor-intensive, down to the simplest decision. For example, air handling in buildings operating with different HVAC systems differs, resulting in the need for different operational plans. Another example is in determining classroom capacities. While this may seem to be a simple formula, as each student was required to maintain a six-foot perimeter, few classrooms are conveniently shaped like a rectangle. Many have curved rows of seats and odd nooks and crannies. The result is that often someone had to physically go to each room and measure or work with the individual architectural drawings for each room in order to determine room capacity and seating arrangements under social distancing guidelines.

Areas like recreation centers and libraries needed reopening strategies as well. Would the computer laboratories and makerspaces be open? If so, what would their capacity be and how would they function? IHEs contain a variety of offices and services, and reopening is not simply a matter of determining how many students can fit into a socially distanced classroom. Every single office and every single work environment needed its own reopening plan, factoring in safety, physical space, resources, and the degree to which it is essential to the institution's mission and core functions.

Institutions first had to decide if the resumption of face-to-face instruction, in part or in whole, was possible. Once that decision was made, the next question to consider was how to reopen residence halls for those IHEs that had them. The optimal plan would be to have single-occupancy rooms with each student having their own bathroom, but few dormitories are set up like that. While most institutions ruled out triples, doubles remained a more complicated question. One option was to consider the roommates in a double as a "household," for quarantine purposes. Since the dormitories could not be fully occupied, not all students could be accommodated in campus housing. How could the available rooms be equitably distributed? Some institutions booked rooms at nearby hotels, but that solution was both expensive and uncertain.

One mid-size public research university chose to run a small summer undergraduate research program as a test case. A few weeks into the program, housing and residential life staff were reporting that many of the students were not following the social distancing guidelines or wearing masks in the public areas. Reopening plans attracted skeptics, including Laurence Steinberg, a psychology professor who specializes in adolescents and young adults. In a widely shared and discussed *New York Times* op-ed piece, Steinberg argued for the unlikelihood of the young to make careful science-informed choices during their college years. (Steinberg, 2020). All the elaborate contingency planning would be for naught if students stopped following the safety guidelines.

LESSONS LEARNED

One of the most significant lessons learned from the move to remote operations in spring 2020 was that IHEs would need robust contingency plans for reopening in the fall and for future operations. In higher education, where contingency planning was not a well-established practice, the primary concern in March 2020 included not only continuity of the academic mission but also ensuring the safety of students, faculty, and staff. While "safety first" was the guideline that all IHEs professed to be following, the lack of information about COVID-19 and the shifting and sometimes contradictory guidelines from government and healthcare authorities made it difficult for leaders to know what the safest approach would be, and how to balance such decisions with practical considerations. Since every academic term requires months of advance planning and preparation in the higher education sector, institutions needed to learn how to plan for the unplanned.

Facilities and auxiliaries shouldered the major burden of extracting and implementing health guidelines in a shifting landscape. Their staff remained on campus, keeping both the literal and metaphorical lights on when many other areas were able to operate remotely. Bearing the very real risks of exposure at a time when little was known about either the short- or long-term effects of COVID-19, it was critical for the facilities and public safety staff to have faith in the decisions that were being made by the administration. COVID-19 provided many IHEs a quick lesson in why and how to invest in emergency operations planning, so that leaders can offer practical guidance on how to maintain the core function of the academic mission while responding to safety concerns, especially in situations where information is incomplete. EOC teams and campus leadership needed to communicate effectively to keep plans clear and personnel motivated (see Chapter 2 on communications).

Operating safely under COVID-19 conditions required a detailed understanding of the physical space and of normal campus operations. Leadership had to balance the risks of exposure to COVID-19 with the risks of shutting down operations, often with no clear path to follow. Prior to the COVID-19 crisis, few senior staff at any IHE had spent a lot of time discussing the minutiae of air handling in various campus buildings or how to source disposable gloves. Given the nature of this particular crisis, such topics became common points of conversation across leadership teams. Thus, leaders who engaged voices from across the functional units of their campus were in a stronger position to make informed decisions and be able to get them implemented.

REFERENCES

American Campus Communities, Inc. (2020, July 20) Quarterly Earnings Analyst Package Q2 2020. Retrieved from https://s21.q4cdn.com/407815868/files/doc_financials/2020/q2/2Q20-supp.pdf

Busta, H. (2020, April 16). Colleges use empty dorms to house first responders, healthcare workers. HigherEdDive.com. Retrieved from https://www.educationdive.com/news/colleges-use-empty-dorms-to-house-first-responders-healthcare-workers/576213/

Cromar, A. (2020, March 11). *UPDATED: How Boston-area colleges are approaching refunds after asking students to vacate campus housing. Boston.com*. Retrieved from https://www.boston.com/news/local-news/2020/03/11/heres-how-boston-colleges-are-approaching-refunds-after-asking-students-to-vacate-campus-housing

Diep, F. (2020, March 19). If coronavirus patients overwhelm hospitals, these colleges are offering their dorms. *The Chronicle of Higher Education*. Retrieved from https://www.chronicle.com/article/if-coronavirus-patients-overwhelm-hospitals-these-colleges-are-offering-their-dorms/

Fain, P. (2020). *Higher Education and Work Amid Crisis*. Inside Higher Ed. Retrieved from https://www.insidehighered.com/news/2020/06/17/pandemic-has-worsened-equity-gaps-higher-education-and-work

Farris, D. & McCreight, R. (2014). The professionalization of emergency management in institutions of higher education. *Journal of Homeland Security and Emergency Management*, *11*(1), 73–94. Retrieved from https://doi.org/10.1515/jhsem-2013-0074

Harper, S. R. (2020). Covid-19 and the racial equity implications of Reopening College and University Campuses. *American Journal of Education*, 127(1), 153–162. Retrieved from https://doi.org/10.1086/711095

Kerr, E. (2020, April 8). COVID-19 closed dorms. Will students get a refund? *US News and World Report*. Retrieved from https://www.usnews.com/education/best-colleges/paying-for-college/articles/will-colleges-closed-over-coronavirus-offer-room-and-board-refunds

Larkin, M. (2020, March 13). As college students leave dorms during coronavirus, mix of fear and resignation. *WBUR News*. Retrieved from https://www.wbur.org/news/2020/03/13/coronavirus-dorms-empty

Leckrone, B. (2020, April 21). Turn buildings and parking lots into Covid-19 testing sites. *The Chronicle of Higher Education*. Retrieved from https://www.chronicle.com/article/turn-buildings-and-parking-lots-into-covid-19-testing-sites/

Mervosh, S. & Swales, V. (2020, March 10). Colleges and universities cancel classes and move online amid coronavirus fears. *The New York Times*. Retrieved from https://www.nytimes.com/2020/03/10/us/coronavirus-closings.html

Redden, E. (2020, April 7). Stepping up and helping out. *Inside Higher Ed*. Retrieved from https://www.insidehighered.com/news/2020/04/07/universities-and-their-students-are-helping-coronavirus-response-myriad-ways

Silvy, T. (2020, April 9). SSU providing hundreds of beds to handle anticipated surge of local coronavirus patients. here's where they will go. *Santa Rosa Press Democrat*. Retrieved from https://www.pressdemocrat.com/article/news/sonoma-state-university-to-provide-at-least-580-beds-for-local-coronavirus/

Steinberg, L. (2020, June 15). Expecting students to play it safe if colleges reopen is a fantasy. *The New York Times*. Retrieved from https://www.nytimes.com/2020/06/15/opinion/coronavirus-college-safe.html

Suffolk University dorm transformed into shelter for homeless during coronavirus crisis. (2020, March 29). WCVB5 ABC. Retrieved from https://www.wcvb.com/article/boston-mayor-walsh-coronavirus-update-march-29-2020/31968871

Chapter 10

Human Resource Leadership

Meeting the Needs of Faculty and Staff in the Early Pandemic

Rachael A. Kipp, Kara M. Rabbitt, and Suzanne Wilson Summers

At its core, higher education is a deeply human and relational endeavor. While some campuses may be justifiably proud of their buildings, technology, locations, or facilities, it is the people who deliver their educational and research missions and who keep campuses safe, clean, operational, and relevant. As of fall 2019, national data indicated that American colleges and universities employed roughly 4.2 million faculty and staff members (Lederman, 2021). Across all higher education sectors, from community colleges to research universities, personnel costs related to instruction and student support account for the largest percentage by far of institutional budgets. Consequently, the COVID-19 pandemic and attendant financial stresses, while affecting all operational units, had a deep impact in the area of Human Resources (HR). Without support for the transition to remote instruction and work by faculty and staff, institutions of higher education (IHEs) could not sustain their mission. Yet the move to remote work and instruction required HR units to significantly revamp procedures to accommodate work performed in a largely remote environment.

HR units often serve as key soothsayers, needing to anticipate future requirements to assist their institutions in continuing to achieve their missions. On many campuses, for example, HR departments were among the first to recognize and to begin planning for the pandemic's disruption. As early as January 2020, some HR leaders performed environmental scans to evaluate and recommend mission continuity plans even while operating with incomplete information regarding the emerging pandemic. To do so, they drew upon experience with past crises while adapting to a public health crisis whose effects proved far more momentous and wide-ranging than previous localized events. HR units became key drivers of campus success in mitigating employee anxiety and uncertainty when so much was unknown and daily decisions felt so monumental and consequential. These units sought to balance concern for employees with a need to ensure the availability of personnel to continue institutional missions.

This chapter focuses on two overarching themes. First, it explores the personnel impacts of the transition to remote work in early spring 2020, which required HR departments to work with administrative units to identify essential employees and to transition others rapidly to remote work. It also explores how IHEs worked to maintain morale and to support the mental health and wellbeing of employees as it became clear that the pandemic would not be a short-term situation.

TRANSITIONING OPERATIONS TO FACE COVID-19

HR leaders found the period of January to March 2020 extremely challenging as institutions responded to and attempted to anticipate personnel needs through a fluid and uncertain situation. Although no one could have predicted the scope or length of the COVID-19 crisis, past experience with emergency planning provided a place for HR units to begin envisioning next steps as it became clear in spring 2020 that the pandemic would impact all institutional operations. Relying on experience from prior events such as hurricanes or fires made sense in early modeling, as most IHEs expected that the March campus shutdowns would be a temporary phenomenon lasting, at most, a few weeks.

Early Phase: Initial Transition to Remote Operations

By late February and early March 2020, planning accelerated as the move to remote teaching and support work for most campus units became imminent. HR departments spearheaded the preparation for a possible move to remote operations by asking each campus office to consider what and whom they would need to maintain mission continuity. As one HR leader of a regional comprehensive institution shared, "HR and Legal departments were among the first to note the potential ramifications of this outbreak across campuses." The foresight of HR leaders about the implications of the pandemic meant that they spent much of their early effort persuading leadership teams that the emerging threat of COVID-19 could be serious.

HR leaders also worked with other administrative units to revise business continuity plans, review standing protocols, and consider profound changes in how units conducted work. At William Paterson University, a public regional comprehensive university in New Jersey, the HR division had, by early March 2020, reworked the business continuity plan to place quarantine protocols for those who may have traveled abroad and, later, to other states. Recalling the experience of planning for an anticipated H1N1 outbreak a decade prior, the Vice President for HR had already begun outreach across the campus to encourage supervisors to create plans to move employees to remote work, if possible.

HR leaders received little initial guidance at the federal level and faced wide variation in state guidance, thus complicating their planning efforts. As reports began to flood news outlets and social media about the horrific experiences of COVID-19 victims, employees' fear and anxiety increased. Such media reporting rendered essential the need for institutional planning focused on clear and transparent communication to all employees based on what was known at any given time, though the paucity of knowledge about COVID-19 and mechanisms of transmission and treatment in this period inevitably rendered the information environment incomplete.

Across the nation, IHEs responded in a remarkably similar manner over a very brief period of time. Most institutions operating on a semester calendar took advantage of their spring breaks, often extended, to plan for and to implement the transition to remote work. Like IHEs across the US, at Clemson University, a southeastern public research university, HR leaders initially assumed that any move to remote work would last weeks rather than months. By February 2020, the university had activated an Emergency Operations Center (EOC) that included HR personnel and began planning for a potential shutdown.

By March, as states implemented shut-down orders, IHEs confronted the need to determine which job functions were "essential" and which could be performed remotely. These negotiations—cross-divisional and complex—continued throughout the first weeks of the evolving pandemic. Most HR departments have existing categories of employees whose work is deemed essential when there are emergency conditions. They reviewed these standing designations quickly with an eye toward ensuring that critical functions could be performed while maintaining a bare minimum on-campus presence.

While such a process made sense in terms of quickly formulating lists, at far too many campuses the racial and class stratification and differentiated health outcomes of the workforce created concerns that "essential workers," such as custodians and maintenance staff, were disproportionately low-income and employees of color. Requiring these employees to continue to work on campus exposed them to increased risk of COVID-19 at a time when most faculty members and clerical and student support staff were making the transition to remote work. That the communities from which these essential workers came were also disproportionately impacted by COVID-19 cases spoke to the high costs of increased exposure for service workers across employment sectors.

HR leaders began to engage different campus units in systematic identification of essential and non-essential personnel, of critical functions, of work that could be carried out remotely, of necessary technological support, and of needed training. This process involved many offices: HR, IT, risk management, and, for unionized environments, leaders of the collective bargaining units. (The question of continuity of instruction is addressed extensively in Chapter 4.) One of the immediate tasks of HR units across campuses, in coordination with IT and line supervisors, was to ensure that non-essential employees who would be shifted to remote work had computers, access to enterprise software, and WiFi (see Chapter 8 on IT). HR personnel coordinated with frontline supervisors, as well as IT departments, to ensure that those employees in non-essential classifications possessed the necessary equipment and technology to work at home, and to set up reporting processes for a remote environment.

The shift to remote work affected employee morale in multiple ways, and HR leaders quickly realized that attending to employee morale and mental health, and addressing concerns in a compassionate manner, would shape the success of IHEs as they navigated the pandemic. For example, as the pandemic progressed, personnel policies and contexts became more complex. Clemson employees, like faculty and staff at many IHEs, worried about the potential for job losses during remote operations. To alleviate these concerns, in early March, Clemson established a policy that no one would lose their job, although employees would be required to complete training in preparation for remote work. Other institutions began to look at shifting or repurposing employees into different positions so that they would remain useful and maintain employment.

Remote Work Becomes the Norm

By April 2020, it had become clear that the shutdown would last longer than first imagined and that campuses would not reopen during the rest of the spring semester. HR departments tracked and implemented developing public health information, as well as federal and state employment policies when available. Working with supervisors across their campuses, HR departments played an essential role in building remote work competencies within their institutions. The shift to remote work necessitated that supervisors change their mindset about how tasks could be accomplished, how they could supervise employees remotely, and what "work" meant when it was not being conducted on campus. In units where physical presence had traditionally been the norm, many supervisors found it challenging to conceive of what remote work could mean and to imagine how they could trust or monitor the workdays of employees they could not see. HR departments helped managers to develop team building, communications, workflow, and managerial skills for a remote environment, including implementing remote platforms for shared workflows and team communications and utilizing project management software to track progress on goals.

The challenge of life outside of and in relation to work posed a particularly tricky dilemma. Many remote employees, particularly women, shouldered disproportionate care responsibilities for children who were attending school remotely due to the shutdown of K-12 schools or of elderly relatives pulled from at-risk nursing homes (NASEM, 2021). This meant that employees caring for family members might be able to work primarily early in the morning or late at night rather than during traditional business hours. The traditional line between home and work blurred as employees became used to seeing family members and pets in the background of virtual meetings. HR leaders reported often needing to encourage supervisors to extend flexibility and empathy to employees who struggled with family responsibilities.

Some institutions found, nevertheless, that remote work was surprisingly effective. At William Paterson University, for example, in a survey conducted by HR in late spring 2020, 95 percent of managers reported that they were pleasantly surprised that their employees did more, not less work, while working remotely. This experience was replicated at other IHEs. In some places, supervisors needed to encourage employees not to work overtime as remote work erased the line between on and off duty. Such evidence of productivity ultimately gave supervisors confidence that remote work would succeed, even as HR departments encouraged supervisors and employees to navigate the tension between work requirements and a work–life balance.

It was important, however, to find means to offset the loss of the casual contact that functions to bond employees and create connection to the unit's mission. The HR department at Clemson University, for example, held virtual Friday "happy hours" to maintain employee morale and to promote team-building across the 60 people who worked in the unit. They also published bimonthly HR newsletters and held a monthly all-HR meeting where, among other issues, they could engage in fun, team-building activities or bring in speakers to address stress.

Subcontractors and Vendors

Such strategies served, if imperfectly, full-time institutional employees. Many IHEs, particularly smaller institutions, however, frequently subcontract certain functions such as dining services, maintenance, housekeeping, and shuttle bus services. Such contracts relieve the institution of the administrative burden of managing those employees, the majority of whom are lower income and often from minoritized populations (Burke, 2020). Institutions with performance-based contracts pay the vendor based on the number of meals served or on adequate cleaning of the buildings, but do not specify within these contracts the number of employees needed to do so. In some cases, agreements like these resulted in some savings for the institution: if no meals were served, for example, the institution had no obligation to pay the vendor.

The jobs of people hired by the vendor to produce or serve these meals, however, were collateral damage after the pandemic closed such campuses, a phenomenon that became increasingly evident in light of the emerging focus on systemic racial injustice in spring 2020 and would lead by the following academic year to student protests against use of vendors on campuses (Anderson, 2021). When reporting the impact of COVID-19 on employment at their institution, most IHEs did not consider employees who were furloughed or laid off by vendors. In one widely-publicized case, Harvard University contemplated laying off its contract dining and catering employees without pay (Bolotnikova, 2020; Douglas-Gabriel, 2020). Ultimately, the university changed its mind and did offer contract employees regular pay and benefits through the end of the semester (Doyle, 2020), but this was the exception and not necessarily the rule.

Equity Concerns in Staff Transition to Remote Work

Considering the complex nature of modern IHEs with their wide array of functional units, contract workers represented just one vulnerable population of employees. While faculty, students, professional and clerical staff, and many administrators were able to make the rapid transition to remote teaching and learning and related support functions, many physical plant, housekeeping, and food service staff positions were defined by responsibilities tied to the workers' physical presence on campus and/or to directly serving in-person students. These roles faced the greatest challenges in the rapid changes that followed the shuttering of campus facilities and classrooms in the wake of the pandemic. Like administrators and faculty, some professional and support staff were able to continue the same work, albeit remotely. For many staff positions, however, the shift to remote work changed the essential nature of their functions, as in the case, for example, of media services staff who were no longer needed to support classroom technology and were instead moved to online IT support.

The ability to work remotely also often reflected the hierarchical nature of campus support roles, with higher-salaried and more technologically prepared managers or staff able to shift their functions to virtual delivery, while less skilled and hourly workers faced greater uncertainties for continuing their roles. During this same period, there was a more direct physical impact on staff working in facilities, maintenance, housekeeping, and residential life who were needed to deal with the planning and execution of the students' move out for those institutions with residential housing. Far from being able to isolate themselves from potential contact with others who might be infected with COVID-19, these employees worked face to face with each other and, in some cases, with students and family members to address the practical needs of moving students out and shutting down buildings and laboratories.

For those employees whose functions required an on-campus presence but whose circumstances made this challenging due to family or health concerns, HR units needed to develop specific policies and support aligned with emerging federal and state policy. Some IHEs were able to offer alternative options including paid time off, a transition to alternative work assignments that could be performed remotely, or hazard pay for remaining on campus. Other campuses required such employees either to report to their on-campus units, charge their time against banked leave, or move to unpaid status.

Given the short period of time to accomplish everything needed for the transition to remote work, most institutions advised adaptability and patience to supervisors. Generally, HR units encouraged managers to be flexible, to be generous with time off if needed, and to be mindful about arranging meetings during times employees were likely to have other family members at home. A public university that operated in a highly unionized environment dealt with those essential workers who could not work from home, such as campus police and physical plant workers, by convincing units to prioritize non-maintenance tasks and by moving these essential workers to a rotating two-week on/two-week off schedule while assuring full pay. While the decision cost the institution in terms of salary dollars spent without benefit of work, it provided an important morale boost for those employees needing to come to campus while others could work remotely.

Role of federal and state policy

The unprecedented nature and scope of the health threat elevated the role of federal and state policy on new HR policies and provided the legal parameters for emerging personnel policies. Monitoring new policy directives and legislation, developing implementation plans, and communicating new policies to employees and supervisors—activities undertaken during normal times—became an even more critical function of HR departments throughout the pandemic.

The creation of new COVID-related federal legislation allowed IHEs to adopt more generous leave policies that reflected the complicated situations that both employees and institutions found themselves in during the pandemic. In March 2020, Congress passed the Families First Coronavirus Response Act (FFCRA), in effect on April 1, 2020 through December 31, 2020, which afforded workplace protections to all employees (Nelson Mullins Riley; Scarborough LLP, 2020). Additionally, the Emergency Family and Medical Leave Expansion Act (EFMLEA) allowed employees to take up to 12 weeks of job-protected leave under the Family Medical Leave Act (FMLA) for a qualifying leave related to a "public health emergency," defined as an emergency declared by federal, state, or local authorities regarding COVID-19.[1]

The Emergency Paid Sick Leave Act required employers with fewer than 500 employees and employees of governmental agencies of any size (including public IHEs) to provide paid sick leave when employees were unable to work (or telework) due to a COVID-related federal, state, or local quarantine or isolation order in the following cases: if an employee had been advised by a health provider to self-quarantine; if the employee was experiencing symptoms of COVID-19 and sought a medical diagnosis; if the employee was caring for an individual who was subject to a quarantine or isolation order; and/or if the employee was caring for a minor-age child in the event that the child care provider of their child(ren) was closed or unavailable due to COVID-19. Moreover, employers could not require employees to use other pre-accrued leave before using COVID-19 paid sick leave.

At the state level, policies varied widely. According to the National Conference of State Legislatures, states passed over 100 bills related to COVID-19 and higher education between March 2020 and the following fall term. The largest impact of state and regional policies on IHEs in the early phases of the COVID-19 pandemic were the strictures on movement and the ability to be open (due to stay-at-home or shelter-in-place orders) that began in March in many states, but were delayed in others, such as South Carolina, until mid-April.

CONTINUITY

By May 2020, budgetary pressures deepened from the cost of transitioning to remote instruction and work even as most institutions also faced the prospect of fall semester enrollment declines and reduced public funding. Campus leadership teams grappled with the question of whether or not to institute hiring freezes. The hiring cycle for faculty in higher education generally begins in late fall each year and, by March, is fairly far along with offers being made or negotiated around that time. Considering the immediate and future budget impacts of the pandemic, many institutions enacted hiring freezes for the rest of FY 2020, filling only critical positions or those searches that were nearly complete.

The pandemic would ultimately result in a historic shedding of jobs across higher education. Institutions that had already been facing a precarious financial future, which was then compounded by the pandemic's impact on enrollments and revenues, had little choice but to reduce personnel expenditures. A *Washington Post* study revealed that, nationally, higher education unemployment grew from 3 to 8 percent between February and April 2020 (Douglas-Gabriel & Flowers, 2020). By April 2020, a survey of 142 presidents of two- and four-year institutions revealed that over half expected to have to make budget cuts, including laying off full-time faculty and staff (Bauer-Wolf, 2020).

Other IHEs looked for different ways to cut expenses. By the time of the pandemic, a growing reliance on contingent faculty had become a common part of IHEs' budget models. Adjunct faculty offer institutions needed professional expertise at a low cost while also providing IHEs the flexibility to respond to shifts in enrollment. Contingent faculty and administrative staff bore the brunt of layoffs in the early pandemic as IHEs grappled with budget shortfalls. The City University of New York (CUNY) system, for instance, laid off 2,800 part-time instructional faculty in late June 2020 (Valbrun, 2020), roughly a quarter of those it had reported employing in fall 2019 (CUNY, 2019). Although conventional wisdom holds that adjunct faculty are cheap labor, the cost of their employment is the easiest for IHEs to trim. In this period, many IHEs calculated that the fastest means to achieve rapid personnel reductions in the face of declining enrollments was to reduce the number of contingent faculty, particularly since such cuts generally come with less reputational cost than laying off full-time faculty. These decisions came with their own equity consequences, particularly for institutions whose adjunct faculty disproportionately come from underrepresented groups compared to those in tenure ranks.

In unionized environments, although everyone involved understood why certain processes were delayed in the spring of 2020, collective bargaining agreements often specified notification dates for promotion, tenure, and review decisions, and faculty and staff needed to be informed of delays and engaged in planning for personnel reviews. Specific HR processes whose delays or changes during this period were renegotiated with collective bargaining units included post-tenure reviews, sabbatical leaves, promotions and planned pay increases, annual performance reviews, and faculty reappointment processes. Many institutions moved rapidly to create new electronic methods to handle personnel processes that had previously been passed through channels in paper form. Those with collective bargaining units also needed to work with their representatives to assure that membership accepted and understood the new procedures and timeframes.

Not all IHEs had the flexibility of reassigning and retaining personnel. At one campus that was part of a larger state university system and already facing financial challenges prior to the pandemic, union contract provisions and system determinations limited their ability to repurpose positions to avoid layoffs. Consequently, this institution first implemented a hiring freeze and then attempted to repurpose existing employees to fill most of their open positions. This effort was proscribed, however, by union contracts that prohibited the institution from moving people into new employment classifications. Additionally, before they could lay off individual employees, under the terms of their union contracts they would have to lay off an entire classification of employees. This meant that they ended up firing front-line, low-wage and low-skill employees, which generated a great deal of public criticism. This institution was also able to strategically "non-retain" some administrative positions, which were not protected within a bargaining unit.

While some institutions faced a dire financial future as the pandemic persisted, many were in difficult, but not extreme positions. They found themselves unable to pay the employees to stay home but unwilling to furlough them. This meant that managers on many campuses were forced to find alternative work for those employees who needed to report to campus. For institutions operating within collective bargaining units and for civil service-defined roles, these alternate assignments had to fall within title to avoid a basis for grievance.

Preparing for Fall 2020

As institutions began planning for the fall 2020 semester, beginning as early as April 2020, and as COVID-19 cases spiked across the US, institutional leaders reckoned with the very real prospect of a long-term health crisis. They found increased employee anxiety over whether remote work and instruction would continue. Some institutions, like Purdue University, boldly asserted as early as April 2020 that their campuses would be fully open in the fall (Daniels, 2020). Others, like the entire California State University system and Paul Quinn College, an HBCU located in Dallas, Texas, determined by the end of the spring term that they would operate remotely for the coming fall (White, 2020; Sorrell, 2020). Most colleges and universities, however, delayed such decisions in the hope that the trajectory of the virus' spread would soon be better understood. This lack of clarity fed employees' anxieties, and these sentiments often surfaced in Town Hall forums or other sessions supported by HR divisions to share planning updates and to inform employees of support, policy changes, and expectations.

Nationally, by virtue of their relative job security and front-line position interacting with students, tenured faculty voices were often loudest in raising safety and wellness concerns.[2] While staff voices made fewer national waves, they highlighted similar concerns in campus dialogues. Working in cross-divisional teams with leaders in academic affairs, operations, and student life, HR leaders developed, vetted, and communicated a range of new protocols and policies to ensure effective implementation of the campus plan for continuity, whether in person, remote, or combined.

As campuses projected needs for the fall term, the realities of working parents came into play as various states and K-12 school districts weighed different scenarios for schools and childcare facilities. Uncertainty around K-12 plans also created stressors for both faculty and staff parents. Most parents found remote K-12 instruction challenging while working from home, but if schools did not reopen for the fall, it would be even more challenging to address childcare needs if IHEs required these employees to return to campus (Bateman & Ross, 2021).

Public institutions struggled to balance state policies that often had a political tinge with the needs of employees. In June 2020, after Governor Ron DeSantis of Florida announced that public schools would reopen for classes in the fall, Florida State University responded by announcing that it would no longer permit parents working remotely to care for children during work hours, citing a standing policy that had been suspended in March at the start of the pandemic (CNYCentral, 2020). Following a swift national backlash, FSU specified that the policy only "applies to employees whose job duties require them to be on campus full-time during normal business hours," and that it specifically excluded professors (Miami Times, 2020). This statement, however, only made more evident the equity disparities impacting staff and faculty without the security of employment, rank, or tenure. Within a few weeks, after a national uproar, the university further softened its stance, though it appeared that, as at many public institutions across the country, the pressures to reopen and to affirm a commitment to normalcy were driven as much by state politics as by concerns for employee welfare.

These kinds of issues made clear that remote work, while necessary, raised multiple equity issues that institutional leaders and HR divisions needed to address. For example, just as not all students possessed the required technology and internet access for remote classes, so, too, not all employees had laptops or the WiFi access needed to work remotely. HR offices worked with Business Services and IT to set policies on what could or could not be provided, from laptops to office chairs, to support remote work needs across different units.

At William Paterson University of New Jersey, a primary task of HR as the crisis continued was to equalize the application of its remote work policy across institutional units. The existence of the federal statute detailed above (FFCRA) helped. Like many IHEs, the university required employees working from home to sign a professional code of conduct specifying expectations and standards. The HR department took the position that if employees could work from home, they should be allowed to do so within operational considerations. At this public regional university, the union contract governing custodial workers allowed them to stay at home if needed for two-thirds pay. In some cases, the university used the institutional portion of the CARES Act monies (see Chapter 13) to maintain people in paid status.

Supporting Employee Wellbeing

Just as the pandemic increased institutional concerns over students' mental health needs, so, too, it triggered concerns regarding employees' mental wellbeing. An ACE survey of higher education presidents across all sectors in July 2020 revealed that 33% of respondents recognized the mental health impact on faculty and staff as a major concern (Turk et al., 2020). As one study cautioned, "It is understandable to think about our students' mental health first and foremost, but faculty and staff are frequently the first and primary points of contact for students with the institution. Supporting faculty and staff mental health can directly impact the student experience" (ACE, 2020). For institutional leaders, balancing the tensions between a student-focused mission and the needs of employees proved one of the most challenging aspects of leadership during the pandemic.

Many employees reported increased stress, anxiety, and depression as they faced fears around not only their physical health, but also that of their families and communities. Although many IHEs have some form of Employee Assistance Programs, HR departments worked to identify additional means to address the high levels of stress and anxiety. Some institutions contracted with local providers or with new online services to provide mental healthcare. Many expanded wellness offerings on topics such as meditation, exercise, diet, and coping with stress.

Anxiety and fear around contracting COVID-19 was also grounded in real physical health concerns. For those positions that required employees to work on campus, one of the most challenging issues managers and administrators faced was that of addressing concerns from employees who wished to continue working remotely but lacked a qualifying medical reason not to return. If an employee without a documented accommodation refused to work, they lost eligibility for unemployment benefits in most states. HR departments thus grappled with a situation for which there was no compassionate and equitable "one-size-fits-all" solution. One approach was to base all decisions on job function. Accounts payable staff, for example, could more easily work remotely than university nursing staff. One HR head pointed out that although there was no way to eliminate such inequities, they could try to support the staff as best they were able within the parameters of the job function. Even the most hands-on job function on campus usually includes some need for research or reporting, and so this leader strove to offer the occasional work from home day to perform those functions, even if they were rare.

LONG-TERM IMPACTS TO HR

In assuring continuity of institutional operations, HR divisions needed to address not only how to ensure personnel were available to carry on institutional missions in drastically changed circumstances, but also how to help employees navigate remote work during a pandemic with profound and far-reaching impacts on their personal health and wellbeing. Doing so required the recognition that while most college and university employees now worked remotely, they did so in dramatically different personal, as well as professional, contexts. In higher education, as in the economy as a whole, the line between "work" and "personal" became increasingly blurred as faculty and staff juggled Zoom meetings and classes with child/elder care from home in vastly different socio-economic circumstances.

HR divisions played a key role in helping IHEs reflect on and, in many cases, change, how they supported employees and how employees worked, and what modifications to both would need to be kept or made in the post-pandemic future. According to one HR professional at a research-intensive university, the pandemic offered a number of lessons for the future of remote work in higher education. The use of widely available technology made ensuring productivity and efficiency possible. Virtual HR appointments proved more efficient for employees who no longer had to visit in person. Moreover, many employees became more self-sufficient and less likely to rely on HR personnel to provide them with answers they could research themselves.

If remote work offered advantages, it posed challenges, too. The lack of a clear division between work and home meant that employees had to learn to protect their time outside of normal working hours. The question of managerial trust in employees was paramount. Supervisors simply could not be omnipresent; they had to learn to trust and empower subordinates, and they had to work to develop policies and office cultures that would support this trust and empowerment. Some HR units, recognizing the impact of changed living and family circumstances on employees' work lives, played a leading role in pushing institutional units to reexamine assumptions about the need for employees to be constantly accessible and "on" even as technology made this a possibility. One outcome of the pandemic experience is the growing awareness in higher education that employers cannot ignore work–life balance, particularly in times of crisis. As employees began working in a remote environment, often in shared spaces with additional family responsibilities, supervisors had to redefine their expectations of productivity and demonstrate higher levels of sensitivity to employees' personal situations. Farsighted HR units encouraged both employees and managers to respect the need for downtime.

In many ways, the post-pandemic workplace at some IHEs may look more like emerging workplaces in other industries. Many IHEs in this period began looking to implement future flexible/hybrid work plans with fewer employees expected to come to campus for a traditional Monday through Friday, 9-to-5 schedule. As we interviewed HR leaders for this chapter, many expressed that they felt such flexibility would become key in future talent strategies and employer branding. When Boston University began discussions about the possibility of a hybrid work plan, one employee noted: "BU has two options. Adapt and remain competitive in order to retain its top staff and attract the future workforce, or, don't adapt, and witness a wave of staff leave and struggle to hire the next generation" (Ellis, 2021).

LESSONS LEARNED

The fiscal impacts of the COVID-19 pandemic brought to the fore structural issues for many institutions. Prior to the pandemic, many IHEs had delayed "rightsizing" their workforce in the face of changing demographics due to contract considerations, employee opposition, and inertia. The budgetary severity of the pandemic pushed many do what they had previously avoided doing: make hard decisions about programs and positions. Unfortunately, for institutions in this position, the need to make major decisions resulting in historic layoffs deepened the trauma to not only those who lost their jobs, but also to those who were left behind. The reactive severing of programs and faculty and staff positions, although necessary to sustain financial viability, will likely have long-term morale consequences. "Survivor's guilt" is real.

News of institutional layoffs in the *Chronicle of Higher Education* and elsewhere fed faculty and staff anxiety about job security through this period. HR teams grappled not only with the immediate impacts of the pandemic, but also the need to address long-term morale by striving to be transparent, compassionate, and even-handed when personnel and pay decisions were being made in an already tense COVID environment. Leaders understood, or were made to understand in some cases, that how they handled and communicated about these kinds of close-to-the-bone personnel issues would have long-term impacts. Academic institutions tend to have long memories and change slowly. How HR units worked with employees during the pandemic, or how or if they provided transition services to faculty or staff whose positions were eliminated, will undoubtedly continue to play out across colleges and universities in the coming years. IHEs would do well to take a cue from progressive businesses that offer some kind of transition support to those employees they must let go. Such measures send an important message to remaining employees that, even in cases where layoffs prove necessary, affected employees are cared for and shown respect and sensitivity.

Perhaps one of the most important leadership lessons from this pandemic and the resulting move to remote work was a recognition of the need to acknowledge the whole employee, such as appreciating family demands or recognizing the differing resources available to employees. In so doing, many HR leaders gained an opportunity through the pandemic to help their institutions to reimagine work. Moving beyond the early crisis period, many IHEs began instituting hybrid work arrangements for eligible employees in response to employee preference. Many IHEs reported that they were so pleased with the performance of remote employees that they would maintain some form of remote and/or hybrid work options after the pandemic had ended. As the Vice President of HR at a large community college system noted, the pandemic revealed that remote work in some form was here to stay. That college was in the process of identifying positions that could continue to work remotely or in a hybrid configuration even after the pandemic ended. Some saw the continued option for remote work as a recruiting and retention strategy. The pandemic created opportunities to envision a new workplace that reshapes traditional ideas about where and when people work. Such change requires new skills and mindsets. Although IHEs will clearly emerge from this period changed, they can also emerge from it stronger.

Equity Insight: The Impact of the Pandemic on Women in Academia

During the early pandemic, much was written about the impact of the pandemic on women across the workforce. Remote work heightened the disproportionate burden that women face societally as caregivers everywhere, including in higher education. Gender equity advocates in the workforce worried over the impact on employment and stress levels for women, particularly working mothers (see Mahajan et al., 2020; Titan et al., 2020). Higher education possessed no immunity to the gendered impacts of the pandemic. For female faculty, staff, and administrators, gender inequities surfaced quickly as women wrestled with the disproportionate burden of both family caregiving and institutional service. For women of color who faced additional stressors and, in some cases, fewer resources, these challenges were exacerbated (Pettit, 2020).

One study of the pandemic's impact on women faculty found that, "Although institutions typically value service less than research or teaching when it comes to tenure and promotion, service consumes more time for women faculty compared with their men counterparts. Plus, students approach women faculty more for mental health support and expect them to be more nurturing" (Malisch et al., 2020). Women faculty and staff of color often feel a commitment to advance institutional and personal equity goals and, therefore, shoulder an additional burden.

As Malisch et al. noted, "A pandemic naturally highlights privileges, such as financial security and access to mental health care. It also amplifies the mental, physical, social, and economic impacts attributable to pre-existing inequities in academia. Making matters worse, in times of stress such as pandemics, biased decision-making processes are favored, which threaten to deprioritize equity initiatives" (2020). For example, while people of color made up only 25% of the higher education workforce, they would account for more than half of the layoffs within the following year (Bauman, 2021). Moreover, the often-hierarchical nature of the academic workplace and outsized voice of faculty in IHEs meant that the impact on women staff, who faced most of the same environmental effects of COVID-19, often went unconsidered (Skallerup Bessette, 2021).

While institutions have responded to women's calls for action by attempting to address these concerns, it is clear that IHEs can no more afford "gender-blind" policies than they can "race-blind" policies. Colleges and universities reside within broader social and economic structures, and their policies must reflect this awareness. Mentoring programs, flexible scheduling, and policies for retention, promotion, and tenure are all areas ripe for reconceptualization to support the complex gendered realities of faculty and staff.

The pandemic made clear that the intersection of gendered and racialized expectations of women and BIPOC employees created unsustainable burdens on certain members of HE communities. Moreover, "the traditional reward system and lack of work-life integration initiatives are not consistent with the values of engaging in meaningful academic work while also experiencing a fulfilling personal life—values important to the younger generation of both men and women in academia" (Hermann & Neale-McFall, 2020). Women scholars at Northwestern, Purdue, and other colleges and universities across the US, sought to raise awareness of the challenges that COVID-19 exacerbated, but did not create. Moreover, they suggested policy changes, such as delayed tenure and promotion clocks, to ensure that women faculty continued to advance professionally and to create a more equitable post-pandemic future (Organization of Women Faculty, 2020; Susan Bulkeley Butler Center for Leadership Excellence, 2020).

A Close-up Lens on Leadership

Culture Building as an Asset in Institutional Resilience: The Valencia College Experience

One large, urban community college in Orlando, Florida, Valencia College, had adopted an organizational development (OD) model for organizational change and performance several years prior to the pandemic. This approach shaped its institutional response to COVID-19. When President Sandford "Sandy" Shugart arrived in 2000, the college had a traditional HR department. The college leadership made the change of moving traditional HR functions under a new Office of Organizational Development and Human Resources led by Vice President Amy Bosley, who previously served as a faculty member at the college and, therefore, understood the primacy of Valencia's student and academic missions. The OD office not only included traditional personnel functions, but also focused on creating a student-success culture by addressing employee morale, professional development, and internal communications in a highly collaborative and matrixed structure for decision-making.

The work and vision of this more interdisciplinary unit positioned the college well in its efforts to help employees navigate the upheaval of COVID and the move to remote work while respecting the guiding principles that anchored the college's culture. For example, when the college held its first COVID planning meeting on March 3, 2020, it identified two anchoring priorities: employees' and students' health and safety; and the continuity of student learning. The OD unit provided members of the President's Senior Team with the tools to help them embed these goals in internal planning processes and to operationalize them.

Organizational units, assisted by the OD office, continued to identify employees who needed to come to campus to meet institutional needs. During this period, 10 percent of the approximately 5,000 employees were working onsite while the rest worked from home. By July, 2020, the college had developed a "talent sharing program" to allow employees who were not needed on campus and could not fulfill their traditional functions remotely to shift to areas where there was a need. Those who could not be "repurposed" were still paid, a benefit relatively few IHEs could afford, but one that fit into Valencia's history of supporting non-traditional career paths and of permitting employees to work on problems of interest. This practice allowed the college to escape the "tyranny of the org chart," particularly since their employees were not unionized. The campus ethos of collaboration and "people first" meant that everyone could act as both a leader and a contributor. As Vice President Bosley described it, "Equity is not equality or sameness. Institutions have to respond to human uniqueness and circumstances."

The college also partnered with a local hospital network for medical and scientific advice on which to base decisions. Leadership acknowledged to the college community that this reliance on emerging health expertise, rather than political pressures, "will cause us to pursue a more conservative path than our peers." This decision gave employees confidence that their safety and welfare, as well as that of students, would drive decision-making.

Early on, college leadership also reassured employees that everyone who could would work from home and that there would be no layoffs or furloughs. This, employees heard, "will require unbelievable flexibility and care for each other." Valencia's public commitment to maintaining employment stability at a time when many IHEs were laying off or furloughing staff and faculty was a critical component of the college's response and efforts to help employees navigate an already uncertain situation and to maintain high morale.

That flexibility is evidenced in understanding that many employees faced unprecedented challenges in working from home, including family care, requiring that supervisors accept that employees would work when they could, even if this work fell outside of "normal" business hours. The college pursued a practice of generosity in regard to FFCRA policies in order to give employees who needed it time off to fulfill family responsibilities without a heavy burden of documentary proof. The result of communicating trust in employees' performance of their duties in a remote environment enhanced, rather than diminished, productivity. Additionally, in an environment of extreme uncertainty, the college offered employees opportunities to maintain their identification with the institutional mission, a critical element in maintaining morale. For example, those workers who were unable to perform their normal duties were engaged in a phone campaign to contact and communicate care to all of the college's 42,000 students.

The shift to remote work required the development of new skills. When front-line supervisors needed help learning how to manage remotely, the OD department used its internal communications channels to provide it, as well as its Employee Assistance Program and coaching capabilities. At Valencia College, the response to the pandemic was built on an existing culture that places the human element at the foreground of employee relations.

NOTES

1 To take advantage of this measure, employees needed to be on the payroll for at least 30 days compared to the normal requirement of 12 months and/or 1250 hours. Employees would take the first ten days as unpaid leave, although they could use accrued sick leave or vacation time. Additionally, employees could stack this new source of leave on traditional FMLA leave, if they qualified for it. Their jobs would be protected and employers would have to guarantee them the same or equivalent position upon their return.
2 See for example, Prof. Laurence Steinberg's widely-read opinion piece in the *New York Times* (Steinberg, 2020).

REFERENCES

American Council on Education. (2020). *Mental health, higher education, and covid-19: Strategies for Leadership to Support Campus Well-being*. Retrieved from https://www.acenet.edu/Documents/Mental-Health-Higher-Education-Covid-19.pdf

Anderson, G. (2021, March 31). Movement against corporatized campus dining services renewed. Retrieved from https://www.insidehighered.com/news/2021/03/31/movement-against-corporatized-campus-dining-services-renewed

Bateman, N., & Ross, M. (2021, January 6). *Why has Covid-19 been especially harmful for working women?* Brookings. Retrieved from https://www.brookings.edu/essay/why-has-covid-19-been-especially-harmful-for-working-women/

Bauer-Wolf, J. (2020, April 7). *College Presidents Anticipate Cost Cutting, Layoffs from Coronavirus, Survey Finds.* Higher Ed Dive. Retrieved from https://www.highereddive.com/news/college-presidents-anticipate-cost-cutting-layoffs-from-coronavirus-surve/575647/

Bauman, D. (2021, April 19). *Here's Who Was Hit Hardest by Higher Ed's Pandemic-Driven Job Losses.* Chronicle.com. Retrieved from https://www.chronicle.com/article/heres-who-was-hit-hardest-by-higher-eds-pandemic-driven-job-losses

Bolotnikova, B. N. (2020, March 26). *What happens to Harvard's workers? Harvard Magazine.* Retrieved from https://www.harvardmagazine.com/2020/03/what-happens-to-harvard-s-workers

Burke, L. (2020, October 27). Black workers at universities often are left out of conversations about race and higher education. Retrieved from https://www.insidehighered.com/news/2020/10/27/black-workers-universities-often-are-left-out-conversations-about-race-and-higher

CNYCentral. (2020, June 30). *Florida State Will Not Allow Some Employees to Care for Children While Working Remotely.* WSTM. Retrieved from https://cnycentral.com/news/nation-world/florida-state-will-not-allow-some-employees-to-care-for-children-while-working-remotely

CUNY Office of Human Resource Management. (2019, November). *Fall 2019 staff Facts - City University of New York.* Retrieved from https://www.cuny.edu/wp-content/uploads/sites/4/media-assets/Fall-2019-Staff-Facts.pdf

Daniels, M. E. (2020, April 21). *A Message from President Daniels Regarding Fall Semester.* Office of the President - Purdue University. Retrieved from https://www.purdue.edu/president/messages/campus-community/2020/2004-fall-message.php

Douglas-Gabriel, D. (2020, April 17). Students are pressing colleges to keep paying campus workers. Colleges are listening (for now). *The Washington Post.* Retrieved from https://www.washingtonpost.com/education/2020/04/17/college-contract-workers-coronavirus/

Douglas-Gabriel, D., & Flowers, A. (2020, November 20). The lowest-paid workers in higher education are suffering the highest job losses. *The Washington Post.* Retrieved from https://www.washingtonpost.com/education/2020/11/17/higher-ed-job-loss/

Doyle, T. (2020, March 27). *Harvard agrees to Compensate Furloughed Contract dining and Catering Workers.* Eater Boston. Retrieved from https://boston.eater.com/2020/3/27/21197182/harvard-compensating-furloughed-dining-hall-contract-workers-covid-19-pandemic

Ellis, L. (2021, June 17). *'A Mass Exodus': Inflexible Remote-Work Policies Could Bring Major Staff Turnover.* chronicle.com. Retrieved from https://www.chronicle.com/article/a-mass-exodus-inflexible-remote-work-policies-may-bring-major-staff-turnover-for-colleges

Hermann, M. A., & Neale-McFall, C. (2020, December 1). *Covid-19, Academic Mothers, and Opportunities for the Academy*. AAUP. Retrieved from https://www.aaup.org/article/covid-19-academic-mothers-and-opportunities-academy#.YM9_QmhKjtR

Lederman, D. (2021, December 14). Higher ed workforce shrank by 4% in fall 2020. Retrieved February 4, 2022, from https://www.insidehighered.com/news/2021/12/14/higher-ed-workforce-shrank-4-fall-2020

Mahajan, D., White, O., Madgavkar, A., & Krishnan, M. (2020, September 16). *Don't Let the Pandemic Set Back Gender Equality*. Harvard Business Review. Retrieved from https://hbr.org/2020/09/dont-let-the-pandemic-set-back-gender-equality?autocomplete=true

Malisch, J. L., Harris, B. N., Sherrer, S. M., Lewis, K. A., Shepherd, S. L., McCarthy, P. C., Spott, J. L., Karam, E. P., Moustaid-Moussa, N., Calarco, J. M. C., Ramalingam, L., Talley, A. E., Cañas-Carrell, J. E., Ardon-Dryer, K., Weiser, D. A., Bernal, X. E., & Deitloff, J. (2020, July 7). *Opinion: In the Wake of Covid-19, Academia Needs New Solutions to Ensure Gender Equity*. PNAS. Retrieved from https://www.pnas.org/content/117/27/15378

Miami Times. (2020, July 15) FSU clarifies remote-work and childcare. *The Miami Times*. Retrieved from https://www.miamitimesonline.com/education/fsu-clarifies-remote-work-and-childcare/article_31b038e0-c6c5-11ea-8563-3f861c7fdba1.html.

National Academies of Sciences, Engineering, and Medicine (NASEM). 2021. *The Impact of COVID-19 on the Careers of Women in Academic Sciences, Engineering, and Medicine*. Washington, DC: The National Academies Press. https://doi.org/10.17226/26061

Nelson Mullins Riley; Scarborough LLP. (2020, March 24). Higher education Coronavirus advisory. *JD Supra*. Retrieved from https://www.jdsupra.com/legalnews/higher-education-coronavirus-advisory-68167/;%20https://www.passhe.edu/inside/HR/syshr/Pages/COVID_FAQ.aspx

Organization of Women Faculty. (2020, September 21). *Eleven Things Northwestern University Leadership Can Do Right Now to Protect Gender Equity in the Face of COVID-19*. Northwestern University.. Retrieved from https://cpb-us-e1.wpmucdn.com/sites.northwestern.edu/dist/0/2419/files/2020/09/OWFCallforImmediateActionSept2020-final.pdf

Pettit, E. (2020, May 26). *Being a Woman in Academe Has Its Challenges. A Global Pandemic? Not Helping. Chronicle.com*. Retrieved from https://www.chronicle.com/article/being-a-woman-in-academe-has-its-challenges-a-global-pandemic-not-helping?cid2=gen_login_refresh&cid=gen_sign_in

Skallerup Bessette, L. (2021, January 20). *Same Covid Stress, Different Benefits*. Chronicle.com. Retrieved from https://www.chronicle.com/article/same-covid-stress-different-benefits

Sorrell, Michael J. (2020, May 15). *Colleges are Deluding Themselves*. The Atlantic. Retrieved from https://www.theatlantic.com/ideas/archive/2020/05/colleges-that-reopen-are-making-a-big-mistake/611485/

Steinberg, L. (2020, June 15). Expecting students to play it safe if colleges reopen is a fantasy. *The NewYork Times*. Retrieved from https://www.nytimes.com/2020/06/15/opinion/coronavirus-college-safe.html

Susan Bulkeley Butler Center for Leadership Excellence. (2020). *Special issue: Higher Education and COVID-19*. Working Papers Series Purdue University. Retrieved from https://www.purdue.edu/butler/working-paper-series/2020/special%20issue.html

Titan, A., Doeptke, M., Olmstead-Rumsey, J., & Tertilt, M. (2020, March). *Covid-19 gender March 2020 - Northwestern University*. Retrieved from https://faculty.wcas.northwestern.edu/~mdo738/research/COVID19_Gender_March_2020.pdf

Turk, J. M., Soler, M. C., & Chessman, H. M. (2020, July). *College and University Presidents Respond to COVID-19: July 2020 Survey*. ACENet. Retrieved from https://www.acenet.edu/Documents/Presidents-Respond-COVID19-July2020.pdf.

Valbrun, M. (2020, July 6). *Economic Fallout of Pandemic Leads to Layoffs at CUNY and UNION Lawsuit*. Inside Higher Ed. Retrieved from https://www.insidehighered.com/news/2020/07/06/economic-fallout-pandemic-leads-layoffs-cuny-and-union-lawsuit.

White, T. P. (2020, May 12). *CSU Chancellor Timothy P. White's statement on Fall 2020 University Operational Plans*. The California State University. Retrieved from https://www.calstate.edu/csu-system/news/Pages/CSU-Chancellor-Timothy-P-Whites-Statement-on-Fall-2020-University-Operational-Plans.aspx

Part III
Planning and Preparation for a Post-COVID World

Chapter 11
Admissions and Enrollment

Kristi N. Hottenstein and Rosalyn Hobson Hargraves

THE CONTEXT

In an April 2020 pulse point survey conducted by the American Council on Education (ACE), 192 presidents from all sectors shared their most pressing concerns regarding the COVID-19 pandemic and their institutional capacity and needs with respect to financial impacts, remote learning, and student mental health. From a list of 14 issues, presidents indicated that the top-ranking concern selected across all sectors was "fall or summer enrollment numbers." The second-ranked concern across all sectors was "long-term financial viability" (Turk et al., 2020). These top two concerns are clearly and inextricably linked. In fact, one of the most pressing issues facing many IHEs prior to the COVID-19 crisis was the projected "enrollment cliff" in the Northeast and Midwest as institutions there grappled with maintaining financial viability in the face of declining enrollment due to reduced numbers of 18-to-21-year-olds and the impact on college enrollments (Conley, 2019).

A number of pre-pandemic factors increased the complexity and challenges admissions officers and enrollment managers faced in the spring of 2020. For example, the preceding year, the National Association for College Admission Counseling (NACAC) ratified revisions to the Code of Ethics and Professional Practices that allowed institutions to offer incentives to applicants who applied under binding early-decision programs; to recruit students once they had submitted a deposit to another institution; and to solicit transfer applications from previous applicants or prospective students regardless of whether they had inquired about transferring (NACAC, 2019; Jaschik, 2019).

Furthermore, as college enrollments often fail to mirror the demographics of the US, institutions grappled with admissions practices that could produce a more diverse student body while also adhering to Title VI of the Civil Rights Act (US DoE, 2020). Many universities had begun the move to test-optional and need-blind admissions, while others implemented race-conscious admission practices.

However, these practices were not without controversy and legal challenges (Raymond & Stempel, 2020). While the most highly successful enrollment management officers could look at predictive factors to gauge fall enrollment numbers, even pre-COVID, the 2020 admissions cycle was like no other. As one former ACE Fellow who served as Vice Chancellor for Enrollment Management at a Midwest urban comprehensive public university expressed,

> I've spent 15 years priding myself on my ability to accurately predict not only the size of the incoming freshman and transfer cohorts but also the ability to predict retention using historical data, predictive analytics, and algorithms for student retention. Typically, we can get within a half a percent of where our overall university enrollment will be for both graduate and undergraduate programs. Any thought of this level of accuracy for the class of 2020 is completely out the window. The trends that we're seeing in student behavior are as unprecedented as COVID-19, and rightfully so.

In short, the onset of the COVID-19 pandemic in spring 2020 further complicated an already complex admission cycle. In a national student survey conducted by SimpsonScarborough in April 2020, 1 in 4 high school seniors who had decided on where they would enroll in the fall 2020 said COVID-19 affected their college choice. Twenty-four percent of these seniors said that "they may change their minds about the college they want to attend as a result of COVID-19." While the majority of high school seniors surveyed who had planned, prior to COVID-19, to enroll at a traditional four-year college or university in the fall still planned to enroll, admissions officers had to be prepared for that number to change as the financial fallout from COVID-19 continued to affect families across the country. The environmental complexity of student decision-making about enrollment created by the pandemic threw traditional admissions and enrollment calculations out the window.

Differential Impacts on Student Populations

In fall 2019, 90% of full-time undergraduate students enrolled in US public universities were under the age of 25, and over half of them identified as White (NCES, 2021). Yet the majority of US post-secondary students did not fit the above demographic, and IHEs had to approach their admissions and enrollment processes to accommodate the impact of the pandemic on their own specific student populations. Adult learners, part-time students, international students, graduate students, professional and continuing students, Pell-eligible students, dual credit/enrollment populations, and minoritized students all experienced broader impacts from the virus. The impact of the pandemic on various student populations had profound implications by sector, and it is important to explore how COVID-19 impacted the admissions and enrollment of these various student populations. For example, regional comprehensives and community colleges have historically attracted large numbers of adult learners, as well as those who are low income and from minoritized groups. These sectors, particularly community colleges, felt COVID's effect on enrollment immediately and deeply.

Likewise, communities of color experienced the impact of COVID-19 disproportionately. This impact extended beyond health implications to financial and educational effects. Numerous national surveys highlighted the disparities of COVID-19's impact on minoritized communities. Black and Latinx populations were far more likely than Whites to have been laid off and to have canceled or changed their educational plans. A study conducted by SimpsonScarborough in April of 2020 indicated that 41% of high school seniors of color said it was likely they would not attend college in the fall or that it was "too soon to say" compared to 22% of White students. "Nearly two-thirds of minority students (64%) said their plans were being affected by COVID-19, compared to 44% of white students" (SimpsonScarborough, 2020). Similarly, lower-income students were more likely to delay graduation than their higher-income peers. These statistics alarmed chief enrollment management officers (CEMOs) as there was very little that could be done that late in the recruitment cycle to reverse these looming statistics. A number of institutions extended their decision/deposit deadlines to try to allow admissions counselors more time to connect individually with students in the hopes of trying to convince them to attend.

Admissions and enrollment officers understood the dire personal and national consequences of fewer students beginning and completing college. In recent decades, the number of students from historically-underrepresented populations attending and graduating from college had made significant gains. A college degree provides increased opportunities, increased wages, increased economic vitality within communities, and lowers the likelihood of unemployment. Moreover, a college education remains our country's most direct path to increased economic and social mobility (Synder et al., 2019), and COVID-19 directly threatened this opportunity in the most disadvantaged communities. By contrast, the cost of dropping out of college measured by lost earnings alone is $3.8 billion nationally in a single year, and research suggests that those students who stop out or delay are far less likely to finish. As shutdowns spread across the US in an effort to protect public health and safety, unemployment rose dramatically in the spring. No one could predict how the economic downturn would impact students' ability to afford college. Nor could anyone predict how students' health concerns, the demands of those in "essential worker" status, or familial obligations would impact students' decisions to attend college. Higher education leaders such as ACE President Ted Mitchell voiced concerns that US higher education risked losing 20 years' worth of gains in access for first-generation and minoritized students.

The pandemic, he warned, "is a perfect storm that could wash away hard-won progress" (Mitchell, 2020).

Admissions and enrollment officers faced many questions for the coming year's class: Would the disproportionate health and economic impact of the pandemic on African American and Latinx communities result in a decrease in the number of students from these communities accepting offers of admission? Would travel restrictions still be in effect, preventing international students from enrolling (see Chapter 3)? Would parents want their college-aged children to stay close to home? Would graduate enrollment increase due to the lack of jobs, or decline due to family economic challenges? Would community college enrollments increase due to students taking a gap year, but wanting to maintain some academic engagement or because the economic downturn impacted their ability to afford a four-year option? Or would the converse happen with community college enrollments declining because their typical students could not afford to pay tuition due to job losses? Would financial aid packages have to change? What would be the impact on students' choice to enroll if the institutions needed to operate remotely for the fall? The list of questions on admissions officers' minds seemed only to grow with each passing day in the early weeks and months of the pandemic (Carnegie Higher Ed, 2020.).

THE COVID-19 ADMISSIONS CALCULUS: MEETING ENROLLMENT TARGETS

The COVID-19 pandemic necessitated the creation of a completely new game plan by admissions officers and strategic enrollment administrators to meet enrollment targets. One of the first challenges admissions officers faced was deciding whether or not to change the "admissions calculus," which included: the number of students to admit; the profile of the admitted students (domestic/international, in-state/out-of-state, majors, social identities, socioeconomic status, etc.); the ways in which admissions decisions were made; and the size of the waitlist. Lacking a set of "best practices" to address such a far-reaching crisis, Jon Boeckenstedt, an enrollment official at Oregon State University, noted in an opinion piece from May 2020, that "now might be the best time to think about eliminating archaic rules and processes that exist simply because no one has ever thought to change them, and to focus on how your students might benefit from changes" (Rhyneer et al., 2020).

With so much uncertainty, some colleges chose to increase the number of students being offered admission, while others decided to continue moving forward with the same decision rubric as prior years. One prestigious public R1, for example, decided to open its waitlist up to an additional 500 out-of-state students to offset any potential admit-to-enrolled yield loss. This decision was strategic in that it not only increased the admit-to-enrolled pool by 500, but also potentially doubled tuition revenue because of the difference between in-state and out-of-state tuition rates.

Many admissions officers spent long hours in the final two weeks of March facing great stress to get the admissions calculus right, although this calculation looked quite different across the various sectors of higher education. They had to rethink the long-held metrics previously relied upon to determine who would be admitted. For example, according to a NACAC study conducted in late March and early April 2020, of 637 responses only 13% of institutions indicated they would continue to require the SAT/ACT (NACAC, 2020). An overwhelming 61% indicated that they would not, while the rest remained undecided. Twenty-seven percent of respondents indicated they would accept third quarter or first semester transcripts (last completed before physical school closure) for the 2020 graduating seniors as final, while 30% said they would not collect transcript information and 43% were still undecided. These decisions rested in a growing understanding of the impact of the pandemic on prospective students.

Equity Insight: Standardized Testing and The Need to Change Admission Processes

For years, IHEs have debated whether or not to require standardized tests for admissions. These debates included arguments citing the lack of efficacy of standardized tests in predicting student academic success and the racial and class biases inherent in standardized testing practices. Some argued that these tests effectively excluded certain racial and socio-economic groups while actively favoring others. Studies have shown over time that high school grade point averages (HSGPAs) are stronger predictors of college outcomes than are test scores (Allensworth & Clark, 2020). In fact, despite claims made by the College Board and ACT, test scores appeared closely linked to socio-economic factors and not predictive of college success.

Prior to the pandemic, hundreds of schools had already begun dropping their SAT/ACT requirements. In 2015, Virginia Commonwealth University (VCU) decided to drop the SAT requirement. In his State of the University address that year, President Michael Rao announced that VCU would no longer require applicants with a high school GPA of 3.3 or higher to submit SAT scores, following a national trend toward relying on the GPA as a better predictor of student success. Rao defended the decision: "We are not denying a transformative education to students who we know would flourish here just because they don't have a certain SAT score. ... So, beginning this fall, your ability to succeed at VCU will no longer depend on your ability to pass a test that's fundamentally flawed" (VCU News, 2015).

Once the pandemic hit, COVID-19 had a similar impact on testing as it did for so many other aspects of higher education. While thousands of schools still used standardized tests in their admissions decisions, COVID-19 "forced the hand" of higher education institutions, accelerating decisions that would have been, in all probability, another decade in the making. The College Board and ACT, Inc. had to cancel administrations of their exams (Strauss, May 2020a), and colleges and universities decided to suspend testing requirements for 2020–21. Some universities went as far as stating they would not require tests for a few years as an experiment to see how the admissions process would do without them.

One of the announcements that had a major impact was the May statement made by the Regents of the University of California (UC) system that it would phase out SAT/ACT testing requirements through 2022 and citing factors such as the limiting effects the tests had on diversity of the student body, COVID-19, and equity (UC Office of the President, 2020).

> In March, UC temporarily suspended the current standardized test requirement for fall 2021 applicants to mitigate impacts of COVID-19 on students and schools, effectively making UC "test-optional" for that year. UC will now keep tests optional for an additional year through 2022. ... The University's response to the pandemic has provided an opportunity in the coming years for UC to pause and analyze additional, real-time data on the impacts of test-optional and test-blind admissions. The suspension allows UC to address concerns about equitable treatment for all students regardless of whether they submit a standardized test score. The Regents' vote also acknowledges the likely ongoing impacts of the COVID-19 pandemic on students, families and schools.

While this decision created controversy (Strauss, April 2020b), it opened the door for several other institutions to follow suit. By mid-June, every Ivy League school had agreed to drop SAT/ACT requirements for students entering in the fall of 2020 as had more than 2,000 other colleges and universities in total.

ADMISSIONS AND ENROLLMENT

A Close-up Lens on Leadership

At the University of Michigan-Flint, we have historically required a standardized test score for admission. Pre-COVID, our admissions process required both a high school transcript GPA and a standardized test score. Despite the requirement of both, any student with a 3.0 GPA or higher was admitted to the university regardless of the test score, thus the only test score requirement for students with a 3.0 or higher was simply to turn a test score in, which would not impact their admission decision. For students with a high school GPA below a 3.0, standardized test scores *were* taken into account in their admissions decision.

As the Chief Enrollment Officer, I recommended we move to test optional for 2020 to meet the needs of prospective students. I recommended this process to my faculty advisory committee to take back to each of their respective five schools and colleges to consider. Data were key to getting faculty buy-in. These data indicated that students with a 3.0 cumulative GPA, regardless of their standardized test score, are successful at the University. We defined success as having a 2.0 GPA at the end of their first semester of their freshman year. After careful review of these data and taking into consideration early surveys indicating how COVID-19 may impact students and their college decisions, faculty supported the recommendation to move to test optional admissions. The decision took into account necessary changes to the admission process that would promote student success after enrollment and would maintain the integrity of the class profile. The quick reaction not only of the admissions team to embrace this but by our faculty and staff to understand the severity of the situation and the need at an enrollment-driven institution to make swift changes was impressive.

In addition to test-optional admissions, we also worked with College Board to secure ACT residual testing on our campus. ACT residual testing allows students to take the ACT test on campus, proctored within that campus testing center. The caveat is that the test score may only be used by that university. Our strategy for the addition of ACT residual testing is to get students admitted to the university as quickly and easily as possible based on their high school GPA, not worrying about standardized test scores. Then, the residual testing option allowed us to get students to campus, not only for them to test to qualify for a merit scholarship, but also for us to use their visit to campus as a yield opportunity.

Flexibility in the Admission Process

Admission leaders quickly embraced the need for flexibility in such uncertain times. One decision requiring a quick turnaround to accommodate applicants was the need to change the admissions requirement of official high school transcripts for an admissions decision. Because many high schools, like college campuses, shut down in mid-March, applicants struggled to get copies of their official high school transcripts. So, many institutions made the decision to admit based on unofficial transcripts but informed students that they would need to provide official transcripts before they could begin classes in the fall. UM-Flint implemented this exception not only for high school students but also for transfer students, who made up about 50% of their incoming new student population each fall. Universities also took into consideration the financial implications that COVID-19 created for students, particularly the possibility that some transfer students would not be able to access official transcripts because of account holds from other institutions where they still had remaining balances.

One request that quickly came in from the local community colleges was that four-year transfer universities honor pass-fail grades on transcripts because of their desire to move to a pass-fail system for students who were forced to move from seated courses to distance learning. This grading shift required changes to procedures to accommodate these students, elucidated IHEs' need to be flexible about enforcing long-held norms, and to think creatively about how to adapt to the changing reality of college admissions in the COVID-19 era.

The choice on many campuses to move the deadline for students to make their college decision from the traditional May 1 to June 1 represented another example of collaboration and coordination across institutions and across the field of higher education admissions. In some ways, this delay helped to mitigate the impact of NACAC's policy change to allow for post-deposit recruitment (with deposits coming later) and a shorter uncertainty period for summer melt. Enrollment managers at many institutions had to collaborate with the "competition" to settle on a new June 1 deadline for deposits. For open access institutions and some public and private institutions without deposits, however, this extension created new problems for predicting yield as their competitors extended deadlines. In addition, with standardized testing centers and fourth quarter or spring semester grades in limbo, undergraduate, graduate, and professional programs had to adjust or waive long-held entrance requirements.

CLOSING THE DEAL

With campuses and high schools shuttering their doors to the public, students, and all but essential personnel, admissions offices and enrollment management divisions became hotbeds of innovation, creativity, and collaboration. Institutions faced a slew of difficult questions: How do we close the deal with future students? How do we convert admission offers to enrolled students? In many tuition-dependent schools, the fate of the institution rested on getting to that "yes" and keeping it a "yes" through the "summer melt" (attrition of students who submit an enrollment deposit but subsequently withdraw).

Institutions addressed these issues based on their missions and resources. For example, William & Mary University, a small public liberal arts university in Virginia, had decided prior to COVID-19 to phase in modest enrollment growth via a larger freshman class. Therefore, the decision to engage in a strategy of more aggressive admission offers proved to be important to sustaining progress toward that goal. "We saw more summer melt in our freshman class by early June than we had seen in full for the prior cycle by the August move-in date," said Vice President for Strategic Initiatives & Public Affairs Henry R. Broaddus. "The competition for students was fiercer than ever."

Pre-COVID, for many four-year institutions, the admissions visit or tour often sealed the deal, particularly for students seeking a residential or on-campus experience. Higher education research highlights the importance of a sense of comfort and belonging to student retention, and that often begins when a student visits campus, feels comfortable, becomes excited, and decides that a university is "a good fit." Some would argue that replicating this on-campus feeling virtually is impossible, but given the COVID-19 pandemic, institutions had to do their best to create the same reaction from potential new students using virtual means by creating virtual campus tours and visits. Admissions officers found creative ways to connect prospective students and their families with alumni, faculty in their major, current students, and other future students through this period. Virtual campus tours, campus videos, and video chats became the new normal way to engage with students. This shift required quickly setting up platforms to engage prospective students and to highlight campus features. As an immediate response to an emergent situation, this switch was, and would continue to be, critical to the enrollment process.

Marketing and Communication

Marketing and highlighting academic programs and features of institutions remained vital during the COVID-19 era given the unknowns of how students would respond to the pandemic. In March, the *Chronicle of Higher Education* (Hoover, 2020) gave some sobering statistics: 17% of student respondents were considering an alternative to attending a four-year college, with over 20% of those students considering taking a gap year or enrolling part time. Additionally, some students considered rural universities as a means to continue social distancing while other students considered staying closer to home for financial reasons.

As the end of the spring semester neared and admissions officers looked ahead to securing a fall class, they tried to comprehend and respond to the new realities of recruitment and the decision patterns of prospective students. This meant that they needed to remain agile in their marketing and recruitment strategies. Enrollment officers had to continue to monitor the patterns and trends of prospective students and to interpret how those new trends might impact their institutions. Intentional recruitment with a message that drew those students in was key. For example, a regional public comprehensive could promote their location, affordability, and the transferability of their courses to other larger institutions that may have been students' first-choice destinations prior to the onset of COVID-19. Additionally, regional public universities that primarily serve a commuter population within a regional area needed to create financial aid packages that would make them competitive with local community colleges for the next few years.

For institutions recruiting students based on their ability and desire to play collegiate athletics, closely monitoring NCAA guidance proved critical, especially for small private institutions that had traditionally leveraged extracurricular involvement (athletic and non-athletic) as a means to justify private school tuition. These colleges had to be especially mindful of students who based their college decision on the ability to participate in extracurriculars. When sports seasons became limited or canceled, such shifts impacted college choice as students who might have historically chosen institutions to continue their extracurricular activities feared they would not be able to participate in those sports, particularly fall athletics.

The colleges that appeared to garner the most success were those who communicated with their prospective students frequently and were able to provide meaningful information so that students could make well-informed decisions. A May 2020 Carnegie report showed that about 40% of students wanted weekly updates from their school of choice and about 25% wanted multiple updates. The study revealed that interest in communication increased for African American students from March to May, as well as for those intending to go to public institutions. Colleges needed to be careful about information overload and platform choice, as well as dissemination of useful and new information.

Remaining engaged with key recruitment stakeholders was another critical strategy for admissions leaders through this period. For example, with high schools being shut down, admissions counselors found it impossible to recruit in previous traditional ways. Here, student engagement trends that predated the pandemic assisted. Over the preceding decade, social media and digital outreach surpassed traditional high school visits in terms of effective marketing to high school students. Yet this shift did not entirely replace the importance of high school visits for connecting with students and, especially, with high school guidance counselors. Those counselors play a critical role in recruiting students as they guide and recommend institutions to the students they work with based on their knowledge of institutional fit. In order for them to do this, they needed to remain informed about various colleges and universities and their offerings. One strategy used by colleges and universities during the COVID-19 pandemic was to set up new or additional webinars for students, parents, and high school counselors to participate in the various stages of the admissions process. Counselor-specific webinars with content focused on what high school counselors need to know about the college or university proved to be successful, as were webinars for parents and those that addressed FAFSA and scholarship opportunities.

New Student Orientations

How and when new student orientation is handled varies greatly from institution to institution, but like almost everything else, this important preparation for successful onboarding of the incoming class also needed careful evaluation during the early stages of the pandemic. For many institutions that had traditionally held in-person orientation sessions and had not, up until COVID-19, significantly invested in resources to support online options, the transition proved much more difficult. They had to quickly put together online orientations for students, often homegrown, to create the best and fastest virtual experience. The pandemic accelerated innovations that many institutions had under consideration and that would expand their reach. As an example, UM-Flint approved a new $63,000 online transfer orientation learning platform not only for 2020, but moving forward to help recruit transfer and out-of-state students who could not physically visit the campus.

VCU, a public urban research institution with over 30,000 students including 3,800 first-time freshmen, created a series of online "Ram Ready" modules for all new students including first-year students, transfer and adult learners, as well as international and returning students. Admissions staff also encouraged the participation of parents and family members. These self-paced modules covered a wide range of topics, including housing, dining, transportation, health and safety issues, and financial aid. In addition, students were required to meet with VCU staff and student orientation leaders using the Zoom digital video teleconferencing platform. The university also required students to schedule a virtual meeting with their academic advisor after completing the online modules.

Small liberal arts colleges and universities, such as William & Mary (W&M), faced both unique challenges and different opportunities in connecting with students. W&M, for example, is a university steeped in tradition whose mission and values reflect the importance of relationship and human connection. Traditionally, the campus had worked to establish the connections core to their mission even prior to a new student stepping onto campus. With the pandemic, W&M had to determine how to build such connections virtually. To address this goal, W&M

enlisted alumni, students, parents, and friends from all over the world to engage with future W&M students. In addition to making a decision to bring first-year incoming students to campus before other students returned, the university used social media, digital video teleconference platforms, and videos to create critical relationship-building with the incoming class. These innovations opened the pathway to an innovative partnership with the Posse Foundation, a national non-profit committed to providing scholarships to diverse students with outstanding academic and leadership potential. This relationship allowed W&M to become the first institution to enroll a statewide Posse cohort the following year (Warters, 2020).

Graduate and Professional Programs

Traditionally, economic downturns and/or tight labor markets have resulted in increased enrollment in graduate degree programs. Students completing undergraduate degrees often consider masters programs as an alternative to the job market, and individuals who have recently been laid off might go back to school to earn a degree in an emerging field or one where job prospects are better. However, most of the jobs lost during the early pandemic were positions from the service industry with low educational requirements. It was thus difficult to predict how this particular labor change might impact enrollment in master's degree programs given that the majority of employees in this sector did not hold a bachelor's degree. Even though it was anticipated that enrollment in master's degree programs could be expected to increase, it was uncertain how a pandemic and budget crises might temper that growth.

Non-Traditional Students

Much of the research and media coverage of the impact of COVID-19 on college students focused on traditional-aged college students packing up and heading home from their residence halls or on high school seniors on their way to college. Relatively little attention was initially paid to adult learners on whom the pandemic's impact was as significant or greater. Many of these students were working full-time jobs while facing significant family care responsibilities, including suddenly overseeing the K-12 education of their at-home children (Dill, 2020). Latasha, a first-generation college student in Ohio and mother of three who was studying to be a nurse when COVID-19 hit, shared that "The hardest thing is trying to juggle school while homeschooling one kid, getting another one ready for kindergarten, and having a 20-month old running everywhere." Despite the struggles, she planned to continue her education.

The impact of COVID-19 on adult learners in the early pandemic was significant, just as campuses around the country were freshly engaging an important population in light of demographic shifts for projected college enrollments. Some institutions recognized the unique circumstances faced by non-traditional students in this period and took measures such as emergency funding or childcare grants to help keep these students in school, which became important efforts to both recruit and retain adult learners. One of the features of the COVID-19 pandemic was the blurring of lines between the needs of students and the needs of employees.

LESSONS LEARNED: THE CHANGING LANDSCAPE OF ENROLLMENT MANAGEMENT

COVID-19 may have been the catalyst that higher education needed to change archaic admissions requirements. Despite significant research indicating standardized tests' bias against BIPOC students, it was a long, slow process to move institutions to test-optional admissions practices. In this, and in other areas impacting enrollment and retention, pre-existing trust and collaboration between CEMOs and faculty allowed some institutions to pivot more quickly than others when it came to making changes to admissions requirements and processes.

Another lesson from the early pandemic for IHEs and enrollment management was the need to focus on the intersectionality of higher education, access, and equity. COVID-19 brought to the forefront that while we have made great strides in access and equity in higher education, we still have a long way to go. Measures such as moving toward test-optional admissions allowed institutions to put into practice their stated equity commitments, but this is only the beginning. Barriers like transportation, childcare, food insecurity, and housing continue to disproportionately impact already marginalized populations.

Enrollment has always been important at tuition-driven institutions, especially for small privates, but as the landscape has changed, and as more and more public institutions find state appropriation dollars being cut, the importance of enrollment has drawn greater attention in the public sector, as well. In case the pressures surrounding enrollment were not high enough before the pandemic's appearance, its impact, including the unpredictability of yield and growing financial needs of students with increased tuition costs, drove many CEMOs to function in quasi-development roles, seeking grant funding for incentive and completion programs and courting foundations for scholarship dollars. As one of the authors noted in this period, "I never thought of myself as a development officer, but that has certainly changed. I used to always say recruitment and retention are everyone's problem, and now, development is too. I find myself meeting with foundations and donors to increase scholarship dollars to ensure we are affordable for students and competitive with our peers" (Kristi Hottenstein, Vice Chancellor for Enrollment Management, University of Michigan-Flint).

If CEMOs entered the 2019–2020 academic year facing unprecedented changes to long-standing practices in the admissions cycle and processes, the early pandemic exacerbated the volatility of the enrollment landscape and accelerated innovations. The coming years will tell whether the resulting changes increase access and success and how IHEs will meet new and different admissions and enrollment challenges.

REFERENCES

Allensworth, E. M., & Clark, K. (2020, January 27). *High School GPAS and ACT scores as ... - sage journals*. High School GPAs and ACT Scores as Predictors of College Completion: Examining Assumptions About Consistency Across High Schools. Retrieved from https://journals.sagepub.com/doi/10.3102/0013189X20902110

Carnegie Higher Ed. (2020, May 14). *Senior Fall Decision: The After May 1st COVID-19 Study*. Retrieved February 27, 2022, from https://www.carnegiehighered.com/wp-content/uploads/2022/01/Carnegie_COVID-19_Senior-Decision-Study.pdf

Conley, B. (2019, September 6). *The Great Enrollment Crash*. Chronicle.com. Retrieved from https://www.chronicle.com/article/the-great-enrollment-crash/?cid=gen_sign_in

Dill, E. (2020, April 2). *Coronavirus Complicates an Already Tricky Balancing Act for Adult Learners*. Chronicle.com. Retrieved from https://www.chronicle.com/article/coronavirus-complicates-an-already-tricky-balancing-act-for-adult-learners/

Hoover, E. (2020, March 25). *How Is Covid-19 Changing Prospective Students' Plans? Here's an Early Look*. Chronicle.com. Retrieved from https://www.chronicle.com/article/how-is-covid-19-changing-prospective-students-plans-heres-an-early-look/?cid2=gen_login_refresh&cid=gen_sign_in

Jaschik, S. (2019, September 19). *Inside higher ed*. NACAC agrees to change its code of ethics. Retrieved from https://www.insidehighered.com/admissions/article/2019/09/30/nacac-agrees-change-its-code-ethics

Mitchell, T. (2020, August 11). *Opinion: The risk of losing 20 years of access to Higher Education*. The Hechinger Report. Retrieved from https://hechingerreport.org/opinion-the-biggest-danger-to-u-s-higher-education-losing-20-years-worth-of-gains-in-access-for-first-generation-and-minority-students/

National Association for College Admission Counseling (NACAC). (2019, September). *Code of Ethics and Professional Practices*. Retrieved from https://www.nacacnet.org/globalassets/documents/advocacy-and-ethics/cepp/cepp_10_2019_final.pdf

National Association for College Admission Counseling (NACAC). (2020). *Ensuring all students have access to higher education: The Role of Standardized Testing in the Time of COVID-19 and Beyond*. NACAC Task Force on Standardized Admission Testing for

International and US Students. Retrieved from https://www.nacacnet.org/globalassets/documents/knowledge-center/nacac_testingtaskforcereport.pdf

National Center for Education Statistics (NCES) (May, 2021). *Annual Reports: Undergraduate Enrollment*. Retrieved from https://nces.ed.gov/programs/coe/indicator/cha#:~:text=In%20fall%202018%2C%20total%20undergraduate,enrollment%20was%2013.2%20million%20students

Raymond, N., & Stempel, J. (2020, November 12). *U.S. Court Upholds Harvard Race-Based Admissions; Supreme Court Appeal Expected*. Reuters. Retrieved from https://www.reuters.com/article/harvard-admissions/u-s-court-upholds-harvard-race-based-admissions-supreme-court-appeal-expected-idUSKBN27S26G

Rhyneer, M., Boeckenstedt, J., Niles, S. D., Pérez, A. B., & Clark, R. A. (2020, May 7). *The Coronavirus Enrollment Crash: Five Admissions Leaders on the Pandemic's Impact — and What Can Be Done About it*. Chronicle.com. Retrieved from https://www.chronicle.com/article/the-coronavirus-enrollment-crash/?cid2=gen_login_refresh&cid=gen_sign_in

SimpsonScarborough. (April 2020). *Higher Ed and COVID-19: National Student Survey*. Retrieved from https://f.hubspotusercontent30.net/hubfs/4254080/SimpsonScarborough%20National%20Student%20Survey%20.pdf

Strauss, V. (2020a, May 30). *Testing Giants Act and College Board Struggle Amid Covid-19 Pandemic*. The Washington Post. Retrieved from https://www.washingtonpost.com/education/2020/05/30/testing-giants-act-college-board-struggle-amid-covid-19-pandemic/

Strauss, V. (2020b, April 24). *Analysis| University of California Academics at Odds with Each Other Over Using SAT/ACT Scores to Admit Students*. The Washington Post. Retrieved from https://www.washingtonpost.com/education/2020/04/24/university-california-academics-odds-with-each-other-over-using-satact-scores-admit-students/

Synder, T. D., de Brey, C., & Dillow, S. A. (2019, December). *Digest of Educational Statistics 2018*. National Center for Education Statistics (NCES). Retrieved from https://nces.ed.gov/pubs2020/2020009.pdf

Turk, J., Soler, M., & Vigil, V. (2020, April 23). *College and University Presidents Respond to COVID-19: April 2020 Survey*. American Council on Education, Research & Insights. Retrieved from https://www.acenet.edu/Research-Insights/Pages/Senior-Leaders/College-and-University-Presidents-Respond-to-COVID-19-April-2020.aspx

UC Office of the President. (2020, May 21). *University of California Board of Regents Unanimously Approved Changes to Standardized Testing Requirement for Undergraduates*. University of California. Retrieved from https://www.universityofcalifornia.edu/press-room/university-california-board-regents-unanimously-approved-changes-standardized-testing

US Department of Education (ED). (2020, January 10). *Education and Title VI*. Retrieved from https://www2.ed.gov/about/offices/list/ocr/docs/hq43e4.html

VCU News. (2015, January 27). *VCU to Drop SAT Requirement*. Retrieved from https://news.vcu.edu/article/vcu_to_drop_sat_requirement#:~:text=Virginia%20Commonwealth%20University%20President%20Michael,better%20predictor%20of%20student%20success

Warters, N. (2020, October 15). *William & Mary Launches Innovative Partnership with the Posse Foundation*. William & Mary. Retrieved from https://www.wm.edu/news/stories/2020/william-mary-launches-innovative-partnership-with-the-posse-foundation.php

Chapter 12

Advancement through a Pandemic

Kara M. Rabbitt and Jennifer A. Ostergren

KEEPING THE FUTURE IN VIEW THROUGH A CRISIS

During the early pandemic, the long-term work of college and university advancement and development divisions (e.g., cultivating future donors, stewarding gifts meant to sustain scholarships over time, building endowments toward strategic goals) seemed less pressing than assuring program completion by current students, providing for the immediate needs for the shift to remote work and instruction by staff and faculty, and ensuring the health and security of campus communities. However, one truth held by those working in advancement and development is that, regardless of the crisis, capacity building for future giving must continue. As leadership cabinets across the country responded to the COVID-19 crisis in spring 2020, many of their collective discussions focused on immediate student and institutional needs. Advancement leaders, however, also quietly continued to build toward long-term goals even as they addressed institutional decisions to establish emergency funds and engaged in canceling or postponing planned development events. They worked with their teams to pivot operations and strategized how to maintain stewardship, expand virtual outreach, and keep in close contact with valued donors through an unprecedented period. Leaders in this area were well aware that it would be too late to restart their work when this crisis was over and that their efforts during the early months of the COVID-19 pandemic need to assured the capacity to secure future gifts that would be crucial in helping institutions survive and even thrive in a post-pandemic world.

Advancement and development units maintain an important ear to external stakeholders and play an essential role in bridging community needs and providing feedback loops for the crafting of messages external stakeholders need to hear in times of crisis. Within the four-frames model of leadership (Bolman and Deal, 2013), advancement leaders often function in the realm of the Symbolic. This capacity to frame meaning was of critical importance in the early pandemic. While IHE leadership teams as a whole operated within the Human

Resource frame in their focus on the needs of different campus constituents and in the Structural frame in a need to establish new systems and protocols, the Symbolic functions of meaning-making, inspiring, and providing a collective sense of identity and purpose were core to the work of advancement teams as they sought both to secure needed crisis support for their institutions and to assure the long-term connections necessary for future growth. Innovations that advancement teams created by necessity during this period would also likely change how they will conduct their work in the future, as development officers learned new ways of engaging and connecting alumni and donors with the campus and with each other.

PRE-COVID CHALLENGES AND GOALS

Prior to the COVID-19 crisis, philanthropy and partnership development were of growing importance to most higher education institutions grappling with declining public funding, deepening tuition discounts, and increased competition for tuition dollars (McGee, 2015) as many faced the beginnings of the "demographic cliff" as the pool of traditional-age students began to decline (Grawe, 2018). According to the National Center for Education Statistics (US Department of Education, n.d.), educational endowments, however, were performing well in the pre-pandemic period. Most had been on the rise, with the average endowments for all US institutions up 9% in the fiscal year 2018 over the previous year. Many struggling smaller private institutions had begun to increase endowment spending prior to the pandemic. This trend accelerated rapidly in 2020 (Massachusetts Institute of Technology, 2017).

Leading up to the pandemic period, development and advancement work in higher education had begun to reshape the broader landscape of philanthropy and charitable giving to institutions. According to the National Association of Independent Schools (2019), trends in this area included tax reforms and a shift to larger and less frequent donations, the growing use of online giving and crowd-sourced funding (especially among younger donors), fewer and wealthier donors accounting for a larger share of giving in the US, and a growing emphasis in social conscience giving, as well as an expectation of transparency in expenses and use of donations (Orem, 2019).

THE IMMEDIATE AFTERMATH—SPRING 2020 PIVOTS IN THE WORLD OF PHILANTHROPY

As campuses across the country closed their doors in March 2020, advancement units quickly moved their operations and teams to remote formats and reprioritized their agendas. As the crisis continued, teams also began to lay the groundwork for future actions and a shift of strategic priorities. Several leaders noted the importance of restraint through this period. While most teams reached out to support student emergency funds, one vice president of a large public institution noted that they did not wish to be "too loud" in these requests, as they knew that some of their key foundation funders were providing significant support to the community, as well.

Events

Difficult and often expensive decisions to cancel, postpone, or move to a virtual format any planned upcoming advancement events, such as galas, alumni reunions, or fund- and friend-raising opportunities planned for the coming weeks or months, occupied advancement teams during the early phase of the pandemic shutdown. Early in the crisis, like other campus units who hoped the shutdown would prove short-lived, some advancement teams simply crossed their fingers and hoped that pushing back events a month or two would prove sufficient. However, by mid-April, as campuses began to cancel spring commencement exercises, it became clear that such important networking events could not reasonably run in-person and meet continuing state and local social distancing protocols. Advancements teams, therefore, began to cancel, push for even later dates, or restructure into virtual format their planned events through the fall as regional and federal health guidelines made it increasingly unlikely that they would be able to hold gatherings in the foreseeable future.

Campus Giving Days

The pandemic also impacted Planned Giving Days. One regional comprehensive in the West, set to launch its first giving day in fall 2020, quietly canceled the plan before announcing it. Instead, they shifted their team's focus to emergency fund development because they wanted the first year of the Giving Day to be a successful launch they could build upon, not a further complication in a turbulent period.

Wabash College, a small private men's college, opted to reschedule and refocus the theme of their 7th Annual Day of Giving scheduled for early April. The college moved from a suddenly problematic theme of "spreading the fame" (wishing to avoid any reference to "spreading" during a pandemic) to a more unifying concept of "Wabash Together." The institution shifted the intended April date in favor of the date in May when commencement would have occurred had it not been postponed. Building on its highly engaged alumni network, the college ended up with its most successful giving day to date. This event proved strikingly successful and created higher yield due to lower related costs despite being the first entirely virtual event. Organizers managed to create a high-touch feeling for alumni, current students, and the entire campus community despite its virtual format. Since the college also usually used the event to cultivate a philanthropic awareness among current students (with student clubs representatives traditionally going door to door in the dorms to encourage college residents to donate laundry money as their first gift), the advancement team worked to provide equivalent, low-impact opportunities for current students. College leaders gave the Student Senate the student fees intended for a refund due to COVID circumstances. The Student Senate then opted to use those monies as a fund marker for the day of giving, to be "unlocked" as a donation back to the college upon sufficient student engagement with the day's goals. Additionally, some students donated their housing refunds back to the campus during this day. Across many campuses, what the advancement teams needed to do to innovate through the early pandemic would likely change how they would run such annual events moving forward.

> **Equity Insight**
>
> Colleges and universities serving a large percentage of minoritized students and/or those from lower socio-economic status who were particularly impacted by the COVID-19 crisis faced emergency fundraising concerns through this period that made campus giving days of vital and pressing importance. Securing support for students facing food and housing insecurities, helping students cover moving costs, and providing the breadth of student services necessary to assure persistence to degrees through this period demanded new revenues just when campuses were shutting down and losing auxiliary funding sources. The pivot to online instruction, for example, was further complicated for HBCUs because "34% of Black Americans don't have high-speed internet and 42% are without personal computers" (Charles & Dobson, 2020), which created a need for advancement teams to secure additional resources for students being pushed off campus. Prairie View A&M University, an HBCU within the Texas A&M University system, shifted their Giving Tuesday fundraiser in this period to seek emergency aid for students in an online-only event through social media and email marketing. According to an interview by Carme Williams, vice president of development at Prairie View, with *Inside Higher Ed*, the event succeeded better than expected specifically due to the impact of the pandemic: "Given the demographic of our students – and our alumni know the demographic of our students because it was once them – this was one of our best Giving Tuesday efforts that the university had" (Whitford, 2021).

Gala Costs—Actual and Opportunity

While debates abound in philanthropic teams about the benefits of galas, and not all institutions make use of such events, for some colleges and universities these annual events are key drivers of scholarship funding as well as important occasions to build or foster relationships with current or future donors. At William Paterson University, a regional comprehensive, the April Legacy Gala had long functioned as an important opportunity for the Foundation to fundraise for their annual scholarship funds. Like many such events, the gala also served to cement important relationships by allowing the university to recognize key philanthropic partners, engage new potential donors, and showcase student accomplishment to highlight the impact of giving. In March 2020, the advancement team negotiated with the venue to move the planned gala from April to June, in the hope that gatherings would be possible by then. In the end, the Foundation would hold the planned 2020 gala virtually in April 2021 with the same honorees. Rather than proposing refunds to attendees in spring 2020, the Office of Advancement assured those who had purchased event tickets that these would be honored the following year and asked if they would wish, instead, to turn the ticket contribution into a donation, which many did. The loss of the 2020 gala meant that the Foundation was unable to make its usual transfer of scholarship funds to the university. More significantly, losing the event meant losing its symbolic and political opportunity for networking with potential donors, for connecting students with alumni, and for building a collective sense of belonging. Vice President for Advancement Pamela Ferguson shared that communications with alumni and donors around the event helped many to realize that scholarship support was more important than ever before, however. Though her team faced a need to build new alumni pipelines on the other side of the pandemic, they found that those who could give gave more through this period. They also planned to take elements of what they learned to change future events, even if in-person, such as using brief pre-recorded videos of donor messages or alumni profiles rather than the traditional series of speeches from the podium. As with campus giving days, advancement teams had the opportunity through this forced pause to reconsider the purpose and formats of long-standing annual events.

Alumni Engagement

The goals for working with institutional alumni remained the same through the early pandemic even as teams looked for new ways to engage with and add value to the alumni experience. Several campuses sent mass surveys to target alumni needs during this time. A few launched webinars by April or May 2020 on home-schooling, stress/anxiety reduction, strategies for working from home, increasing LinkedIn activity, and sharpening resume and interview skills. One urban regional comprehensive campus noted that their attendance rate for these events was almost double the percentage of registrants who typically showed up to in-person gatherings. At another institution, a vice president shared that pandemic conditions offered a significant opportunity to reach out and offer something of value to alumni and donors (such as mindfulness tips, virtual wellness checks, and career advice sessions). In the early crisis, this institution was careful to have their team avoid making any request until people asked what they could do and only then did they offer options to help that would best meet the current student and institutional needs.

Some colleges and universities took the opportunity to find new ways to serve alumni and to increase engagement during this period. Advancement professionals had to get creative in fostering a sense of community that honored the relationships their alumni had with the institution and built a culture of giving. At the same time, social distancing diminished the ability to have genuine and personal interactions with prospective major donors. Some development officers found ways to individualize their outreach and demonstrate sincerity and value to their constituents. This form of outreach is a trend that may strengthen advancement efforts in the future. As one leader noted, her team realized that they were making too many assumptions about alumni and would not know what these individuals cared about unless they asked. They found that the head of the alumni association had more of an impact on former students than the president. She noted, "We're at MACH-3 all the time. It takes strength to say, 'wait.' We won't get more money by doing it poorly." This campus, like many others, developed a selection of free online courses over the summer for their alumni in such options as human resource management, communication strategies, or other areas that might attract mid-career alumni looking to "sharpen a saw" during a relatively quiet period in their professional lives. This strategy served to connect to alumni and build relationships with them that could lead to future giving or graduate enrollment. Such efforts to build virtual connectivity to the campuses were vital in light of projected declines in likely philanthropic giving (Daniels, 2020). If most donors were projecting giving less, more potential donors would need to be engaged downstream to offset likely losses.

SHIFTING OPERATIONS AND PRIORITIES

Rebuilding and Reactivating Teams

As advancement teams moved to remote work during this period, not only did they have to cancel or postpone planned events, they had to reprioritize their units and reimagine their work. Where a major gift officer might typically spend much of the week setting up or traveling to one-on-one meetings with donors or prospects, there is only so much cultivation work that can be accomplished at a distance. One advancement leader shared during this period that his team immediately reviewed their donor and prospect lists, dividing these up among team members by names they knew or had some connection to, and began to create outreach plans to check in systematically with those with whom they had established relationships—including foundation board members, college board members, regional business leaders, key alumni, and long-time donors—to see how they were doing and to let them know what the campus was doing in service to its students. This shift basically, he noted, reprioritized team efforts from cultivation to stewardship and relationship building, the very components of advancement work that could too easily fall away when identifying and cultivating prospects became the main focus. A leader at another campus echoed this strategy, noting her team almost immediately determined to view this period as stages of a natural disaster—event, recovery, rebuild. In the crisis phase, they prioritized individualized touches to every major donor and asked how they could be of service: "Just making sure you and your family are okay. Let us know what we can do for you."

Several advancement leaders shared that this shift in focus was difficult for their teams for several reasons. First, the culture of development work is fairly territorial and competitive, with gift officers gaining professional standing and satisfaction from the gifts they "close." Stepping away from a focus on closing gifts and building a new collaborative, relationship-nurturing strategy required a different form of emotional work. Second, since fundraising focuses so much on the relationships one builds with donors, the virtual shift brought frustrations to those used to having very personal, direct interactions and visits with people. Fundraising work is rarely remote: most fundraisers are very socially orientated, and many gift officers found the shift to remote engagement both challenging and isolating. More than one advancement leader used the term "grieving" to speak about how their teams felt in this period. Several leaders shared that they worked carefully in team meetings through the early pandemic to acknowledge their challenges with remote work and to provide emotional check-ins as staff grappled with the grief and frustrations of the time.

In keeping with the Symbolic leadership frame, one vice president, knowing how forward-facing her advancement team generally was, sent them a picture of a flower on the first gray day of remote work as a symbol of future blossoming and wrote that they would get through this together. Based on the team's very positive responses to this outreach, she would end up sending a virtual bloom every day until they returned to campus, creating through that photographic bouquet ultimately both a documentation of the length of their time apart and a symbol for their continuing connection. Advancement teams needed to develop similarly creative strategies to maintain connections with donors or prospects. Some met such individuals in parks, where they could be socially distanced outside together. Others went on hikes with donors or even went shopping for some who were shut-in. They made "old-fashioned phone calls" and sent hand-written notes as vital forms of human contact during a period when they could not meet.

Since most development officers also track visits as part of their operational goals, leaders also needed to figure out ways to help these individuals "count" virtual visits in their records. One major Southwestern university worked with SalesForce through this period to create a better tracking system with causal proposals (beyond a single silo) that permitted advancement personnel to share interdisciplinary work and goals across units in ways that provided "credit" for assists in these lifts. Another institution created a "Virtual Visit" button for staff to track their calls or Zoom meetings just as they would in-person visits. So effective was this change for several teams that a few vice presidents shared by late spring and summer 2020 that they fully intended on continuing to operate more virtually even after the virus was no longer a threat. As one campus leader noted, moving forward this shift would change how contacts are made, in that officers could see more people virtually than they could contact while sitting in an airport waiting for a plane. This leader reported that the number of substantive contacts being tracked by his team had risen substantially, with the highest number for the entire fiscal year logged in May 2020. He also noted that the move to remote work accelerated the process of moving from qualification to cultivation. However, he anticipated that the final stages of working toward an ask would still likely take place in person. At a national level, many teams reported increased online giving through this period and projected a far more digital future for their work (Whitford, 2021).

Some campuses also took advantage of the crisis to reexamine the organizational structures of their development teams. In shifting operations, development officers worked to find ways to mobilize donor engagement at a centralized and coordinated level and away from unit-specific and multi-layered or competing levels. For example, a few campuses reported operating under a highly decentralized development model prior to the crisis, with predominantly unit-centric efforts (i.e., centers or schools fundraising for their specific programmatic needs, or athletic programs operating outside the purview of general advancement efforts for the campus). Leaders from a few such campuses noted a need to shift from unit-specific efforts to an institution-wide or "one voice" effort to function remotely. Doing so avoided having competing voices contacting outside stakeholders as advancement units across campus worked to assure that they refrained from, as one leader stated, "bombarding people with information." As she stressed, teams in this period needed to frame clearer arguments and "not take up so much air." While the coordination of communication schedules, for example, had not occurred at this institution prior to the COVID-19 crisis, it was a game-changer that created better open rates and greater responses. A key takeaway shared by several leaders was a plan to move permanently from previously decentralized staff models to centralized structures that would continue beyond the early crisis period.

Pausing, Refocusing, or Shifting Capital Campaigns

According to a May 2020 poll of 110 university advancement leaders (EAB, 2020), prior to the COVID-19 crisis, nearly two-thirds of institutions were involved in some phase of an ambitious capital campaign. Most opted to move these campaigns forward, despite the challenging economic climate posed by the pandemic in the US. Over three-quarters of institutions that had been planning to enter the quiet phase of a campaign during the next fiscal year opted to do so, while acknowledging that they might have to change their projected timeframes for publicly launching planned campaigns. Across all institutions currently engaged in a campaign in May 2020, 45% stated that they were still deciding whether or not to delay their closing date and over 10% had already pushed the close date back a year or more.

For institutions that had already launched comprehensive campaigns, most quietly continued. As Michelle L. Janssen, CFRE, Dean for College Advancement at Wabash College, shared, "Philanthropy is elastic and will snap back." She noted that people who are charitable generally "are optimists at heart and want to help," a view shared by many advancement leaders. Though this was not necessarily the time to acquire new donors or to make new asks, some institutions closed some of their largest gifts during the early phase of the COVID crisis as committed donors reached deeper in the face of increased need.

Strategizing Voice and Communication

Many units opted to deploy staff to reach out individually to key donors and prospective supporters to check in on how they were doing, update them on campus news, and invite them to share their feedback on current efforts to support programs and students. Others created virtual meetings with small groups to share updates and to solicit input into planned activities. Some creative teams engaged deans, students, or key faculty researchers to share what was going on in their areas and to lead Zoom discussions with key donor groups, such as foundation board members or alumni leaders. One advancement leader from a large university shared that "Zoom will change the work forever moving forward." She noted that the virtual platform provided important democratization of the dialogue that permitted, for example, alumni or donors from scattered geographic regions or diverse personal circumstances equal access to interact with the president at one of their most successful events ever. "Everyone was in their home, comfortable together," she observed.

As the campus established new outreach plans, these teams and advancement leaders also needed to decide how and when to deploy key figures, such as presidents or chancellors, or beneficiaries, such as students or faculty. Additionally, they needed to determine which virtual means best served the message, the audience, and the symbolism of the event. As the president of a philanthropic management consultancy firm shared in a March 2020 *Chronicle of Philanthropy* article,

> it is important to consider which channel an executive uses to communicate. For example, email provides a formal assurance that your institution is prepared and following precautions, while social-media platforms offer a more human touch to reassure people that you are taking immediate action and are responsive to their needs.
>
> (Hilser-Wiles, 2020)

Given that the pandemic caused strained budgets, this was a challenging time to invest in new resources, but many tools and platforms provided crucial means both to shift operations virtually and to engage differently and with different populations during this period. For example, one college campus rolled out a new "ThankYou" video messaging tool to send individualized messages to graduating seniors and to use student videos to reach out to donors. Using social networks allowed campuses to crowdsource emergency funds and to create new engagement with year-end goals.

The COVID crisis also required advancement teams to articulate how the established emergency funds responded to the needs of students, the broader campus community, and the region. One of the California State University campuses, for example, launched "hero stories." These included the work of faculty to call almost all of the institution's students after early data showed that roughly 34% of students were not engaging in courses online. The results were inspiring: 99.6% of students remained enrolled and the average GPA increased by .3–.4 for the term. This story, highlighting the dedication of faculty and staff to student success, along with such data points as the fact that 81% of the university's students were on financial aid, helped the team make a compelling case for continued giving. The campus also rolled out Zoom "luncheons" of 8 to 10 key donors with deans in early summer 2020 to share stories of how faculty were continuing to advance research and work with students and of creative strategies and successful outcomes from the spring pivot to remote learning.

The role of coordinated and centralized communication efforts represented an important area of focus for some teams, with development leadership working to time communication to donors in relationship to other campus-wide outreach. A major Southwestern university created a communication calendar stratified by themes to avoid diluting the impact of communications and asks through the early pandemic. Each week, units and central offices focused their communications to alumni and donors on specific topical areas. This allowed the campus to move forward strategically with a solicitation week, an information week, a utility (or resource-sharing) week, and a gratitude week. This coordinated plan helped the campus channel communication flows, prevent information overload, and decrease competing communications. The "gratitude" theme week also shaped campus-wide communication to align with the institution's core values.

Operating without Athletics

As institutions and regions made health-based decisions that canceled games or whole seasons for athletic teams, advancement units from colleges and universities with a strong sports identity faced a new challenge: operating without what one vice president termed the "lubricant" of sports events to engage donors. Campus sporting events provide an important environment for fundraising, so the loss of this space through the early pandemic resculpted the social landscaping of fundraising. As teams looked forward to the 2020–2021 year, they also needed to develop contingency plans for another year without athletics. For some campuses, this period provided an opportunity to integrate athletics fundraising with centralized advancement teams to assure, as one leader shared, that "the tail was not wagging the dog." One such campus shifted reporting of the Athletics Department's fundraising team to the Foundation, noting that they use athletics because it is comfortable for donors, but that the institution, not the team, should be the meaning of the giving. Another advancement leader from a Big Ten school shared that this period taught the teams to be donor-focused rather than unit-focused. Though this institution would not be moving to a completely centralized model, they did create through this period a more hybrid advancement model that connected support for athletic facilities and teams to institutional goals linked to specific donors.

Reprioritizing Solicitations

While giving priorities shifted and most teams moved their focus from cultivation to outreach, long-term fundraising goals continued in quieter phases and dialogues continued to support previously developed proposals. As one vice president explained, the goal was "not to press, but to keep strategic conversations going." However, the early phase of the pandemic was not generally viewed as a time to be making new asks. Advancement teams quickly shifted their giving priorities to meet the emergent needs of the most at-risk students, sending out requests to friends and alumni to contribute to emergency funds established to help students fly home, ship their things, purchase the materials they would need to continue their education remotely, or otherwise respond to the exigencies of the crisis. Most campuses rolled out emergency fund opportunities within the first week or two of campus closures. Advancement teams quickly researched the needs and the contextual levers that could be utilized to help meet these needs, such as the tax changes passed by Congress as part of the CARES Act that included a $300 tax deduction for charitable giving without requiring itemized filing. They helped to sculpt strategies for broader, if not deeper, giving as teams alerted potential donors of this fiscal incentive for support (Killen, 2020).

The impact of the crisis on college athletes also created a new need, as some campuses launched appeals for 5th-year scholarships for students whose eligibility was extended due to policy changes at the National Collegiate Athletic Association level (for further discussion of this issue, see Chapter 7). Campuses with strong college sports programs scrambled to meet the extended scholarship needs of these students through extensive outreach to boosters and alumni. Virginia Tech University, for example, launched a "Keep Jumping" fundraising campaign in summer 2020 to address the financial shortfalls due to canceled sports events and to assist the continuing student athletes' scholarship needs (Kauffman, 2021).

PHILANTHROPY MOVING FORWARD: CALCULATING LONG-TERM IMPACTS AND PLANNING FOR THE NEXT PHASES

Every leader of an advancement division we spoke with for this chapter stressed the long view of their units. Keeping a future-oriented mindset, stewarding gifts to serve later generations, assuring growing opportunities – these were the goals the divisions kept in mind even as those around them responded to the central and pressing priorities of the crisis. Advancement leaders understand that their goal is to support the long-term excellence and viability of the institutions they serve.

Projected declines in donor dollars, combined with the pressing financial contexts addressed in Chapter 13, including reduced state funding and projected drops in tuition income due to declines in enrollment, created real concerns for many campuses (Busta, 2020). In pulse point surveys of college and university presidents conducted throughout the spring of 2020, the American Council on Education (ACE) asked respondents to choose their most pressing issues at various moments of the crisis. "Long-term financial viability of the institution" ranked consistently high, with "Ability to fundraise at this moment" less pressing but still noted by most presidents (Taylor, 2020). In the end, the pandemic itself would generate an unprecedented 9% year-over-year increase in educational contributions in 2020 (Hadero, 2021). Despite this short-term gain, the long-term fiscal health of IHEs had never been more tenuous. Advancement teams witnessed an uptick in planned giving bequests as people updated their wills during the initial phases of the pandemic in spring 2020. Yet the outcome in terms of likely estate gifts remained unclear through this period in light of potential long-term portfolio losses due to COVID-related economic stressors on the market (Stiffman, 2020).

Managing Endowments

Since many advancement units determine their drawdowns for endowed scholarships on a three-year trailing average, the fact that the pandemic hit after a solid year of stock market gains meant that most institutions faced little early impact. According to an April 2020 National Association of College and University Business Officers (NACUBO) survey of 333 institutions, even though most endowments experienced first-quarter losses in 2020, most were able to fully award planned 2020–2021 scholarships (NACUBO, 2020a). Seventy-two percent of institutions responded that they expected to maintain their current spending rates, with an additional 8% planning to increase spending to meet increased need, and only 7% planning to decrease spending in the coming academic year (National Association of College and University Business Officers, 2020b). However, many endowments face limits on drawdowns tied to donor restrictions on use and designed to ensure that endowment revenues are spent toward the purposes for which the monies were received and protect the corpus for continuing yields for future generations.

In a troubling trend, survey respondents noted that 20% of endowment funds were underwater at the end of the first quarter of 2020, meaning that their value had fallen below the original gift amount and placing ongoing revenue from the funds at risk. NACUBO noted that,

> Some institutions consider it prudent to spend from an underwater endowment, as long as there is reasonable confidence the endowment will at least return to its threshold value at the end of an appropriate time horizon; they maintain a long-term outlook regardless of current market conditions. Other institutions will increase spending from older funds with healthy appreciation margins as a way of fulfilling their spending policy rate while allowing time for underwater funds to recover value
> —National Association of College and University Business Officers, 2020b

The early impact of the pandemic on endowments was undoubtedly a cause for concern (NACUBO, 2020b). However, most healthier institutions had pre-established mechanisms to monitor and adjust payouts in accordance with investment policies designed to ensure the long-term viability of their accounts. While these adjustments—taken globally—had not yet affected projected spending for the 2020–2021 academic year, moving forward institutions would face the likelihood of weaker investment returns and reduced gifts in light of COVID-related employment declines and profit losses. In the early months of the crisis, some institutions already reported lost planned gifts, particularly stock transfers, due to early drops in the stock market. As institutions struggled with maintaining enrollments and the added costs of campus closures, this extreme market volatility negatively affected endowments.

Added to declining revenues from investments, institutions faced political pressures as both internal and external stakeholders questioned why IHEs did not dip into their endowments to help cover budget shortfalls. However, as defined by NACUBO, "endowments are not rainy-day funds. Endowments are managed to provide colleges and universities with a steady and reliable source of funding over the long term" (National Association of College and University Business Officers, 2020a). Additionally, legal agreements with donors often limit IHEs' ability to use gifts other than for their donors' intended purpose. In some cases, both donor agreements and state law forbade the use of endowments to fund annual operating expenses. Still, some states did allow special appropriations which IHEs can use for emergency student aid, and some institutions with large endowments, such as Yale and Princeton, did opt to increase endowment investment payouts. Even so, given smaller returns, as Princeton Provost Debbie Prentice announced in a published email in April 2020, revenue gaps also required reduced hiring, salary freezes, and cuts in "non-essential" expenditures even on such a well-endowed campus. Relatively few IHEs could boast of such large endowments or had the cushion to increase payouts, however, making the financial challenges wrought by pandemic conditions and needs even greater.

In the near term, experienced investment managers advised IHEs to avoid emotional decision-making in managing endowment investments that could lead to the liquidation of portfolios in response to market volatility. Instead, they were advised to adhere to their Investment Policy Statement (IPS) and use it to rebalance portfolios. Organizations such as NACUBO advised endowment managers to check institutional liquidity sources and to develop low-/medium-/high-planning scenarios. Additionally, they encouraged IHEs to analyze relationships with key donors to determine if they might want to loosen spending restrictions on gifts or give more. IHEs could also obtain liquidity through short-term secured or unsecured lines of credit. As the budget and enrollment picture became more apparent for the fall, institutional investment managers would need to revise their IPS to evaluate and recommend changes based on new conditions.

Pipeline Impacts

In a survey of college and university advancement officials run by EAB in May 2020, "41% of institutions [were] projecting declines of 10% or more compared to FY2019. More than 1 in 5 [were] expecting the revenue drop to surpass the 20% mark" (2020). The most significant percentage of projected declines were in the small- and mid-sized gift range. Of potentially greater concern to advancement officers during this period was the downstream effect of suspending or reducing cultivation visits. The "prospecting pipeline" dropped off precipitously during the 2020 COVID-19 crisis, with 20% of schools anticipating 30% or more declines in numbers of prospect visits and a likely subsequent decline in FY 2021 gift dollars.

Higher education was not, of course, alone in the challenges of adjusting their philanthropic activities during the COVID-19 outbreak. As the *Chronicle of Philanthropy* (2020) detailed in numerous toolkits, opinion pieces, and articles throughout the spring of 2020, the costs of and contact losses due to canceled events and the adjustments in operations for units working remotely rendered it difficult to continue to engage donors and provide effective stewardship. Identifying and cultivating new donors proved even more challenging through this period.

The challenge across higher education was to find the means to move, after the initial stages of the pandemic, toward building for the future. After the first few months, most advancement leaders began to loop their teams back toward exploring possible new cultivation opportunities. They gradually changed their messaging from the immediate needs for students and programs and focused on key strategic priorities for their institutions. As one vice president shared, "We don't know what we don't know yet. But we need to be ready to hit the ground running when this is over. If you are just picking yourself up, you'll be behind when the path opens back up." Most institutions faced budget cuts, declining enrollments, and a pressing need to support the initiatives that would make their programs compelling and successful. After the initial shutdown, advancement teams needed to be future-focused and positive during a period when the present contexts were the most difficult and the outlook the most negative.

LESSONS LEARNED

In its very mission, advancement always looks beyond the "now" toward the long-term sustainability of key strategic initiatives and core institutional goals. Through the cultivation of alumni, fundraising initiatives, donor identification and recruitment, institutional marketing support, and connections to strategic communication initiatives, advancement and development offices, almost more than any other campus unit, work in support of the campus of the future, of the next generations of students and programs, and for the health of the institution beyond the current moment. As such, while working to support crisis needs in the early pandemic, advancement leaders also needed to focus on the long view. Most of the interviewed participants shared that they did so quietly in spring 2020, fully recognizing that their cabinet-level peers were focused on concerns of "now." While other institutional leaders focused on issues such as ensuring student retention and completion and the welfare of employees, the leaders of advancement and development teams needed to think in terms of ten to twenty years down the line and beyond, even as they joined their peers and supported their institutions in responding to the crisis: How do we engage future donors, now? How can we serve alumni during this pandemic, now, in a way that will connect them to the institution for the future? How can we steward existing gifts even as we seek additional, crisis-focused contributions? How can we pivot our cultivation efforts in a period of social distancing and local lockdowns? The strongest teams continued to play the long game, even as they altered planned events, created new virtual initiatives, and launched key campaigns—through new technologies and under current crisis conditions.

A key outcome of the early pandemic for college and university advancement teams is likely to be a continued shift toward virtual engagement initiatives and a trend toward drawing teams away from in person contacts and back to phones, virtual platforms, and written communications. As institutional resources become more restricted, advancement leaders are less likely to send their gift officers off on fishing expeditions and road trips. Many learned through this period that more could be accomplished remotely, and at a lower cost, in terms of cultivation than via traditional prospect visits.

A final lesson learned by all the advancement leaders we spoke with was the key need to coordinate and to strategize communications across divisions. Through this period, the speed of communications—from presidents, vice presidents, athletic directors, alumni teams, and others—forced a level of strategic collaboration and coordination that many campuses noted was more effective than past practice.

A meaningful outcome in the interviews for this chapter was the quiet nature of the first two points above: most vice presidents for advancement we spoke with shared that they recognized that their Cabinet colleagues faced pressing, immediate, crisis-related concerns through this period. However, they also knew that their presidents or chancellors and their boards would soon be looking at the fiscal realities ahead (Taylor, 2020). Beyond the need to reschedule, cancel, or reconceive planned events and respond to emergency fundraising needs, most advancement leaders knew that they needed to pivot teams to maintain long-term work that would sustain their institutions. Accordingly, advancement teams quietly focused in early spring 2020 on a period that many other higher education leaders could scarcely envision through the early pandemic: the future.

REFERENCES

Bolman, L. E. E. G., & Deal, T. E. (2013). *Reframing Organizations: Artistry, Choice, and Leadership.* San Francisco, CA: Jossey-Bass.

Busta, H. (2020). *College Fundraisers Brace for Declines in 2020 and 2021. Higher Ed Dive.* Retrieved from https://www.highereddive.com/news/college-fundraisers-brace-for-declines-in-2020-and-2021/579410/

Charles, S., & Dobson, B. (2020, June 9). *Historically Black Colleges Fight for Survival, Reopening Amid Coronavirus Pandemic.* USA Today. Retrieved from https://www.usatoday.com/story/news/education/2020/06/09/coronavirus-hbcu-colleges-fall-semester-2020/5286165002/

Daniels, A. (2020). Foundations under pressure. *The Chronicle of Philanthropy*. Retrieved from https://www.philanthropy.com/article/foundations-under-pressure

EAB Survey Points to Dramatic Decline in University Fundraising. (2020, June 26). EAB. Retrieved from https://eab.com/insights/press-release/advancement/covid-19-fundraising-decline/

Grawe, N.D. (2018). *Demographics and the Demand for Higher Education*. Baltimore, MA: Johns Hopkins University Press.

Hadero, H. (2021, June 15). Americans gave more in 2020 than ever before. KARE11.com. Retrieved from https://www.kare11.com/article/news/nation-world/charitable-giving-all-time-high-us-2020/507-2dc5f8e1-eb53-401f-bb3f-8e791e443d9f

Hilser-Wiles, S. (2020). 4 ways to ENGAGE major donors during the Covid-19 Crisis. *The Chronicle of Philanthropy*. Retrieved from https://www.philanthropy.com/article/4-ways-to-engage-major-donors-during-the-covid-19-crisis/

June, A. W. (2021, February 25). College endowment spending rose and returns fell as the pandemic set in. *The Chronicle of Higher Education*. Retrieved from https://www.chronicle.com/article/college-endowment-spending-rose-and-returns-fell-as-the-pandemic-set-in?cid=gen_sign_in

Kauffman, P. (2021, May 4). Help for college sports during covid-19. *GoFundMe*. Retrieved from https://www.gofundme.com/c/blog/help-college-sports-during-covid-19

Killen, E.T. (2020, December 20). Special tax deductions available this year for cash donations to charities; IRS works to raise awareness. *Internal Revenue Service*. Retrieved from https://www.irs.gov/about-irs/special-tax-deductions-available-this-year-for-cash-donations-to-charities-irs-works-to-raise-awareness

McGee, J. (2015). *Breakpoint: The Changing Marketplace for Higher Education*. Baltimore, MA: Johns Hopkins University Press.

Massachusetts Institute of Technology (2017, August 16). Endowment spending: Goals, rates, and rules. *Forum for the Future of Higher Education | A Community of Academic Leaders and Scholars Who Explore New Thinking and Ideas in Higher Education*. Retrieved from http://forum.mit.edu/articles/endowment-spending-goals-rates-and-rules/

National Association of College and University Business Officers (2020a, April 10). *What Does the Recent Market Downturn Mean for College Endowments?* Retrieved from https://www.nacubo.org/Topics/Risk%20Management%20and%20Campus%20Security/Emergency%20Preparedness/Coronavirus%20Relief%20Advocacy/Endowments

National Association of College and University Business Officer (2020b, June 12) *COVID-19 endowment impacts and Stewardship Strategies*. Retrieved from https://www.nacubo.org/Research/2020/COVID-19-Research/Q1-2020-Endowment-Survey

Orem, D. (2019, June 18). *5 Trends Driving the Future of Philanthropy*. National Association of Independent Schools. Retrieved from https://www.nais.org/learn/independent-ideas/june-2019/5-trends-driving-the-future-of-philanthropy/

Stiffman, E. (2020, November 19). Planned-gift donors are pledging bigger gifts during the pandemic. *The Chronicle of Philanthropy*. Retrieved from https://www.philanthropy.com/article/planned-gift-donors-are-pledging-bigger-gifts-during-the-pandemic-new-report-says

Taylor, M. (2020, May 21). College and university Presidents respond to COVID-19: May 2020 Survey. *Research & Insights*. Retrieved from https://www.acenet.edu/Research-Insights/Pages/Senior-Leaders/College-and-University-Presidents-Respond-to-COVID-19-May-2020.aspx

US Department of Education. (n.d.). *The NCES Fast Facts Tool Provides Quick Answers to Many Education QUESTIONS (National Center for EDUCATION STATISTICS)*. National Center for Education Statistics (NCES). Retrieved from https://nces.ed.gov/fastfacts/display.asp?id=73

Whitford, E. (2021, February 23). Pandemic forces college fundraisers to abandon tried-and-true strategies, go digital. *Inside Higher Ed*. Retrieved from https://www.insidehighered.com/news/2021/02/23/pandemic-forces-college-fundraisers-abandon-tried-and-true-strategies-go-digital

Chapter 13

Moving the Institution Forward

Contingency Planning in Extreme Unpredictability

Suzanne Wilson Summers and Gabriela Cornejo Weaver

"College" in the popular imagination often presumes a residential campus experience and many aspects of campus life beyond academic programs, begging the question of the value balance between a "college education" and a "college experience." This calculation varies widely depending on the needs of students, as well as on institutional mission and sector. Institutions that have built their brand (and their budget) around "the experience" in addition to "the education" faced a distinct conundrum once the pandemic shutdowns occurred and the value of the college experience they could provide was diminished in the shift to remote learning. As they looked toward planning for the fall semester, they faced increasing pressure to recreate as much of their face-to-face experience as possible in order to retain students. It became clear over the course of the late spring and early summer that the crisis was not abating, and most IHEs recognized that a return to "normal" operations was increasingly unlikely. The question became: how much of the college experience could be safely recreated under COVID-19 conditions? While institutional leaders may have had their own ideas about this, so did students, parents, faculty, and staff. Balancing the needs and desires of these groups represented the greatest challenge presidents and chancellors faced as they looked toward fall.

By late spring, as IHEs began contingency planning for the fall, campus leaders conducted environmental scans; assessed and mobilized institutional resources, both human and financial; and sought to provide operational transparency and reassurance to students and employees while acknowledging the reality of an uncertain future. Many institutions had experience with at least some level of emergency planning, but both the length and the deadliness of the COVID-19 pandemic went far beyond the normal challenges of planning efforts. IHEs confronted the need to formulate plans that addressed a range of issues from technology access to mental health concerns, and they did so in a looming economic downturn with declining revenues.

As institutions engaged in future planning, the importance of leadership never seemed clearer. As a pair of contemporary observers noted in an opinion piece in the summer of 2020, "So much of what will happen in the next weeks and months will turn on how academic leaders make choices and the ways in which they recognize and adapt long-standing but no longer effective behaviors and habits. The very desire for a return to normalcy may result in choices that prove to be counterproductive to supporting the life and vitality of the academic environment leaders wish to preserve" (Burbules & Gunsalus, 2020).

If, as some have argued, definitions of "crisis" are co-created by stakeholders, consensus about appropriate directions for contingency planning often rests on a shifting mix of institutional mission, culture, history, and stakeholder trust (Gigliotti, 2019). Skillful leaders looked through this period to marshal the support of critical stakeholders, on and off campus, to ensure that decisions could be implemented and would have needed support. The ability to mobilize support for options proposed through planning often rested as much on these intangibles as on more obvious factors, such as budgets. This is where previous institutional culture and trust building made a tremendous difference. *How* IHEs approached planning likely mirrored pre-existing practices, but also needed to reflect the current campus climate. Was that approach going to be collaborative and distributed or top-down? In a prolonged crisis that touched every corner of institutional practice and every stakeholder group in different ways, leaders needed to garner the support of campus constituencies by incorporating and expanding collaborative planning practices and transparent communications. They needed to do this even as faculty, staff, and students reported increasing levels of stress, anxiety, anger, and grief. In a study commissioned by the *Chronicle of Higher Education*, faculty in a variety of sectors representing tenured, tenure track, contingent, and non-tenure track ranks were asked how they would feel if they were required to return to the classroom in the fall semester. Two-thirds "responded that they would be 'very' or 'somewhat' concerned. When broken down by gender, 72 percent of women professors over all [sic], compared with 65 percent of men, replied that way" (Chronicle of Higher Education, 2020, p. 21). Given these concerns, the use of a primarily top-down approach to planning for the fall semester, while offering efficiency, could fracture the campus community as institutions sought to accommodate the reality that COVID-19 would not be a short-term crisis.

INCORPORATING EQUITY CONCERNS INTO PLANNING

Institutional leaders engaged in fall planning in the context of an unfolding racial justice movement across the US and a growing awareness of the disparate equity challenges faced by different employee and student populations. As anger over the racialized health impacts of COVID-19 and police violence against Black Americans exploded in the summer of 2020 and spilled into college campuses, institutional leaders faced calls from their campus communities to address issues of racial profiling and harassment and to do more to respond to the impact of the pandemic on students of color, first-generation students, as well as on women students and employees. The closure of K-12 schools and nursing homes disproportionately burdened women students and employees who bore the majority of parenting and eldercare responsibilities (NASEM, 2021). As leaders and planners looked ahead, they sought to balance concerns about financial and operational sustainability with a growing awareness of the need to ensure more equitable outcomes for students and employees and often explicitly referenced equity and inclusion concerns in their communications around future planning. President Michael Sorrell of Paul Quinn College, an HBCU urban work college that serves a majority Black student body from lower-income backgrounds, announced that it was "too dangerous at this time to allow on-campus living, instruction, and engagement" for the populations they served (Justin, 2020). Not only did the campus opt to continue remote instruction in the fall, they also made the difficult financial calculation to reduce tuition by more than $2,000 and to provide WiFi hotspots and laptops to every student who needed one. Paul Quinn also "joined a historically Black college and university esports network to replace canceled fall sports" (Justin, 2020), thus working to provide alternate and safer means to offer college experiences beyond remote learning.

FROM SHORT-TERM RESPONSE TO LONGER-TERM PLANNING: SCENARIO PLANNING FOR FY21 AND BEYOND

By late spring, with no cure for COVID-19 in sight, institutions' planning timeframes began to lengthen. Whereas in February and March 2020, institutional leaders envisioned a short-term emergency and only expected their decisions to have a shelf life of a few weeks, by April it was becoming clear that the pandemic would disrupt the rest of the spring term and quite likely beyond. As spring gave way to summer, not only did institutions need to begin planning for a longer-term crisis, but in some cases, prior plans for purchasing commitments or space allocation needed to be rolled back, sometimes at a cost. The many unknowns made the exploration of operating scenarios a crucial process. Unknowns included the question of how long COVID-19 might continue to spread, where, and at what rate. Would there be effective treatment and prevention eventually? What financial impact would the pandemic have on institutional resources, including state and government sources? Scenario analyses sought possible answers to the question, "What might the summer and fall terms look like?" While scenarios needed to address familiar concerns, they also necessitated the inclusion of variables outside the control of the institution, such as new impacts on enrollments, health guidelines imposed by policymakers, technological limitations, and the availability of visas and travel.

By the end of the spring 2020 semester, a mix of issues shaped planning for fall. These included a growing awareness of student and employee mental health issues and stress, institutional mission, financial stability, and the composition of the student body. In addition, political pressures shaped the internal planning discussions of many IHEs. CEOs and senior teams debated how to weigh these factors and make the best decisions for their institutions and campus communities.

A May 2020 report revealed that while a majority of recent high school graduates who had intended to go to college for the fall semester remained committed to doing so, some were likely to change this decision if COVID-19 forced IHEs to pivot again to remote instruction (McKinsey & Co, 2020). Students would be more likely to enroll in IHEs that were close to home and would become price sensitive when it came to the amount of tuition they were willing to pay for a remote experience. Many leaders sought to respond to student demand for in-person instruction and worries about lost revenues should they remain closed for the fall by delaying a decision with the hope that they would be able to reopen fully for the coming academic year.

Not all followed this path. As early as May, the entire 23-campus California State University (CSU) system indicated that they would remain remote, basing their decisions on their assessment that COVID-19, which continued to rage across the US, would be unlikely to subside by fall. Most community colleges—whose student body included a high percentage of Black, Indigenous, and People of Color (BIPOC) and low-income students—similarly made the early call to remain virtual. Leadership teams everywhere weighed the health risks with the need for stability and maintaining trust with both students and employees, while coming to very different decisions about reopening for their institutions (Sorrell, 2020).

While institutional and system leaders bore ultimate responsibility for the reopening decisions, they consulted peers formally and informally to share planning considerations. Higher education associations played an important role throughout the pandemic in convening regular meetings of presidents, CAOs, and other key figures to allow opportunities to share approaches taken, insights gleaned, and lessons learned across institutions. These meetings allowed individual institutions to leverage the collective knowledge and experience base of the group. They also provided opportunities for leaders to share their struggles and successes in ways they might not feel comfortable doing within their home institutions.

In varying ways, institutions needed to consider how to develop or shift strategic plans to accommodate new and unknown public health realities; cultivate new sources of enrollment; develop distance learning and hybrid curriculum sharing programs; and implement mitigation strategies to keep their campus and, in many cases, larger communities safe. At the same time, leaders everywhere confronted employee burnout simultaneously with the need to realign programs and repurpose employees while working to improve the racial climate on campus. As COVID-19 infections rose across the US in the summer of 2020, faculty and staff at institutions that publicly declared their intention to reopen in fall led the criticism of these institutional decisions, believing that they indicated a lack of care for students, employees, and the surrounding communities (Redden, 2020). Trust, the critical variable as institutions planned for an unknown future, was tested and strained at many institutions.

Budgetary Considerations

By May, the financial impact of the pandemic hit many institutions hard. In many states, declining tax revenues due to the shutdown of many businesses curtailed state revenues which, in turn, posed the threat of reduced appropriations to public IHEs. For those IHEs that had already faced shaky futures before the pandemic due to demographic changes and subsequent declines in enrollment, the disruptions the COVID-19 brought raised an existential threat. For some, long-term survival would depend on restructuring or merging due to the financial impact of the pandemic and, in the near term, institutions needed to figure out which planned changes were still possible. Some IHEs began the process of eliminating low-demand programs and faculty positions, often igniting campus opposition from those who complained that the pandemic had created political cover for institutional leaders to do what they had already wanted to do.

For residential institutions whose mission centered in-person instruction, the potential losses in auxiliary revenues from housing and dining fees, not to mention the reluctance of parents and students to pay the same tuition for online instruction as they paid for face-to-face, had those schools holding out hope for some form of face-to-face instruction with concomitant resumption of campus life. They had to plan both physically and fiscally where operations and auxiliaries were concerned and find a balance between maintaining a safe environment and having the financial and material resources to enable the execution of that plan.

From a financial standpoint, budget scenario planning was affected primarily through lost revenue, alleviating expenses, and new expenses for the institution. Alleviated expenses included items such as refunding a portion of student aid or employee benefits from a decline in research activity while research facilities were closed. The variables potentially affecting revenues included: reduced enrollments resulting in both tuition and auxiliaries losses; the inability to use funds from sponsored research; lost income from the cancellation of conferences, programs or events; and possible reduced returns on institutional investments due to steep drops in interest rates (for example, see JHU, 2020). These calculations indicated that some institutions would have a shortfall of as little as

5 percent of their normal operating budget—for institutions beginning on a good financial and looking at a "best case" scenario—to as much as 40 percent of their operating budget, particularly for smaller institutions that were already on shaky financial ground or for large institutions with a high dependency on foreign students and/or income from their campus hospital[1] (Whitford, 2020).

As institutions struggled with maintaining enrollments and the added costs of campus closures, extreme market volatility negatively affected endowments (See Chapter 12). Nevertheless, internal and external stakeholders questioned why institutions did not dip into their endowments to help cover budget shortfalls. The reality is that institutions are often barred either by state statutes or donor agreements from doing so (Whyte, 2020).

Many Historically Black Colleges and Universities (HBCUs), Hispanic Serving Institutions (HSIs), regional comprehensives, and community colleges, which serve more low-income students and depend heavily on tuition revenues, lacked substantial endowments and, therefore, a financial cushion when revenues declined. The leader of one HBCU, Makola Abdullah of Virginia State University, noted that "We are largely tuition-driven, and we are largely dependent on the level of financial aid help that our students can get from their Pell grant, from the state, and from philanthropy. And so it puts us in a slightly different situation in that our level of reserves would be lower" (Grayer et al., 2020).

Institutional Planning Architecture

By 2020, many IHEs already had existing crisis management experience with natural dishem to share leadership and to create asters, active shooters, or previous health crises, such as Ebola and H1N1. The previous fall, for instance, severe wildfires had raged through northern California and Oregon, causing campus closures in the affected areas. Institutions in the Gulf states had likewise experienced extended closures due to hurricanes. Institutions that had experienced such disasters were able to build on existing procedures and lessons learned from previous situations to shape their pandemic planning responses. Although the nature of this crisis, as well as its duration and depth, may have differed from previous crises, such institutional experience proved helpful in navigating the pandemic. Campuses that had not previously needed to activate their emergency plans often had a larger lift to create the communication and planning structures necessary to work their way forward from this period.

The contingency planning processes in 2020 often had a core group responsible for making final decisions—usually people at the highest levels of the administration at the institution—with broader circles of individuals with critical information, and an even wider circle of people beyond those who would be making decisions about implementation details. Commonly, the CEO, CFO, COO, and CAO may have begun to outline broad possibilities, but then pulled in those who were responsible for facilities, human resources, enrollment, IT, auxiliaries, and other affected units. Given the interdependence of these functional units, leaders needed to balance the need for comprehensive information with the need to make decisions on a very fast timeline.

Planning at the Institution Level

With the outbreak and spread of COVID-19 in the US in early spring, many institutions formed *ad hoc* planning structures to examine and act on pertinent data reminiscent of the role of Emergency Operations Centers (EOCs) used for on-campus emergencies, such as a fire, flood or active shooters. In an October 2020 interview with institutional leaders at a large campus of a state system in the western US, for instance, they shared that the university already had continuity plans based on an all-hazards approach that included identifying who would perform critical functions in the case their buildings or the campus were unavailable. Additionally, each critical function owner had created unit-level continuity plans. During the early spring, the existence of these plans allowed them to execute existing emergency response protocols. By late spring, they shifted relatively smoothly into continuity planning for summer and fall.

Sensitivities over political and public reaction to the possibility of continued remote operations called for careful positioning of the planning work being done on campuses (and its messaging, see Chapter 2). For example, the University of Michigan-Flint (UM-Flint) adjusted both the makeup and name of the emergency operations team as fall planning occurred. After restructuring, the team's name was changed to the "Return to Campus" committee. While many institutions chose to call them "re-opening" committees, leadership at UM-Flint wanted to communicate clearly that while operations had temporarily moved off-campus, campus had never completely closed, thus the name.

In some cases, existing structures were inadequate to the scale of the pandemic. For example, one large, private Northeastern university created a new committee in early April that consisted of the CEO, CAO, COO, CFO, Vice Provost for Budget and Planning, Vice President for External Affairs, CIO, and General Counsel. These people normally work together on a regular basis, albeit in other groupings. The configuration of this planning cell provided the CEO with rapid access to the information that would directly influence or be influenced by pandemic-related decision-making. Additionally, people from other teams focused on specific areas—such as online teaching, academics, research, health and student life—supplemented the core team as needed. Meetings took place twice per week for each group, with activity among smaller cohorts occurring constantly via emails, text messages, and telephone calls as needed. Such an approach represented a highly organized, yet flexible, one that allowed senior leaders to respond quickly to changing circumstances.

The direct and wide-ranging impact of this crisis made it imperative that CEOs and senior leaders mobilize campus support from students, faculty, and staff quickly by actively and deliberately engaging them in the planning process. This translated into the need both to create feedback loops from key internal and external stakeholders and to ensure transparency as a planning principle. At Valencia College, whose culture is characterized by a high degree of internal collaboration, an Academic Continuity Committee composed of the CAO and faculty and team leaders planned for the transition to remote learning. Planning for fall was conducted by a "Conditions to Reopen" committee headed by the VP of Organizational Development. Identifying guiding principles for planning and implementation kept the college focused on its core mission: ensuring student learning.

Everywhere, a concern with safeguarding the wellbeing of both students and employees as much as possible informed planning efforts. By late spring 2020, as the pandemic wore on, CEOs identified student and employee mental health concerns as a primary concern. One response was to provide as much certainty about the fall semester as early as possible. For example, Valencia College's faculty indicated that they wanted college leaders to commit to a teaching modality early on and the college decided in summer to go online for fall for the vast majority of classes.

Planning at the System Level

Institutions that were part of a state system were able to draw on expertise and resources unavailable to independent colleges. Campus leaders across systems shared ideas and learning with each other, and systems leaders made resources and information available to individual campuses while working with them to formulate policies. The level of operational autonomy within state systems varied considerably, and one of the key challenges for state systems and component campuses was the coordination of responsibilities and sometimes varying levels of urgency on issues based on statewide versus local campus needs. According to the Chancellor of a campus in one state university system in the Southeast, the challenge for planning was that while the state provided less than 20 percent of the budget, they exercised considerably more oversight. The advantages included their role as an honest broker and the assistance they could provide. For example, systems offices assumed an intermediary role with state and national public health and governmental authorities. In some cases, they negotiated with state and federal authorities to procure additional funding for PPE. At times, however, the necessity to coordinate with system directives slowed individual campuses down when they were ready to take an action, such as canceling commencement, but the system as a whole had not yet caught up in making a collective decision.

A Close-up Lens on Leadership

Contingency Planning within a System: the California State University Example

In the early phase of the pandemic, systems leaders generally set policy while leaving operational responses to individual campuses. For example, when the chancellor of the country's largest university system, California State University (CSU), Tim White announced in mid-May that all 23 CSU campuses would remain almost totally in remote instruction in the fall term, shock rippled across the country in this strong signal that COVID-19 was not a short-term crisis. Within the CSU system, this system-level decision required CSU campus presidents to execute remote operations as part of campus contingency planning that aligned with CSU system directives. The Chancellor's Office (CO) specified what decisions would be undertaken by the system—such as in person vs. virtual overall; approvals required for in-person classes; and housing capacity—but left the remaining decisions to campus leaders. Each campus reported key information in an overall repopulation report that the CSU CO then reviewed and approved before the campus moved forward. The CO served as the gatekeeper for decisions about campus access and usage and ensured an equitable division of resources across campuses. It also gleaned information about employees' needs and views from system-wide affinity groups which it could then communicate to campus leaders, an important function in the early phases of the pandemic.

At CSU-Long Beach (CSULB), the pre-existing EOC managed the contingency planning team. It met weekly and included an Emergency Response team. The latter created a repopulation team composed of different functional areas, that included Academic Programs, HR, Facilities, Police, and Student Conduct. Beginning with an incident management team, others were then added as necessary, including an academic dean and a purchasing manager. To ensure the flow of information to senior leaders, the president's chief of staff was added to liaise with the Executive team.

The challenge of coordinating information flows in the midst of an unfolding crisis created the need for a communications plan. At CSULB, "zip calls" served as unplanned conference calls designed to address emergencies. The Repopulation Committee created key subteams; members from the planning team headed up each subteam and brought information back from those groups. The subteams included student conduct, academic programs, housing, facilities, and others.

Although large institutions and systems generally had emergency planning and response infrastructure, many smaller institutions did not. These IHEs looked for other solutions to share knowledge and experience. For example, one solution to overcome this experience deficit came from leveraging national, regional, and sector-specific association. Like other bodies, the Great Lakes Colleges Association, which consists of 13 small liberal arts colleges, provided forums for sharing information between senior institutional leaders. As colleges planned for fall, members considered how to address logistical challenges based on state-level guidance and the implications of the pandemic on FY2020 budgets and employment, as Mickey McDonald, President of the Great Lakes College Consortium, shared in a September 2020 interview for this study.

CONTINGENCY BUDGETING

By summer 2020, almost every IHE faced increasing budget pressures due to the enrollment and financial costs of the pandemic. While campus leaders created contingency plans for the likelihood of a prolonged crisis, they looked to curtail institutional spending through a series of cost-cutting measures, which varied by institution. For example, some IHEs ceased or curtailed capital projects. Many initiated immediate hiring freezes to reduce current and future expenses related to salaries and benefits for employees. Some campuses halted faculty searches or even rescinded job offers for the upcoming fall terms and discontinued spending on professional development and equipment. Some campuses also announced immediate or planned reductions in contributions to employee retirements. For example, Georgetown University, Johns Hopkins, and Boston University, among others, announced either reductions or temporary suspensions to employer contributions to retirement as a cost savings measure.

One private, research-intensive institution established a budget committee with membership from among key senior leaders as well as finance and legal staff. This group began meeting once or twice weekly beginning in early April, 2020, in order to discuss how different scenarios would affect revenues and expenses, as well as to brainstorm and forecast possible cost-saving measures. For example, they needed to consider various levels of graduate student enrollment for the coming academic year because the impacts of the pandemic on the ability of international students to return to, remain, or work in the US were still unknown. The committee considered scaled scenarios, with 10%, 25%, 50%, etc., of full graduate and undergraduate enrollment. They further looked at the various cost-saving measures they could put in place that would not sacrifice jobs, such as freezing hiring for positions not yet filled. As a final variable, they examined how much they would need to make up by cutting current personnel. These intense discussions continued well into June, being refined as more information became available and putting certain parts of the plan in place as they became appropriate and necessary. Their efforts were ultimately successful in leading the institution through the financial impacts of the pandemic, but it was difficult, careful work that required protracted attention.

Using a Symbolic frame, many IHE leaders sought to convey that these decisions represented short-term, shared sacrifices in a time of national and global crisis. Faculty and staff reception of such messages, however, depended on levels of campus trust as leaders relied heavily on the community they had built before the onset of crisis. Some gave careful thought to ensuring that sacrifices were seen to be shared. For example, a letter by the President of Boston University in April, 2020 indicated that the President and Provost would each take a 20% salary reduction and that the Deans and Vice Presidents would each take 10% salary reductions (Brown, 2020). With respect to salary reductions across faculty and staff, some institutions chose to execute these equally across the board. At others, reductions and furloughs were stratified based on salary levels and positions in order to provide a more equitable approach (Sinek, 2020).

To further reduce costs, some institutions also sought to renegotiate the terms and conditions of existing debt from bond issues. As the University of Michigan (UM), for instance, sought to meet an anticipated budget shortfall of between $400 million to $1 billion across its three campuses, in May 2020, its Board of Trustees decided to issue $1 billion in general revenue bonds to refinance debt and to pay for previously planned construction projects. The proceeds would provide UM a cushion for its general operations budget given the uncertain financial climate created by the pandemic. As security, the university would be supported by a pledge of the university's general revenues from a variety of sources, including athletics, housing, parking, unrestricted gifts, grants, and investment earnings (Marowski, 2020).

Although IHEs across the nation struggled to absorb the costs of the spring shutdown and move to remote instruction, some found that the closure of physical campuses resulted in some operational savings. Valencia College found, for instance, that the closure yielded a substantial reduction in energy expenses. Even so, these savings were swallowed up by the need for emergency student aid, the cost of enhancing technological capacity, such as purchasing laptops and WIFI hotspots for both employees and students, and increased liability insurance premiums.

COVID's Impact on Federal and State Funding

As the costs of the COVID response became clearer in the early pandemic, institutions, many already in precarious financial shape after years of state disinvestment and enrollment declines, worried how they would manage and survive.

Higher education organizations, including the American Council on Education (ACE), lobbied Congress for emergency aid to both public and private IHEs to help them weather the added costs of converting to remote instruction and to provide emergency student aid. Some larger and financially stable institutions began to prepare for the possibility of requests for merger to come from smaller institutions.

In late March, 2020, Congress responded with the Coronavirus Aid, Relief, and Economic Security (CARES) Act (HR 748, 2020), which provided IHEs with $14 billion of aid distributed through the US Department of Education (DoE) in two allotments. Of this amount, $12.5 billion went directly to IHEs based on a formula that favored residential institutions that primarily provided in-person instruction to full-time students. In recognition of their greater institutional and student needs, DoE provided an additional $1.4 billion for HBCUs, HSIs, Tribal Colleges and Universities (TCUs), Asian American and Pacific Islander Serving Institutions, and small institutions primarily serving low-income students. An additional $350 million was earmarked for smaller institutions who were not included in the other allocations, but still demonstrated significant unmet need (Schwartz and Busta, 2020).

The legislation mandated that institutions use at least 50 percent of the total funds they received to provide direct emergency aid to students within one year. Such direct aid could include grants for student food, housing, course materials, technology, healthcare, and childcare (Schneider, 2020). Many institutions had already used their own resources to provide emergency student aid and the cost of moving classes online prior to the passage of the act, but could not use CARES Act funds to reimburse themselves for aid given prior to passage of the law. Facing the likelihood of state cuts and enrollment declines, many institutions expressed through higher education associations under the umbrella of ACE a desire for greater flexibility to keep CARES Act funds in reserve to shore up their financial state (Blum, 2020).

The CARES Act funding formula favored institutions with larger percentages of full-time, low-income students. These restrictions inadvertently penalized IHEs with an access mission, particularly community colleges, or institutions with a high percentage of adult learners, whose students are more likely to attend part-time, online, and are less likely to successfully complete FAFSA. Sixty-five percent of community college students, for instance, are enrolled part-time and are more likely to be nonwhite, low-income and first-generation students than their full-time counterparts. They are also more likely to be working full-time and taking care of family members while enrolled. A *Washington Post* piece estimated that the DoE's guidance would effectively bar 1.5 million students from receiving aid (Douglas-Gabriel, 2020).

A later tranche of funds was intended to help IHEs pay for the move to remote instruction, the purchase of personal protective equipment (PPE), and other instructional and operational expenses. Institutions could not reimburse themselves for other expenses until they had given at least 50 percent of the first allocation as cash grants to students. Moreover, the law required that institutions receiving funds retain current employees to the "maximum extent practicable." The DoE struggled to disperse funds quickly even as its interpretations of the act generated enormous controversy, and this became a source of frustration as IHEs bore the staggering costs of pivoting to remote operations. Slow dispersals hamstrung them as they attempted to plan ahead for summer and fall terms (Redd, 2020).

The CARES Act did allow institutions to choose how to spend the institutional portion, based on local needs. Many colleges recognized the precarious economic conditions that students and their families faced and that meeting these needs would help stabilize enrollments while adhering to institutional missions. At one large community college, which already offered 30 percent of its courses online before the outbreak of COVID-19, this meant dedicating $18 million to direct aid to help students. The leadership team created an internal task force that included internal auditors and financial aid staff to figure out how to identify eligible students and to connect them quickly with funding.

Although almost all IHEs gave high priority to training faculty on remote instruction and ensuring they and staff had access to needed technology, they also had to meet emergency COVID safety requirements. At one state-system institution that we interviewed, much of the $20 million in CARES institutional funds went to replace air filters, install plexiglass dividers, and purchase PPE and COVID tests. The committee composed of the CAO, CFO, the President of the Academic Senate, and representatives from the Academic Senate prioritized the types of spending and put out a call for spending proposals. In an interview for this study, campus leaders shared that composition of this committee meant that those who might have slowed the decision-making process were involved from the beginning, which allowed for rapid implementation.

The CARES Act and other federal funding to higher education proved a critical "cushion" for financially stretched and stressed institutions as they addressed the consequences of the early pandemic wave. As noted above, however, an overly traditional understanding of college students' identities and needs hampered the effectiveness of this support. Higher education advocates sought to rectify this discrepancy by lobbying for additional funding to institutions that primarily served minoritized and low-income students. The highly politicized nature of the Trump administration's DoE also resulted in policy interpretations that limited institutions' ability to aid some student populations, such as Deferred Action for Childhood Arrivals (DACA) recipients, who already had the least access to public assistance to remain enrolled. Many IHEs sought to address the inequities contained within federal policy. For example, some institutions used CARES funds to provide aid to their non-DACA students while raising private donations dedicated to ensuring that their DACA students had the aid they needed to remain enrolled.

For public institutions, the precarious nature of state budgets added to the complexity of scenario planning. Some state legislatures had already completed the regular annual budget development and approval process before campuses shut down in March. Institutions in these states, facing the impact of a worsening economy and declining public revenues, confronted the possibility that states might seek to rescind initial allocations. For example, in Indiana the state budget had been approved in late February before campus shutdowns, but Indiana's commissioner for higher education later warned college and university leaders to prepare for the possibility of state funding cuts (Loughlin, 2020). In late May, the President of Indiana State University alerted trustees to expect state funding reductions. The experience of Indiana public institutions was replicated in other states and CEOs, along with their External or Government Affairs staffs, needed to keep a watchful eye on the shifting policy landscape and to exercise influence when possible.

LESSONS LEARNED

One of the most significant lessons learned from the responses to COVID-19 disruptions in the spring of 2020 was that IHEs needed contingency plans for reopening in the fall that included best- and worst-case scenarios, along with something in between. Many institutions fixated on achieving a "best-case" scenario, which they defined as a return to in-person operations and instruction. This focus spoke to the lingering power and public appeal of traditional models of in-person instruction at many IHEs as representing "the college experience" and to the institutional business models that support them. Not only did contingency plans need to take into account new expenses associated with a mass transition to online instruction (see Chapter 4 on Continuity of the Academic Mission, and Chapter 8 on Information Technology Leadership), but also losses and new expenses associated with students not being housed on campus (Chapter 6), developing and implementing new safety protocols (Chapter 9), and compensating employees who were unable to work (Chapter 10). Informed guesswork was all that IHE leaders could rely on for predicting enrollment impacts for the fall (Chapter 11). Thus, contingency planning benefitted from collaborative approaches to information sharing and analysis. Establishing effective teams that included people with intimate knowledge of different segments of institutional operations was important to developing the hypothetical planning scenarios being explored.

While there was a certain uniformity to the pandemic response of IHEs in the spring 2020—with almost all adopting a remote work and teaching model—the diversity in conditions and institutions across the US made it clear that planning for the fall 2020 term required a more tailored approach. "Safety first" remained the guiding principle, but there was no general consensus on what was considered safe as different municipalities and states advanced different public health directives. The question of "safety for whom?" also arose as campus leaders confronted different concerns from students, parents, faculty, and staff. Each institution needed to plan for its own population of students, its own particular configuration of facilities, as well as its own expected population of faculty, staff, visitors, etc. The need to plan ahead for the fall semester while facing a slew of unknowns taxed the capabilities of institutions and their leaders everywhere. Many of those who succeeded best in navigating this process were those who had previous experience with such planning—either due to dealing with prior crises or due to robust emergency operations planning already in place—and who were able to empower talented teams of people to invest in collaborative decision making and implementation.

While leaders confronted budgetary, personnel, and operational concerns, the need to monitor and respond to the campus climate assumed greater importance as the pandemic wore on and both students and employees faced not only physical, but also increased mental, emotional, and financial stressors. Leadership in this context required planning for an unknown future while ensuring transparent communications with anxious students and employees; monitoring the federal and state policy and budgetary environment; and considering how local policy decisions and planning would affect disparate constituencies. If this crisis made anything clear, it was that a "one-size-fits-all" approach to equity left many behind as it became clearer that campus groups experienced the pandemic very differently (Haley, 2020).

As the COVID-19 pandemic entered the summer and institutions prepared for fall, senior leaders began to reckon with the increasing likelihood that it would be a longer-term crisis than anyone could have imagined in March. Leaders had to sustain themselves and each other. Many did so by drawing on their own personal networks, as well as sectoral and national higher education associations to engage in knowledge sharing. These connections not only allowed leaders to learn from each other, but also helped to normalize the experiences of individual campuses and institutional leaders. Building such communities of support when faced every day with existential and unknown challenges may have been one of the most critical things that leaders learned to do through this period.

NOTE

1 Hospital incomes were adversely affected across the country as non-COVID and non-urgent services were largely canceled/postponed and fewer people were willing to go to hospitals for services.

REFERENCES

Blum, J. (2020, April 22). *Clearing the Path to Stability*. Congress and the Education Department must correct unintended consequences from the CARES Act (opinion). Retrieved September 25, 2021. Retrieved from https://www.insidehighered.com/views/2020/04/22/congress-and-education-department-must-correct-unintended-consequences-cares-act

Brown, R. A. (2020, April 17). *Message from President Brown: Budget Contingencies*. Boston University, Office of the President, Letters. Retrieved from https://www.bu.edu/president/message-from-president-brown-budget-contingencies/

Burbules, N. C. and Gunsalus, C. K. (2020, August 14). *Dealing with the Now*. Inside Higher Ed. Retrieved from https://www.insidehighered.com/advice/2020/08/14/what-happens-next-week-will-turn-how-academic-leaders-make-choices-and-change-no

Chronicle of Higher Education. (2020). *On the Verge of Burnout: Covid-19's Impact on Faculty Well-Being and Career Plans*. Chronicle of Higher Education. Retrieved from https://connect.chronicle.com/rs/931-EKA-218/images/Covid%26FacultyCareerPaths_Fidelity_ResearchBrief_v3%20%281%29.pdf.

HR748 – 116th Congress (2019–2020): CARES Act. (2020, March 27). Retrieved from https://www.congress.gov/bill/116th-congress/house-bill/748

Douglas-Gabriel, D. (2020, April 22). *More Than a Million College Students Will Be Shut Out of Emergency Grant Program*. The Washington Post. Retrieved from October 2, 2021, from https://www.washingtonpost.com/education/2020/04/21/more-than-million-college-students-will-be-shut-out-emergency-grant-program

Gigliotti, R. A. (2019). *Crisis Leadership in Higher Education: Theory and Practice*. New Brunswick, NJ: Rutgers University Press.

Grayer, A., Jarrett L., and Pomrenze, Y. (2020, May 18). *HBCUs Doubly Hurt by Campus Shutdowns in Coronavirus Pandemic*. The Philadelphia Tribune. Retrieved from https://www.phillytrib.com/news/health/coronavirus/hbcus-doubly-hurt-by-campus-shutdowns-in-coronavirus-pandemic/article_e75e32d2-139a-5bcd-bbcc-b0347b2a4b71.html?utm_source=Sailthru&utm_medium=email&utm_campaign=Issue:%202020-05-21%20Higher%20Ed%20Education%20Dive%20Newsletter%20%5Bissue:27454%5D&utm_term=Education%20Dive:%20Higher%20Ed

Haley, E. D. (2020, June 9). *We Are Not in the Same Boat*. Inside Higher Education. Retrieved from https://www.insidehighered.com/blogs/gradhacker/we-are-not-same-boat

Johns Hopkins University (JHU). (2020, April 21). *A Message From Johns Hopkins University President Ronald J. Daniels: April Update on Financial Implications + Planning*. Johns Hopkins University Coronavirus Information. Retrieved from https://covidinfo.jhu.edu/financial-implications-and-planning/april-update-on-financial-implications-planning/

Justin, R. (2020, July 9). *Free Laptops, Esports and Tuition Cuts: How One Dallas College is Pivoting During the Pandemic*. The Texas Tribune. Retrieved from https://www.texastribune.org/2020/07/09/paul-quinn-college-texas-coronavirus/

Loughlin, S. (2020, May 22). *Pandemic Throws Higher Ed Funding into Uncharted Waters*. Tribune-Star. Retrieved from https://www.tribstar.com/news/local_news/pandemic-throws-higher-ed-funding-into-uncharted-waters/article_ab7eaf52-0549-5422-ad39-f946fc71ece0.html

Marowski, S. (2020, June 16). *University of Michigan Sells Nearly $1B in Bonds Due to Uncertainty of Coronavirus*. mlive. Retrieved from https://www.mlive.com/news/ann-arbor/2020/06/university-of-michigan-sells-nearly-1b-in-bonds-due-to-uncertainty-of-coronavirus.html?utm_source=Iterable&utm_medium=email&utm_campaign=campaign_1293100&cid=db&source=ams&sourceId=4805458

McKinsey & Co. (2020, May 21). *The Pandemic has Worsened Equity Gaps in Higher Education and Work*. Insider Higher Education. Retrieved from https://www.insidehighered.com/news/2020/06/17/pandemic-has-worsened-equity-gaps-higher-education-and-work

National Academies of Sciences, Engineering, and Medicine (NASEM). 2021. *The Impact of COVID-19 on the Careers of Women in Academic Sciences, Engineering, and Medicine*. Washington, DC: The National Academies Press. https://doi.org/10.17226/26061

Redd, K. (2020, May 11). *Flash Poll Results: CARES Act Emergency Aid for Students*. NACUBO. Retrieved from https://www.nacubo.org/Research/2021/COVID-19-Research/May-5-Flash-Poll

Redden, E. (2020, August 18). *Higher Ed's Moment of Truth*. Inside Higher Education. Retrieved from https://www.insidehighered.com/news/2020/08/18/after-spring-and-summer-planning-higher-ed-faces-its-moment-truth

Schneider, M. (2020, April 20). *ED Issues Guidance ON Coronavirus Stimulus Funds for EMERGENCY Grant Aid*. NACUBO. Retrieved from https://www.nacubo.org/News/2020/4/ED-Issues-Guidance-on-Coronavirus-Stimulus-Funds-for-Emergency-Grant-Aid

Schwartz, N. and Busta, H. (2020, March 25). *Daily Roundup: Other News From Around Higher Ed*. Higher Ed Dive. Retrieved from https://www.educationdive.com/news/tracking-how-the-coronavirus-is-impacting-colleges/574858

Sinek, Q. (2020, April 17). *UA President Robbins ANNOUNCES EMPLOYEE Furlough, Budget Cuts in Email*. The Daily Wildcat. Retrieved from https://www.wildcat.arizona.edu/article/2020/04/n-covid-robbins-email

Sorrell, M. J. (2020, May). *Colleges are Deluding Themselves*. The Atlantic. Retrieved from https://www.theatlantic.com/ideas/archive/2020/05/colleges-that-reopen-are-making-a-big-mistake/611485

Whitford, E. (2020, April 27). *'Just No Comparison' for Pandemic's Financial Shock*. Insider Higher Education. Retrieved from https://www.insidehighered.com/news/2020/04/27/colleges-rev-cuts-pandemic-related-costs-keep-mounting

Whyte, A. (2020, March 27). *Universities Were 'Not Prepared' for this Crisis*. Institutional Investor. Retrieved from https://www.google.com/url?q=https://www.institutionalinvestor.com/article/b1kybhrtgmnzc8/Universities-Were-Not-Prepared-For-This-Crisis&sa=D&ust=1592574057660000&usg=AFQjCNH4eEuYyusTrF9grUSbYojKWENjLQ

Chapter 14

Reflections on Leadership through Crisis

Gabriela Cornejo Weaver, Suzanne Wilson Summers, Kara M. Rabbitt, and Rhonda Phillips

THE LESSONS SHARED

The organization of the previous chapters may give the impression that each functional unit in IHEs operated independently in its response to the pandemic during spring 2020. This is far from the truth, and certainly not what we observed. For the purpose of simplifying the narrative, it was useful to capture the information in these seemingly siloed themes. Each chapter, however, reveals the connections between functional areas. In addition, each chapter provides a set of lessons learned that emerged from the specific functional responsibilities. Mirroring the chapters themselves, these lessons cross the boundaries of the functional units they are describing. Taken as a whole, a number of important lessons emerge around leadership from the collection of chapters.

1. Leadership decisions proved most effective when teams shared information and collaboratively made and implemented decisions. To develop a full understanding and awareness of the challenges and their impacts across the institution and its stakeholders, leaders needed to ensure communication flows between middle-level managers and upper administration, as well as across functional units. (Chapters 2, 3, 4, 5, 6, 7, 8, 9, 12, 13)
2. Institutions and their leaders need to address issues of equity in its many dimensions and to work to correct disparities of access to opportunities and/or resources. The pandemic raised new awareness of these issues, even as it exacerbated existing inequities. It is important for leaders at all levels to understand the members of their communities as "whole" individuals with intersectional identities. (Chapters 2, 3, 4, 5, 6, 8, 10, 11, 13)
3. The pandemic response led to new modes of working, teaching, meeting, and providing services that challenged perceptions of what was possible even as they raised equity concerns. It became clear that these new approaches provide benefits such as the ability to serve that had

not been predicted before. Some of these changes will remain as part of the post-pandemic "normal," and deliberate planning to support those enduring changes will be beneficial for institutions. (Chapters 3, 4, 5, 6, 8, 10, 12)
4. The institution, and its success, are all about the people and the relationships among them. Communities came together in this time of crisis; they helped create and implement solutions. Centering people in leadership decisions and actions is critical. Yet leaders must think beyond roles to understand the experiences and needs of differing groups within their campuses. (Chapters 4, 7, 9, 10, 13)
5. The shared and traumatic impact of the pandemic reminded everyone of the importance of treating others with compassion. This had consequences for everything from communication strategies, to work scheduling policies, to decisions about job cuts. (Chapters 2, 4, 8, 10)
6. Institutions that had previously engaged in extensive planning and coordination efforts were in a better position to pivot and make difficult decisions when faced with the pandemic. In many cases, institutions need to engage in planning for multiple scenarios as they move into a future where crises are likely to accelerate. This will require developing the capacity to scan the environment for emerging trends and potential crises and to create and test planning protocols long before they are needed. (Chapters 5, 8, 9, 13)
7. Successful leaders were those who had the ability to be visible, adaptive, empathetic, and creative, and who empowered others in their community to also think and act creatively to solve problems. (Chapters 7, 11, 12)
8. Communication was the glue that held together successful pandemic response efforts. This refers not only to communication from a leader out to community members, but also communication across leadership teams and across functional units. Equally important, successful leaders recognized the importance of listening to students, faculty, staff, and others. To be most effective, communications need to occur on a regular cadence. Leaders should demonstrate a willingness to be transparent, including when only partial information is available, and to correct mistakes in communications when those happen. (Chapters 2, 7, 9)
9. The most successful leadership teams made decisions that were guided by core principles: mission, care for all members of the campus community, safety first. The duty of care was central even as institutions wrestled with how to provide the care individuals needed. (Chapters 4, 8, 13)
10. Trust is key. Developing and maintaining trust is tied to items listed above: compassion, communication, collaborative decision-making, awareness of the needs and context of individuals. (Chapters 4, 9, 10)

Returning to and Reexamining the Frames of Leadership

The genesis of this study was the opportunity to observe and learn from leaders as they faced the greatest challenge of their professional lives. The insights shared with us by leaders in higher education institutions across the country helped the editors, authors, and other members of our cohort of ACE Fellows to return to our home institutions or to move on to new roles better prepared to face the changes ahead and with a deeper appreciation of leadership and of the centrality of equity considerations. At the beginning of this book, we pointed to the four frames of leadership outlined by Bolman and Deal (2013): Structural, Human Resource, Political, and Symbolic. Several of the authors of chapters throughout this work found these frames to be useful in considering the decision-making and actions of leadership teams through the early pandemic. In the lessons highlighted throughout these chapters, we note that these frames can also apply to the equity considerations IHEs faced during this period.

Even as institutions across the US confronted the immediate and all-encompassing challenges of responding to a global pandemic, awareness grew quickly regarding the disproportionate and inequitable effects experienced by different student and employee populations. The pandemic heightened and amplified a growing understanding of inequities in higher education. In myriad ways reaching well back into the twentieth century, colleges and universities have implemented programs and initiatives that sought to expand college access and completion rates. The COVID-19 crisis, as discussed throughout this book, threatened to undo years of halting and partial progress in this work for access, equity, diversity, and inclusion. In the first months of the COVID-generated campus shutdowns, institutions, foundations, and state and federal governments recognized this threat and focused on addressing these uneven impacts with new levels of emergency student and institutional aid. If the pandemic affected every area of higher education, addressing the inequities it created for students and the related threat to institutions of losing students enrollment became a unifying theme of the early response. It also highlighted the need for "Equity-minded leaders [who] pay attention to patterns of inequity in student outcomes by different social identities like race, class, gender and gender identity, sexual orientation, and religion, and the systemic, historical, and political nature of such inequities [and who] work to promote awareness and understanding of inequities, dismantle discriminatory policies, and create institutional changes that promote more just and equitable outcomes for students" (Kezar et al., 2021). Over time, the pandemic's differential impacts on faculty and staff would also emerge.

If we consider leadership through the equity lens that this period brought into sharp focus, all four frames in which leaders can operate to bring about organizational change appear to align. The Structural frame demands that we reexamine the institutional systems, policies, and practices that might perpetuate inequities. The Human Resource frame invites us to focus on the people that make up our campus communities—students, faculty, staff, and administrators—and the increasingly visible realities of their complex lives. The Political frame requires us to navigate the competing agendas at play within our communities and in relation to their larger contexts. And the Symbolic frame reminds us to recall our mission and to value the stories that make its purpose clear. Leaders wishing to effect inclusive organizational change with equitable outcomes will need to draw upon all of these tools to engage campus stakeholders in collectively building a path forward. In the words of Adriana Kezar and associates, they need to create "shared leadership," exemplified by "a greater number of individuals taking on leadership roles than in traditional models" and a greater flexibility of roles that allows "individuals with the expertise and skills needed for solving the problem at hand [to] lead." The result, as we witnessed and heard from many leaders during the early pandemic, is that "multiple perspectives and expertise are capitalized on for problem solving, innovation, and change" (Kezar et al., 2021). If the metaphorical "table" is where and how decisions are made, this period taught many in formal leadership roles that we need to grow the table and better assure that its space is inclusive so that we ensure our responses to crises encompass the lived experiences of our entire campus communities (McNair et al., 2020).

The model that Kezar and her associates have created for such collaborative work is "shared equity leadership." Leadership in this model involves more than formal positional authority and may be informal and distributed:

> The shared equity leadership approach has three main elements: (1) individuals who have undergone some sort of personal journey toward critical consciousness or built a critical consciousness, cementing their commitment to equity; (2) values that are shared among members of the leadership team or group; and (3) a set of practices that leaders continually enact which both enable them to share leadership and to create more just and equitable conditions on their campuses.
>
> (Kezar et al., 2021, p. 6)

If IHEs have made well-intentioned public commitments to DEI over the years, yet often failed to see substantial gains in student success measures, the early pandemic brought these discrepancies into stark relief and required most of the leaders we interviewed to question the assumptions behind long-standing practices. This shared equity model (Kezar et al., 2021) would argue that there can be no hope for substantive change without both formal and informal leaders undertaking the personal work of equity transformation. Only then can institutions engage in the creation of collective equity-minded values, followed by specific and effective practices. If a critical function of senior leadership is conceived of as creating the environment for DEI work to happen, these leaders must do their own personal work and invite the campus community to engage with them. The symbolic and substantive importance of presidents and other senior leaders engaging in this work with vulnerability and transparency alongside other campus members cannot be overestimated. Equity work cannot be delegated.

The efforts of institutional leaders, faculty, and staff to meet student needs in the early months of the pandemic were genuinely inspirational. Growing research on student homelessness and food insecurity over the past decade had given us an understanding of the precariousness of the lives of many in our community and of the impacts of these basic needs on students' ability to advance their educational goals. Many institutions had already expanded student support services significantly. Even so, conversations with institutional leaders in April and May 2020 often revealed a sense of shock at the scale and scope of these problems as the pandemic progressed. Many IHEs gained a deeper qualitative and quantitative understanding of who their students are and of the kinds of challenges they face not only in the midst of the crisis, but even in more "normal" times.

A commitment to putting equity in action involved centering the needs of both students and employees in the pandemic response. IHEs worked extraordinarily hard to do this in the early phase of the pandemic in ways that spanned all four frames of the Bolman and Deal analysis. The structures established to distribute CARES Act monies and emergency student aid to meet students' financial and technological needs and the changes campuses rapidly developed in grading or admissions policies operated within the Structural frame. Examples of institutional leaders, faculty, and staff driving to students' homes to deliver laptops and mobile hotspots so that they could continue their classes online provided a demonstration of care in action to the campus community within a Human Resource frame. So, too, the efforts of managers to attend to the practical and emotional needs of their teams as they navigated the unfamiliar world of remote work. Many campuses also used astute Political framing to navigate furloughs or pay reductions to assure shared sacrifices that could allow a measure of fiscal stability despite acute financial losses. Appeals to donors and alumni to support students through this crisis functioned most frequently within a Symbolic frame—often delivered by campus figureheads or representative students—that recalled the intergenerational connection of the campus identity and of the need to keep the figurative torch lit.

Equity leadership also requires us to speak openly and explicitly regarding the distinct realities impacting different populations (Kezar et al., 2021, 24–25). It was significant on many campuses that discussions with Black students during the racial justice protests of the late spring and early summer of 2020 revealed the overlapping impact of racism with that of the pandemic for many BIPOC faculty and staff members, as well. So substantial was the confluence of these realities that the CDC director would declare racism a public health crisis the following year: "the pandemic illuminated inequities that have existed for generations and revealed for all of America a known, but often unaddressed, epidemic impacting public health: racism" (Walensky, 2021). The measurable increase in hate crimes against Asian Americans in 2020 during the pandemic (Barr, 2021) likewise impacted significant percentages of those on campuses, as students, faculty, and staff of diverse Asian backgrounds experienced increased stress, isolation, and fear in face of random acts of aggression against members of their communities. As a result of the pandemic, for the first time in decades, the numbers of female college students declined in proportion to males on college campuses (NSCRC, 2021), a gendered reality that was also playing itself out in the lives of women, transgender, and non-binary staff and faculty. IHEs needed to confront the systemic inequities that affected different campus populations differently. In times of crisis, an equity leadership model ensures that the needs of a range of groups are identified and engaged with and confronts the disparate truths impacting different members of our communities.

WHAT WE CARRY FORWARD

The unfolding of what has surely been the most disruptive challenge that higher education has ever faced has provided many lessons for all to learn. Forged in fire, building the airplane as you're flying it, steering a ship through a storm—these and many other metaphors have been used to describe leadership through the first critical season of the pandemic. These figurative representations reflect the myriad emotions around the uncertainty and risk of trying to respond to crushing, immediate needs—such as moving all of our classes instantly online—while keeping the boat afloat (i.e., continuing to deliver the things we normally do in campus operations).

As ACE Fellows, the experience of the early pandemic finished out a year of already-transformational education with a level of intensity, loss, and learning that we could not have anticipated at our opening retreat in August 2019. The cohort of 2019–2020 Fellows learned more and more quickly than had, arguably, any other prior cohort. It is perhaps, then, fitting that we end this volume with what our peers—several of whom have since moved into new leadership roles as deans, provosts, or presidents—took away from this time.

To that end, we offer an epilogue with some reflections on the lessons of this "unprecedented" year from the 2019-2020 cohort of ACE Fellows and mentors. The following quotes are in response to this question:

> *What is the single most important lesson you've learned for higher education leadership as a result of this pandemic, and how can this be applied in the future?*

The extended COVID crisis exposed the contradictions between the values institutions profess to prioritize and the ones preeminent in practice. It is important for leaders to be clear-eyed, to know the difference, and to understand the impact of this incongruence on decision-making and the messaging around decisions. In failing to do so, leaders sow the seeds of suspicion and mistrust among the communities the institutions serve.

Eileen R. Carlton Parsons, PhD (Fellow)
Professor Emerita
University of North Carolina at Chapel Hill
Host Institution: Johns Hopkins University
Home Institution: University of North Carolina at Chapel Hill

The most important lesson related to the COVID-19 pandemic has been how crucial trust in science and confidence in the findings of scientific inquiry are to university policy. In this moment of socio-political polarization and distrust of leadership, decisions seem often to reflect political beliefs rather than scholarly research. Universities are in the position of helping to drive society towards reasoned decision-making and public policy based upon trust, research findings, and the willingness to think about community benefit. Other pandemics (especially HIV/AIDS) should have taught us that good public health thinking depends upon solid science and trust in institutions and leadership.

Ronald P. Strauss, DMD, PhD (Mentor)
Executive Vice Provost
Adams Distinguished Professor of Dentistry and Professor of Social Medicine
University of North Carolina at Chapel Hill

I have learned that flexibility is the greatest equalizer of all plans. It must be fully embraced if colleges and universities desire to emerge from the pandemic with an unquestionable commitment to students and the community.

Gary B. Crosby, PhD
President, Saint Elizabeth University
Host Institution: Rutgers University-Newark
Home Institution: Alabama A&M University

There was no playbook for operating under COVID-19 conditions, and many schools made different calls despite having the same information available. What I learned from these differences is that, in any kind of urgent situation, you need to be willing to act without having all of the facts and be willing to be wrong and change course later on as new facts emerge. A key piece of this process is clear communication. You need to chart a course of action even if you know it is going to be unpopular and be willing to go back when the situation changes and admit when the right thing to do is to change course.

Rachael Kipp, PhD
Assistant Provost, Academic Planning and Accreditation
Suffolk University
Host Institution: University of Rhode Island
Home Institution: Suffolk University

The pandemic put a spotlight on structural inequities in the United States, many of which are rooted in our history of racism and classism. As we enter into a post-pandemic reality in higher education, we must think more inclusively and holistically about the students and communities we serve and the underlying issues and challenges they confront in their educational journeys. If we fail to process these sobering lessons, then shame on us.

Jeffrey B. Leak, PhD
Director, American Studies
University of North Carolina–Charlotte
Host Institution: Johnson C. Smith University
Home Institution: University of North Carolina–Charlotte

The quick change from face-to-face teaching was a difficult transition due to the lack of technology and preparedness at my institution. However, the sense of difficulty in accomplishing this change was minor when I realized the lack of capacity in my students' homes in terms of their everyday lives, from owning desktops or laptops to the lack of access to broadband in the rural areas where my students live. ... Many of my decisions, not only about distance learning, are now viewed through a lens that is intentional about weighing accessibility, disparities, inequities, and the consequences of these realities on my students' overall success.

Edward Martinez, PhD
President
Luna Community College
Host Institution: University of Nevada, Reno
Home Institution: New Mexico Highlands University

As a result of leading through this pandemic season, I learned that we (as leaders and as human beings) can achieve things we never thought we could. Remote and online teaching, engaging students and leading online, were things higher education institutions never thought they could achieve, until we had no other choice. This can be applied to the future by applying the skills of believing the impossible and approaching challenges with an open mind. This need to be creative, innovative and flexible in higher education underscored the cliché statement that "nothing is impossible."

Pamela Moolenaar-Wirsiy, PhD, MPA
Dean of Innovation and Student Success
University of the Virgin Islands
Host Institution: Hampton University
Home Institution: Georgia State University—Perimeter College

As the pandemic timeline extends, I become increasingly aware of how the "work–life" distinction has been a convenient myth we have told ourselves. The stressors of our lives impact every aspect of our professional practice as leaders, the service of our faculty and staff, and the success of our students. It is critical to build upon this awareness and extend our attention to holistic support and development of students, faculty, staff, and leaders.

Sharon Nagy, PhD
Associate Provost
Clemson University
Host Institution: New Jersey City University
Home Institution: Clemson University

I think the most important lesson is about effective communication with stakeholders in an environment that is ever-changing. The pandemic highlighted places with ineffective communication systems and structures that were unable to effectively disseminate information and get feedback from constituents on the timescale necessary for it to make a difference. This exacerbated the already stressful and uncertain situation for many faculty, staff, students and parents. Institutions that were nimble with websites for dissemination of information and that mobilized communications teams quickly to coordinate feedback were more successful in building trust and keeping up morale. Putting effective communication structures in place will be important for managing crisis situations in the future.

Elizabeth Orwin, PhD
Dean, School of Engineering and Computer Science
University of the Pacific Host Institution: Caltech
Home Institution: Harvey Mudd College

The most important thing I learned during the pandemic is that an organization's ability to change is largely predicted by the people within the organization and their individual levels of comfort and anxiety regarding change. As a leader you need to anticipate this and set a context that allows for everyone in the organization to adapt.

Jennifer A. Ostergren, PhD, CCC-SLP
Dean, College of Education, Health and Human Services
California State University, San Marcos
Host Institution: Arizona State University
Home Institution: California State University, Long Beach

I have learned the importance of emotional leadership. Applied example: a student who sent me a nasty gram later came up to me on campus and apologized. I said I didn't take it personally and they were relieved. How many times do we/I have to learn this lesson? As campus leaders, we are often recipients of anger, hurt, and anxiety, but it is rarely about us. This has been especially true during the pandemic. While it is challenging to take at times, the people doing it just need somewhere and someone to vent to. And later on, after they have settled down, they may even quietly regret doing it. We can be compassionate towards those we serve without taking on their "stuff." The universe of leadership is deep and wide, but a key element for me these past two years has been about managing emotions—both mine and those of others.

Jay Roberts, PhD
Provost and Dean of the Faculty
Warren Wilson College
Host Institution: Lawrence University
Home Institution: Earlham College

Far and away, decisions need to be made from an informed position quickly and communicated with confidence. This confident communication must include the "next step(s)" once decisional impact is assessed. Do we continue as planned? How do we pivot to "plan B" based on what we discover as "plan A" is faltering? What is the appropriate cadence to our communication? As the maelstrom of change continues to cycle in the future, leaders with a handle on complex issues who are able to clearly relay understandable information to stakeholders build trust in decision-making processes. It's finding the flow of the process based on the culture that needs to be—as in Goldilocks and the Three Bears—just right.

Robert Arthur Schultz, PhD
Associate Dean and Chair of the Faculty
Jesup Scott Honors College, The University of Toledo
Host Institution: The Ohio State University
Home Institution: The University of Toledo

During the pandemic, it became evident that communities of color were facing a dual pandemic (disproportionate impact of COVID-19 and racial violence). Higher education is uniquely positioned to promote the public good; yet we do not have the skills needed to foster racial equity and justice.

Artika Tyner, EdD, MPP, JD
Faculty and Director Center on Race, Leadership and Social Justice
University of St. Thomas, School of Law
Host Institution: Hamline University
Home Institution: University of St. Thomas

As noted, the experiences and lessons learned during the pandemic are influencing not only our leadership, but also our lives. As of this writing, the impact of COVID-19 is far from over for IHEs. This book is proffered to the higher education community we serve to provide insights and information about the many facets of leadership needed in a continuingly challenging environment. Its authors encourage you to reach out and connect with each other, whether via ACE or other networks, to advance our shared goals, to learn from each other, and to help our institutions adapt and thrive in a post-pandemic world.

REFERENCES

Barr, L. (2021, October 25). Hate crimes against Asians rose 76% in 2020 amid pandemic, FBI says. *ABC News*. Retrieved from https://abcnews.go.com/US/hate-crimes-asians-rose-76-2020-amid-pandemic/story?id=80746198

Bolman, L. G., & Deal, T. E. (2013). *Reframing Organizations: Artistry, Choice, &Leadership*. San Francisco, CA: Jossey-Bass.

Kezar, A., Holcombe, E., Vigil, D., & Dizon, J. P. M. (2021). *Shared equity leadership*. Retrieved February 28, 2022, from https://www.acenet.edu/Documents/Shared-Equity-Leadership-Work.pdf

McNair, T. B., Bensimon, E. M., & Malcom-Piqueux, L. (2020). *From Equity Talk to Equity Walk: Expanding Practitioner Knowledge for Racial Justice in Higher Education*. New Jersey: John Wiley & Sons, Inc.

NSCRC. (2021, November 18). *Covid-19: Stay Informed*. National Student Clearinghouse Research Center. Retrieved from https://nscresearchcenter.org/stay-informed/

Walensky, R. P. (2021, April 8). *Media Statement from CDC Director Rochelle P. Walensky, MD, MPH, on racism and health*. Centers for Disease Control and Prevention. Retrieved from https://www.cdc.gov/media/releases/2021/s0408-racism-health.html

Index

Abdullah, Makola 218
academic continuity. *see* continuity, academics
academic research 74–75, 85–88; finances 79–80; leadership 83–84; research operations 75–78; researchers 80–83
ACE Fellowship 2–3
admissions 113; calculus 182–185; closing deal 186–192; flexibility 186; student populations 180–182
advancement units: keeping future in view 195–196; long-term impact calculation 206–212; moving operations 196–200; pre-COVID challenges 196; shifting priorities 200–206
advising 65–66
agencies, government 28–29
agility 133
agility, studying 52–60
alumni engagement 199–200
American Council on Education (ACE) 2, 19, 122, 179, 206, 224
American Immigration Lawyers Association (AILA) 46
analysis paralysis, communication lens 29–30
Asian American and Pacific Islander Serving Institutions 224
assessments 61–64; of faculty 64–65
Association for University and College Counseling Center Directors (AUCCCD) 98
Association of International Education Administrators 35
Association of International Educators (NAFSA) 35
Association of Physical Plant Administrators (APPA) 139

athletics 115–121; admissions 113; Division I sports 107–108; finances 112–113; health/safety impacts 109; impact of COVID-19 on 108–115; institutional image 114–115; institutional standards 110–111; operating without 205; recruiting 114
Auburn University 42
audience analysis, communication lens 30–31

Barr, Damian 1
Black Lives Matter (BLM) 8
Black, Indigenous, and People of Color (BIPOC) 7, 62, 216
boards, communicating with 24
Bobkinski, Mike 111
Boeckenstedt, Jon 182
borders, closing 46–47
Boston University (BU) 93, 142
Bowling Green University 112
budgetary considerations 217–218

California State System 78
California State University (CSU) 56–57, 216
campus: community 26; consequences of running 147–151; decision-making on 83–84; facilities maintenance 151; giving days 197–198; human resources impacts 147–148; informing operations on 87; planning for return to 151–154; student housing refunds 148–149; vacant residence halls 149–150
campus buildings: consequences of running 147–151; securing 144
capital campaigns, refocusing 203
capital projects 51

241

INDEX

CARES Act 130
CARES Act Emergency Financial Aid Grants 43
Carnegie Classification of Institutions of Higher Education 74
Centers for Disease Control (CDC) 21, 36, 111
Chancellor for Research (VCR) 74
Chief Academic Officer (CAO) 74
Chief Executive Officer (CEO) 19–20; boards 24
Chief Information Officer (CIO) 20, 122–123; changing role of 132–134
China, COVID-19 outbreak in 34–36
Chronicle of Higher Education 187
City University of New York (CUNY) 102
Civil Rights Act 179
cleaning 145–146
Clemson University 36–37, 46
Clemson's Graduate School 47
commencement 67–69
communication 20–27; external 27–29; lessons learned from 29–32; new models of 22
community college(s) 3, 7, 9, 52, 60, 67, 74, 91–92, 131, 155, 168, 170, 181–182, 188, 216, 218, 224–225
comprehensive internationalization 34
contingency planning 213–214; budgeting 222–229; incorporating equity concerns 214–215; scenario planning 215–222
continuity of operations plans (COOPs) 140
continuity, academics 51–52; commencement 67–69; impact on faculty 60–64; online teaching format 52–60; summer programming 69–70; supporting student academic success 64–67
continuity, HR 162–166
Coronavirus Aid, Relief, and Economic Security (CARES) Act 224–226
Council of Colleges of Arts & Sciences (CCAS) 56
counseling services 97–101
courses, different types of 55–58
COVID-19, impact of 1–16; academic continuity 51–73; admissions 179–194; advancement units 195; athletics 107–121; China 34–36; communications 19–32; contingency planning 213–229; enrollment 179–194; and equity 7–10; Europe 36–38; financial implications 79–80; human resources 155–175; impacting athletics 108–115; implications on research operations 75–78; information technology 122–138; international programs 33–50; leadership reflections 230–240; operations facilities 138–154; research resilience 74–88; response to 4–7; student services 91–106
crisis communication 20–21; boards 24; emergency response protocols 21–22; new models of 22; social media 22–24; toward not quite "normal," 26–27
crisis leadership 10–11

decision-making 83–84
Deferred Action for Childhood Arrivals (DACA) 225
digital equity 127–128
dining 101–102
disability services 67
disruptions, research 75–77
diversity, equity, and inclusion (DEI) 49; doubling down on 86
Division I sports 107–108
Droegemeier, K. 74
dual credit/enrollment 60

early alerts 65–66
education, historical resilience 41
eligibility effects 113
Emergency Operations Center (EOC) 21, 54, 140
emergency operations plan (EOP) 21, 139
emergency remote instruction (ERI) 70
emergency response team (ERT) 21
emergency response, protocols/players 21–22
employee wellbeing, supporting 165–166
employer of record 42
endowments, managing 207–208
enrollment 179–180; closing deal 186–192; meeting targets 182–185; student populations 180–182
entities, government 28–29
equity 45, 54, 80, 117, 198; addressing 7–10; digital equity 127–128; disparate impacts 62–63; doubling down on 86; incorporating concerns of 214–215; new opportunities for 86; safeguarding essential staff 145–146; staff transitions to remote work 160–162; standardized testing 183–184; student technology 129–131; women 168–170
essential services, reconfiguring distribution of 143–144

INDEX

essential staff, safeguarding 145–146
Europe, spread of COVID-19 into 36–38
events 197
Executive Committee of Tenure for the Common Good 63
external communication 27–29; government 28–29; public dashboard 28; statements 28; websites 28

F1 student visa program 44
facilities, operations: campus buildings 144; cleaning 145–146; communications 141–143; EOP plans/procedures 139–141; essential services 143–144; logistics 143–146; planning principles 138–139; timing 138–143
faculty: changes regarding assessing 63–64; impact on 60–64; mobility 41–43; preparing for remote instruction 55–58; reappointment calendars 64; tenure clocks 64
faith 100–101
Fall 2020, preparing for 164–165
fall. *see* programs, cancelling
federal funding 223–226
Federal Opening Up America Again 110
federal policy 161–162
flexibility, admissions process 186
food pantries 101–102
Forum for Education Abroad 35
frequently asked question (FAQ) 22
future, keeping in view 195–196

gala costs 199
Giordano, Chris 99
Global Level 4 Travel Advisory 37
global mobility 33–34; beyond student mobility 41–43; international students 43–44; preparations 34–36; program cancellations 40–41; recalls 36–38
graduate programs 190
Green Cards 46

happy hours 27
health centers 97–98
health services 97–101
HEMHA Guide to College Counseling at a Distance 98
hero storis 204
high density, high contact, sports 112
higher education: and internationalization 33–34; responding to COVID-19 4–7
Hillels of Georgia 100

Hispanic Serving Institutions (HSIs) 218
Historically Black Colleges and Universities (HBCUs) 218
housing 91–93; communication 94; consolidation 93–94; expectations 93; housing-related timeline 96; residence life challenges 95
HR operations, transitioning: early phase 156–158; equity concerns 160–161; federal policy 161–161; remote work becoming norm 158–159; state policy 161–162; subcontractors 159–160; vendors 159–160
Human Resource frame, crisis communication 20–21
Human Resources (HR) 147–148, 155; continuity 162–166; long-term impacts to 166–172; transitioning operations 156–162

incentives, rethinking 87
Information Technology (IT) 122–123, 135–136; access 127–128; connectivity 127–128; infrastructure 123–125; issues for consideration 125; network systems 123–125; security concerns 126–127; strategic leadership lessons 131–132; student technology/access 129–131; supporting teaching effectiveness 128–129
infrastructure 123–125
Inspires and Motivates People to Achieve in College Together (IMPACT) 67
institute of higher education (IHE) 33
Institute of International Education (IIE) 35
institution of higher education (IHE) 1, 19, 33, 51, 155; continuity 51–73; and equity 7–10; international programs of 34–50
institutional level, planning at 219–220
institutional planning architecture 218–219
institutional review boards (IRB) 75
institutional standards 110–111
institutions of higher education (IHE) 107
integration 48
International Council of Fine Arts Deans (ICFAD) 56
international recruitment, risks of 49
international students 43–44
internationalization 33–34; closed borders 46–47; international students 43–44; leadership for 47–48; preparations 34–36; program cancellations 40–41; recalls 36–38
Investment Policy Statement (IPS) 208

243

INDEX

J1 exchange visitor program 44
JOVE 56

Karp, Elliot 100

leadership 101, 111; close-up lens on 25, 101, 105, 111, 170, 185, 221; for internationalization 47–48; reflecting on 230–240
Learning Management Systems (LMS) 52, 124
lessons, communication 29–32

maintenance, facilities 151
Major League Baseball (MLB) 113
Malisch, J. L. 169
mandatory recalls 36
March Madness 112
marketing 187–189
McKinsey & Company 20
Mearns, Geoff 114
Medlin, Lander 139
mental health epidemic, counseling for 98–99
ministries 100–101
mobility 133; alternatives to 49

National Association for College Admission Counseling (NACAC) 179
National Association of College and University Business Officers (NACUBO) 207–208
National Association of Intercollegiate Athletics (NAIA) 107
National Collegiate Athletics Association (NCAA) 107
National Institute for Learning Outcomes Assessment (NILOA) 58
National Intramural and Recreational Sports Association (NIRSA) 104
National Junior Colleges Athletic Association (NJCAA) 107
National Science Foundation, Higher Education Research and Development Survey 74
National Science Foundation, National Center for Science and Engineering Statistics 74
NCAA Guidelines for Resocialization of Collegiate Sports 110
network systems 123–125
new normal 86
non-traditional students 190–191

on-site research, ramping up 77–78
online format, teaching 52–55; dual credit/enrollment 60; policy considerations 58–59; preparing faculty 55–58; remote instruction 55–58; scheduling 59–60
Optional Practical Training (OPT) 46
orientation 189–190
outsourcing 133
overseas partners, reconsidering roles of 48

peer-to-peer mentoring 67
Pennsylvania State System of Higher Education (PASSHE) 92
people, research enterprise 85–86
perparedness 34–36
personal protective equipment (PPE) 95, 224
personnel, reclaiming 34–36
physical campus, remote mode 143–146
pipeline impacts 208–209
policy considerations 58–59
Political frame, crisis communication 20–21
pre-COVID challenges 196
professional organizations, value of 48
professional programs 190
programs, cancelling 40–41
Provost and Associate Provost for Global Engagement 56
public dashboard 28
Purdue University 23

ready-aim-fire, communication lens 29–30
reappointment calendars 64
recalls 36–38; decision communication 38–39; operationalizing 38–40; reentry 39–40
recreation centers 104
recruiting 114
refunds, student housing 148–149
remote instruction, preparing for 55–58
research operations, impact on 75–78
research, emergency planning for 85
residence halls, alternative uses for 149–150
resident assistants (RAs) 95

safety 145–146
Salih, Dema Mohammad 100
Santilli, Nicholas 139
Scarborough, Simpson 180
scheduling 59–60
School of Nursing at the University of Massachusetts, Amherst 57–58
security concerns, IT 126–127
Shaw, G. P. 134
social media, leveraging outlets of 22–24
Society for College and University Planning (SCUP) 139

INDEX

solicitations, reprioritizing 205–206
Sorrell, Michael 215
staff mobility 41–43
standardized testing 183–185
state funding 223–226
state policy 161–162
strategic planning 132–133
Structural frame, crisis communication 20–21
structure, reporting 133–134
Student Exchange Visitor Program (SEVP) 44
student groups 103
student mobility, beyond 41–43
students: activities 102–105; beyond mobility of 41–43; differential impacts on populations of 180–182; dining 101–102; health services 97–101; housing for 91–96; international students 43–44; non-traditional 190–191; organizations 102–105; orientation 189–190; program cancellations 40–41; supporting academic success of 64–67
subcontractors 159–160
summer programming 69–70
summer. *see* programs, cancelling
supplemental instruction (SI) 66–67
Symbolic frame, crisis communication 20–21
system level, planning at 220–222

teaching effectiveness, supporting 128–129
teams, rebuilding 200–202
tele-counseling 98
tenure clocks 64
TimelyMD 99
tone 31
too long-didn't read, communication lens 30

town halls 27
travel, banning 46–47
Tribal Colleges and Universities (TCUs) 224
triggers 31
Trump, Donald 4, 45
tutoring 66

universities, external communication 28
University of California, San Diego (UCSD) 78
University of Illinois, Urbana-Champaign 83
University of Michigan (UM) 140, 223; Department of Psychiatry 99
University of Michigan-Flint 92; Office of Housing and Residence Life 95
US Department of State 37

vendors 159–160
Vice President/Provost for Research (VPR) 74
videoconferencing 56
Virtual Desktop Infrastructure (VDI) 126
Virtual Private Network (VPN) 123
visa programs, suspending 46–47
voice, strategizing 203–205
Vorderstrasse, Allison 58

Wabash College 197
Wieck, K. 11
Wieck, K. E. 11
women 168–170
World Health Organization (WHO) 37

YouTube 23

Zoom 27, 55, 61, 100, 125
Zoombombing 24, 126–127

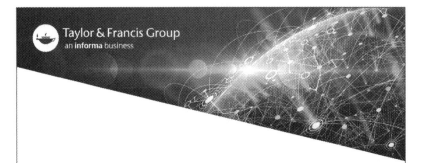

Printed in the United States
by Baker & Taylor Publisher Services